MERGERS & ACQUISITIONS
MANAGING THE TRANSACTION

JOSEPH C. KRALLINGER

McGraw-Hill

New York San Francisco Washington, D.C. Auckland Bogatá
Caracas Lisbon London Madrid Mexico City Milan
Montreal New Delhi San Juan Singapore
Sydney Tokyo Toronto

To each of my business associates:
   Through the years you have been my business mainstay. . .my inspiration. With your help, I continue to enjoy professional service and the challenges of new and changing business horizons.

To each of my children:
   You continue to be the light of my life! Love you Joanne, Diane and Bob. I love your children as much.

Library of Congress Cataloging-in-Publication Data

Krallinger, Joseph C.
   Mergers & acquisitions : managing the transaction / Joseph C.
Krallinger.
      p.   cm.
   Includes index.
   ISBN 0-7863-1166-5
   1. Consolidation and merger of corporations--Management.
2. Business enterprises--Purchasing.   3. Sale of business
enterprises.   I. Title.
   HD58.8.K697   1997
   658.1'6—dc21   97–1463

McGraw-Hill

A Division of The McGraw·Hill Companies

   4 5 6 7 8 9 0 DOC DOC 9 1 0 9

ISBN 0-7863-1166-5

Printed and bound by R. R. Donnelley & Sons Company

This publication is designed to provide accurate and
authoritative information in regard to the subject matter
covered. It is sold with the understanding that neither the
author or the publisher is engaged in rendering legal, accounting,
or other professional service. If legal advice or other expert
assistance is required, the services of a competent professional
person should be sought.

From a Declaration of Principles jointly adopted by a Committee
of the American Bar Association and a Committee of Publishers.

McGraw-Hill books are available at special quantity discounts to use as premiums and sales promotions,
or for use in corporate training programs. For more information, please write to the Director of Special
Sales, McGraw-Hill, 11 West 19th Street, New York, NY 10011. Or contact your local bookstore.

PREFACE

Manage to find the *Fatal Flaw!* At least one exists in every merger or acquisition (M&A). The *Fatal Flaw* may exist on the buyer or seller side . . . more likely both have at least one. Is your M&A effort being managed or is it just happening?

This book is for you. Sellers, buyers, corporate executives, members of the acquisition team, intermediaries, and scholars will benefit from investing time within the pages of this important how-to compendium. Transactions in megadeal size, $100 million, $25 million, or much less than $1 million are covered within these covers.

In order to determine the most critical issues facing both sellers and buyers, the author interviewed many sellers and buyers of businesses. He performed numerous purchase investigations for acquiring corporations and for his own business investments. Your author located, priced, and negotiated the purchase of over 25 businesses and the sale of over a dozen. He has been on both sides of the negotiating table.

This book is different. Many books on acquisitions are written for the scholar or for half-day seminars. This book is different. You have at your fingertips the answers to how to accommodate personal sensitivities, resolve tough negotiating issues, and settle contractual details in every investment involving acquisitions, venturing, and partnering.

This book is specific on managing M&A. This book is designed to bridge the gap between the theory of planning for, finding, and negotiating acquisitions, and the art and skill needed to successfully manage a successful closing for businesses of any size. It is a practical workbook, not a theoretical tome. It is specific, not general. Each chapter and the appendixes are written in easy-to-read detail and cover all of the basic underlying principles and issues you will encounter and need answers for when you invest in, merge with, or sell a business or product line.

Manage people and you manage the transaction. In the real world, financiers are organizing unfriendly takeovers, buying out U.S. businesses, and driving out good management with highly leveraged buyouts. The media have exposed the subject of M&A, but have not informed us how to be successful in this highly sensitive arena where people's lives are impacted greatly by the way acquisitions are managed. The human side is presented in virtually every chapter in this work. The human side of M&A is too often glossed over or ignored; yet nothing is more important to successful acquisitions. You can purchase capital shares of a target corporation, but you cannot purchase people. At best, you only rent people for a time. Yet taxation, capital stock, inventory, machinery, equipment, soft assets, and understated liabilities are given more review and consideration than the personnel needed to succeed in the business. People will generate revenues, profits, and solid cash flow; hard assets cannot! Such assets recorded on the balance sheet tend to depreciate, whereas people, although not recorded as assets, tend to appreciate or depart.

Determine buyer and seller wants and needs. Every acquisition is different because every seller has different wants and needs. When you were a child, you wanted things such as candy and ice cream. But you probably received socks and shoes since you needed them. If you can determine the wants and needs of each party early in the game of mergers and acquisitions, the deal will flow more smoothly or can be ended quickly and painlessly.

To be a good deal, the transaction must be good for both seller and buyer. If either party faces an early loss in the negotiations, those negotiations will terminate. If either loses shortly after the transaction is consummated, the acquisition will probably fail.

Do not fall in love too soon. A word of caution. Too many buyers have such a good understanding of the industry niche they are buying into that they "fall in love" with the target business too soon. These buyers want to grow fast and complete the purchase quickly. They lose their objectivity and do not effectively complete the purchase investigation or business audit of the target company. They will lose more often than they win.

Learn how to find the *Fatal Flaw*. Business owners, key managers, lawyers, accountants, financiers, deal makers, and scholars will find this book complete and easy to read and use. The appendixes provide actual examples of legal documents and a complete purchase investigation program usable in every merger and acquisition. It is better to consider and resolve significant details and potential problems before the acquisition is complete than to run headlong into them afterwards. Approximately 35 percent of all acquisitions succeed (success being defined loosely as exceeding the average growth of the industry niches of the parties). At least the same percentage fail, and the rest are simply adequate at best.

This book is designed to help you vastly increase your chances of success for a fair and good deal as a buyer or seller. Look for the *Fatal Flaw* in every acquisition. Solve it or stop the deal.

Joseph C. Krallinger

CONTENTS

Chapter 10

Sensitive Negotiating Issues   169

Chapter 11

Ways to Structure the Deal and Why   192

Chapter 12

Managing the Closing and Postclosing Issues   217

APPENDIXES

FOREWORD

A largely unwritten part of 20th-century history is how mergers and acquisitions transformed business. When this century began, the concept of an exit strategy, a means for businesses and their owners to create eventual value and/or liquidity, was unknown. A century ago, only the Goliaths of global industry considered M&A to be a realistic *strategy* for growth or competitive superiority. Possibly even these early acquirers were merely reacting to competitive threats or opportunities.

As the next millennium approaches, almost every business at least *considers* M&A in executing its strategic plan. But the subtle, stunning reality is this: M&A actually *drives* many business strategies. M&A has indeed altered the corporate lifecycle itself! What caused this revolution? Technology, trade pacts, deregulation, third world development, capital accumulation, the fall of communism, the growth of vibrant equity capital markets, and many other factors beyond the scope even of Krallinger's fine book.

M&A is so important today because it creates the single greatest uncertainty facing today's business executives and owners. Consider, for example, the two other ways (besides M&A) in which ownership of business assets can be changed: share purchases, and *de novo* investment.

True, when shares are purchased, capital moves literally at the speed of light. But *control* hasn't changed (in most cases), and no new productive asset has been created. Hence the competitive equation remains untouched. Barring a dysfunction in the capital markets, business executives and owners can anticipate the valuation and liquidity impact of those share purchases.

What about *de novo* investment? This is the oldest of the three ways in which ownership is changed; build, rather than buy. And, although *de novo* investment today grows at a pace much more sedate than the rate of growth in, say, the equity capital markets, such investment remains the dominant way to change business asset ownership: creating new productive capacity. Through *de novo* investment, a well-capitalized business can transform the competitive dynamics which it confronts.

But *de novo* investment provides too ample advance notice to competitors. Before ground can be broken, there are often regulatory filings available to anyone with the stamina to wade through them. Irrespective of regulatory delays and data, to buy new equipment or to build a new facility takes time. Competitors can observe, react, and modify their own strategies.

If the investment speeds through regulatory scrutiny and fails to trigger an effective competitive response it must still prove itself. By definition *de novo* investments don't have track records from which to draw comfort. For prospective competitors' executives and owners, such investments may pose a threat, but not one cloaked in great mystery.

Share purchases and *de novo* investment therefore do not comprise the type of event that can suddenly destroy a business—or remove its leaders from their positions. *M&A* does. With perhaps 15,000 deals completed each year globally, no industry is bulletproof.

To focus on how M&A causes uncertainty may seem an awfully negative way to underline why a book like *Mergers and Acquisitions: Managing the Transaction* matters. There are at least two other very practical reasons. First, growth by acquisition has the potential to elevate—or cripple—your own business. Principals and advisors seem to agree that most acquisitions disappoint the purchaser. Careful planning in areas such as those covered by Krallinger in his book ought to improve the odds.

Second, as the 20th century draws to a close, investors and analysts have become skittish about how acquisitions alter shareholder value. If investors or analysts can't understand how the target fits into the purchaser's company, even a reasonably priced purchase (and how rare those can be!) will destroy shareholder value or, worse, encourage litigation if they believe the process was poorly thought through. Conversely, a divester can actually *bolster* shareholder value by ridding itself of a "corporate misfit," even at a bargain-low price. These days, a purchaser can actually enhance its own corporate viability while simultaneously destroying shareholder value. Careful M&A planning may avoid this bizarre situation.

The upshot is that business executives or owners who ignore or avoid studying how M&A deals should work, do so at their own peril. Krallinger has assembled important ideas for those wishing to turn M&A into a strategy for success rather than an ominous uncertainty.

Stephen B. Blum

CHAPTER 1

The Urge to Merge

The average juggler is confident juggling rubber balls or bowling pins, but it takes a great juggler to juggle nitroglycerin bottles.

Anonymous

In a real sense, acquiring, merging, partnering, and venturing with third parties can begin with an easy juggling of strategic plans, priorities, people, and funds, but end in disaster. Merger and acquisition fever continues to cause results similar to those of the Gold Rush in the 1840s. Some people made great returns on their investments, while others lost everything.

The majority of acquisitions are not truly successful within five years if success is defined as equaling or exceeding real growth in value of the combined companies when compared to growth in value of competitors in the same industry. Divorce and separation after acquisitions are all too prevalent after a brief moonstruck honeymoon. So why the urge to merge? Why the desire to grow by external means . . . buying a business? Will the trend continue? Yes!

THE GROWTH IN ACQUISITIONS
CONTINUES UNABATED

The tremendous popularity of acquisitions and mergers of the 1980s is continuing through the 1990s virtually unlimited. Acquisitions in the United States have these features:

- They are allowed by government. Antitrust laws in the United States have not been heavily enforced for years except in matters of defense.
- They are stimulated by abundant supplies of money from both inside and outside of the U.S. borders. The devaluation of the U.S. dollar in relation to a number of stronger hard-currency countries has further exacerbated the acquisition trend.
- They are aided in some industries by deregulation. Deregulated industries that experienced significant mergers and acquisitions in recent years include airlines, banks, broadcasting, oil and gas, telecommunications, and transportation.
- They are pushed to unreasonable limits globally by financial innovations in debt instruments. These include unlimited types of securities used and tailored to purchase particular businesses at previously unheard-of leverage multiples of the equity investments by the principals.
- They are stimulated by greenmailers, who buy blocks of stock in a corporation. These investors are only interested in having the corporation buy the shares back to avoid having to deal with the greenmailer for years. Worse yet, the company may be eventually acquired by the greenmailer and similar cohorts in an unfriendly takeover.

On top of everything else, the U.S. economy has, by and large, remained stable and receptive to the trend. Too much money continues to seek too few good businesses. We have been watching the multiplication of buyouts increase geometrically. Growth by acquisition and merger will go on well into the next decade and beyond.

An abstract of a 25-year statistical review prepared by Mergerstat® Review (a division of Houlihan Lokey Howard & Zukin) is shown in Table 1–1. The table shows steady increases in the number and dollar value of deals announced every year since 1991. Even those over $100 million had similar growth each year after 1991. The number of publicly traded sellers continues to increase every year as well. The type of payment remains about the same with mainly cash deals representing about one-quarter, and with stock-based transactions and combination stock-and-cash deals sharing the balance evenly. Cash deals were predominant in 1990 at 40 percent compared to 25 percent in the four-year period ended 1995. Combination cash-and-stock deals increased from 28 percent

TABLE 1–1

Merger and Acquisition Statistical Review, 1990–1995

	1990	1991	1992	1993	1994	1995
Net M&A announcements	2,074	1,877	2,574	2,663	2,997	3,510
Total dollar value offered (billions)	$108.2	$71.2	$96.7	$176.4	$226.7	$356.0
$100 million+ deals	181	150	200	242	383	462
Method of payment						
Cash	40%	34%	22%	25%	26%	27%
Stock	31%	34%	40%	40%	39%	37%
Combination	28%	31%	37%	35%	34%	36%
Debt	1%	1%	1%	0%	1%	0%
Divestitures	940	849	1,026	1,134	1,134	1,199
Publicly traded sellers	185	148	227	221	344	447
Privately owned sellers	821	757	1,119	1,127	1,324	1,610
Total foreign sellers	266	244	403	400	399	483
Total foreign buyers	266	188	167	190	219	218
Average P/E offered	20.1	20.0	22.7	24.4	24.5	23.8
Average premium offered	42.0%	35.1%	41.0%	38.7%	41.9%	44.7%

Source: Abstracted from Twenty-Five Year Statistical Review, Mergerstat® Review, a division of Houlihan Lokey Howard & Zukin.

in 1990 to about 35 percent for the four-year period ended 1995. The average price earnings ratio (P/E) remains relatively high, in the mid-20 range. Then the matter of paying relatively high prices shows in the average premiums paid over quoted market prices before the announcements staying in the 40 percent range.

This premium is not a problem with privately held companies. Quoted market prices are seldom available. See Table 1–3 for current and past data on P/Es paid to public versus privately held companies. Think about it. Go for some privately held companies of size and save a bundle.

Multiples Vary by Type of Payment and Size

Table 1–2 summarizes the median P/Es by size of acquisition and by type of payment. The smaller acquisitions ($25 million and under) have had the first- or second-lowest P/E multiples in each of the 10 years ended

TABLE 1-2

Median P/E Offered (Base), 1986–1995

Year	$25 MM or Less	Over $25 to $50 MM	Over $50 to $99.9 MM	$100 MM or More	Cash Base	Stock Base	Combination Base
1986	15.8	17.3	20.2	20.5	18.7	18.4	20.6
1987	15.8	18.2	18.5	22.8	22.8	19.7	18.3
1988	14.9	16.5	18.8	19.6	19.7	13.6	17.7
1989	14.3	15.9	17.9	20.4	18.5	15.3	19.2
1990	15.3	13.3	15.6	19.4	13.8	21.3	14.8
1991	11.7	15.5	15.2	17.8	13.8	15.9	11.1
1992	15.5	18.4	21.1	23.2	17.4	16.7	24.0
1993	17.6	20.3	18.1	24.2	19.9	18.9	22.0
1994	17.5	20.3	17.1	21.8	23.3	19.3	17.0
1995	17.0	14.8	19.2	21.1	18.0	20.1	19.4

Source: Abstracted from Mergerstat® Review, 1996, a division of Houlihan Lokey Howard & Zukin.

1995, except for 1990 and 1994 (when they were within a few tenths of a point from the low). These transactions averaged a 15.5 P/E for the 10 years.

Second-lowest P/Es at 17.1 for the 10-year period ended 1995 were paid for those businesses with price tags between $25 and $50 million.

Next in line were those deals averaging between $50 million and $99.9 million in price with an average 10-year P/E of 18.2. Then the megadeals of $100 million or more averaged 21.1 P/E for the same 10-year period. Interesting, isn't it? The larger the deal, the higher the price. Wouldn't it be great to know whether big deals fare better than smaller ones in price 5 to 10 years later? Bet on the smaller ones having a higher percentage return on invested dollar. That is a fact based on experience and on studies made by others over the years since large companies bid up large deals due to competition for the large deals. Higher P/Es do not guarantee higher returns on invested dollars. Not at all. Your own experience tells you that as well—or soon will.

Whether the deal is to be paid in cash, stock, or a combination does not appear to materially influence the P/Es paid. The average P/Es paid by these means for the 10-year period on average were 18.6 for cash deals, 17.9 for stock, and 18.4 for combinations—not that much swing.

PUBLICLY HELD COMPANIES COST MORE THAN PRIVATELY HELD ONES

Many people believe that a publicly held company will command a higher price earnings multiple than the P/Es for privately held businesses. That is supported by the statistics for the past 10 years ending 1995, as shown in Table 1–3. Only P/Es paid for privately held companies for 1993 and 1994 exceeded those publicly held companies' P/Es by about two points—22.0 P/E versus 19.7 and 19.8, respectively, for the public companies.

For the 10-year period ending 1995, P/Es of publicly held companies sold were 3.7 points higher in the multiplier at 19.3, compared to a 15.6 average for privately held companies. This is due to a number of factors, but those businesses with more visibility (public ones) will normally have more buyers interested in acquiring them if all else is equal. Naturally, the type of business as well as its niche, market share, and general financial condition will affect the multiples. Nevertheless, the 10-year record referred to indicates that on average a buyer may acquire more cheaply in the private sector—whereas the private seller must try to convince buyers

TABLE 1–3

Median P/E Offered
Public versus Private, 1986–1995

Year	Acquisitions of Public Companies		Acquisitions of Private Companies	
	Median P/E	No. Transactions	Median P/E	No. Transactions
1986	24.3	259	16.5	105
1987	21.7	191	15.2	25
1988	18.3	309	12.8	50
1989	18.4	222	12.7	42
1990	17.1	117	13.2	36
1991	15.9	93	8.5	23
1992	18.1	89	17.6	15
1993	19.7	113	22.0	14
1994	19.8	184	22.0	18
1995	19.4	239	15.5	16

Source: Abstracted from Mergerstat® Review, 1996, a division of Houlihan Lokey Howard & Zukin.

that the multiplier for the business should at least equal that of publicly held companies for a similar business niche.

DRIVING FORCES FOR ACQUISITIONS

Why this drive to grow by acquisition? Why are the news media over-loaded with articles and discussions about acquisitions? This book in-cludes mergers within the definition of acquisitions.

The driving forces for acquisitions follow:

- Managers and owners of businesses with aging products, those with forecasts for slow or negative real growth in units for whatever reason, or those seeking synergism (vertical or horizon-tal market expansion) with their current products or services or looking for growth from outside.
- Managers and owners who are convinced, sometimes mistakenly, that real growth can be accelerated by acquisitions within or outside of their present product and market niches.
- Anyone who can obtain the financing to buy another business on friendly or unfriendly terms. These buyers are most likely low on cash, high on borrowing, fast on their feet, and smooth-talking. Frequently, they have little operating experience. They are mainly looking to amass capital quickly by borrowing from third parties that may or may not have rights to equity as part of the financing terms. Such buyers almost always expect to turn the acquisition over (sell it) within five years and expect a minimum return on their funds of 35 percent per year. Much higher returns (often mul-tiples of their investments) have been obtained by a number of these buyers.
- Investment bankers with limited or no operating experience have been buying companies. These are portfolio investors that, with new and innovative financing, including junk bonds (which will more and more turn out to equal their name), often price a business by how much it can generate in cash flow to service the debt levels imposed on the net assets.
- Pressures in the international business arena to become global via larger core businesses, increasing numbers of product lines, reduc-ing per-unit distribution costs, and expanding manufacturing and service facilities in multiple locations.

Some Are Targets of Takeovers

The companies that are most susceptible to being taken over by the leveraged buyout investors are

- Large firms with revenues and assets over $100 million.
- Conglomerates with diverse businesses that are not overly in debt in terms of their stockholders' equity and projected cash flows.
- Publicly held corporations that are not well understood by current investors. They have fallen out of favor or never were recognized for their uniqueness.
- Corporations with hefty cash balances or those with small amounts of debt in comparison to stockholders' equity (underleveraged).
- Mismanaged corporations in need of new leadership.

Foreign Investors Want Businesses in the United States

Foreign investors have been almost frantically investing in the United States during the past two decades. They do so because the United States

- Is the single-largest market in the world and it is difficult, time-consuming, and costly to obtain market share there except by mergers and acquisitions.
- Has numerous businesses with special technology and good managers who are capable of efficient production and service at high, or at least satisfactory, quality levels.
- Has many middle-market-size companies.
- Rarely restricts significant imports and exports for their target markets.
- Has few antitrust or regulatory barriers to their investing.
- Offers a public market for their shares and an established market for financing acquisitions.
- Frequently provides higher returns on their net investment than are available over time in their native country.
- Is more politically stable than any other country.
- Tends to have predictable, stable currency exchange and offers discounts to certain foreign currencies from time to time.

Middle-Market Companies Abound and Are Attractive

Middle-market companies (businesses with revenues of $15 to $100 million) exist in large numbers in the United States. They are still totally or partially privately owned or are divisions of larger corporations that are willing to sell them due to lack of fit with their strategic plans, their need for capital, or other reasons. They cover virtually all segments of the Standard Industrial Codes (SICs), including manufacturing, natural resources, distribution, and other services. Many have sizable market share in markets having a total size of not over $150 million.

HOW MANY MIDDLE-MARKET BUSINESSES EXIST?

These middle-market businesses are somewhat less visible and have been less susceptible as takeover targets in the eyes of the large investors and competitors. Data concerning their operations are not as complete as for publicly traded corporations registered with the Securities and Exchange Commission. However, much can be garnered about them to assist in locating and evaluating their position in the industry. Some experts estimate the number of such middle-market businesses at 700,000, while the author believes the number to be about 100,000.

Regardless of the exact number, these businesses can still be purchased at lower net price earnings multiples than larger publicly traded stocks if the buyer is attractive and can be flexible in structuring the acquisition proposal. Private corporations are also more flexible in deal structuring. The negotiations can be done privately and quickly. Usually, these corporations do not require or want much (or any) publicity in advance of the acquisition. Publicly traded corporations must carefully follow the laws and regulations dealing with the sale or merger of their business, especially if the ownership by the new investor reaches or exceeds 5 percent of their shares. Middle-market businesses are surely a viable target for acquirers in the 1990s.

THE PRICES ARE HIGH AND MAY GO HIGHER

Too many good dollars are chasing too few good business mergers and acquisitions. Acquisition prices are not directly tied to the stock market prices for privately held corporations. Nonetheless, all knowledgeable sellers read the newspapers and the stock market prices and try to selectively relate their business value to stock market pricing if it helps their position. Table 1–4 shows how the stock market speculation pricing has varied during a recent 14 year period. These are not conservatively calculated acquisition values; they are the stock market investor speculative trading prices.

Prices for Sellers Continue High

The prices paid by investors for capital stock of businesses as a multiple of the earnings do indeed vary greatly. These prices are fed by an abundance of cash and high-yield securities and a discount on the price of U.S. businesses in terms of many foreign currencies. As noted previously, the buyers of businesses add a premium in almost every case to the P/E prices of between 35 and 45 percent on average. Further, globalization and international partnering are on the rise for many businesses as they look to compete in the international markets.

The pricing for a specific business is addressed in Chapter 8. Suffice it to say, buyers outnumber the sellers of any valuable business. Further, sellers always have a higher value for their businesses in their own minds than prospective buyers have. The future always is presented as bright to buyers. However, realistic buyers may not need to wear sunglasses. Sunrise simply precedes sunset.

TABLE 1–4

Price Earnings Ratios, 1982–1995
S&P 500

Year	P/E Ratio	Year	P/E Ratio
1995	17.5	1988	11.7
1994	15.0	1987	14.1
1993	21.3	1986	16.7
1992	22.8	1985	14.5
1991	26.1	1984	10.0
1990	15.5	1983	11.8
1989	15.4	1982	11.1

Source: Reprinted by permission, Standard & Poor's, a division of the McGraw-Hill Cos., Security Price Index Record Statistical Service (1996 edition).

BUYERS ARE IN THE FAST LANE

R&D Loses to EPS

Research and development expenditures have been and are being cut from U.S. corporate budgets for two reasons. First, the perennial earnings-per-share (EPS) syndrome still influences too many financially driven executives seeking short-term profits. Wall Street addicts add fuel to this fire, and it has raged out of control. Second, the wildly growing, seemingly never-ending leveraged buyouts of large, medium, and small businesses have loaded the domestic balance sheets of many corporations with staggering amounts of debt. Debt must be paid; research, invention, and innovation do not have to be . . . for now.

This insatiable addiction to allowing millionaires and billionaires to be created by the banking industry and financial magicians has come back to haunt investors and employees.

Exporting Technology Stunts Growth

Another problem is the penchant of U.S. business managers to export our technology via sales to Asia, Europe, or elsewhere. With the exception of a few industries, where are the signs of new, broad-based, multi-industry technology being created in the United States? Even announced joint ventures and partnering often appear to give the negotiating edge and advantage to those parties from abroad. It is the giant sucking sound we wake up to in our trade deficit.

Lenders Do Not Lend When Needed

Over the years, bankers insist on exporting money (our money and government guarantees on top of it) and lending it to anyone except our small and midsize companies. Yet, as a group those smaller companies, not the large conglomerates, have been the largest job providers in the past two decades and will continue to be the best job creators in the *next* two decades.

Smaller Companies Create More Employment

These smaller firms number in the millions (between 12 and 18 million, depending on the source of the estimate). The Small Business Administration and others also estimate that smaller firms are creating more new jobs than the larger ones. Large conglomerates go through cycles of changing targeted industrial and commercial niches, downsizing (rightsizing seems the current rage), then expanding and acquiring, and then disgorging and again downsizing, completing the loop often within 10 years or less, and even more frequently if the corporate presidents change with some rapidity.

Global Competition Abounds

Since the late 1970s, the expression *going global* has been in vogue. The economies of many countries are experiencing a surge in internal market growth, a rise in demand for locally produced products from purchasers outside their borders, a need for new or better technology, and the onslaught of foreign competition in virtually all markets throughout the world. These forces will most likely change the competitive environment for niche players in the middle markets as larger foreign and U.S. corporations increase their presence in smaller markets that were previously of considerably less interest to these behemoths.

THE PACE OF FOREIGN INVESTMENTS IN THE UNITED STATES

Global investing for 1995 is shown in Table 1–5. The information is abstracted from an excellent and comprehensive KPMG Peat Marwick LLP publication, *Deal Watch*. Note that net buyers were the United States, Canada, France (which was about even in buying and selling across borders), Germany, Belgium, Italy, other parts of Europe (excluding Russia). Russia and the United Kingdom were net sellers.

According to the Bureau of Economic Analysis of the U.S. Department of Commerce in its *Survey of Current Business* (July 1996 issue), foreign direct investment on a historical cost basis in the United States rose by 11.5 percent in 1995 over 1994 to a level of $560.1 billion, which is over two-and-a-half times that of 1986. Industries attracting the highest percentage growth in foreign investment in the United States were finance, banking, insurance, and manufacturing. Real estate experienced a net decline in 1995. The U.S. direct investment position abroad at the end of 1995 totaled $711.6 billion, up 14.6 percent from 1994. The highest industry niches evidencing such growth were insurance, manufacturing, and finance. Fortunately, this continues a reversal of 1988 statistics when, for the first time, total foreign holdings in the United States exceeded U.S. holdings by $2 billion. Perhaps we are once again investing in growth for

TABLE 1–5

Cross-Border Investments
Calendar Year 1995

Purchasing		Country	Selling	
Number	Value $ Millions		Number	Value $ Millions
1,553	$63,684	United States	849	$60,022
323	14,602	Canada	180	10,625
1,876	**$78,286**	**Total North America**	**1,099**	**$70,647**
664	24,423	United Kingdom	468	35,028
343	12,992	France	332	12,842
15	335	Russia	59	9,730
450	21,190	Germany	322	6,126
55	7,391	Belgium	89	4,971
130	3,640	Italy	162	3,136
1,157	34,673	Europe—All others	1,132	18,010
2,814	**$104,644**	**Total Europe**	**2,564**	**$89,843**
33	198	China	630	12,971
97	5,410	Australia	162	12,599
20	197	India	208	3,235
5	11	Philippines	46	2,966
20	603	Indonesia	82	2,601
12	834	Argentina	112	2,271
1	2	Vietnam	80	2,039
445	15,907	Japan	69	1,574
629	23,276	Others	900	28,622
1,262	**46,438**	**Total rest of world**	**2,289**	**68,878**
5,952	**$229,368**	**Global total**	**5,952**	**$229,368**

Source: KPMG Peat Marwick LLP, *Deal Watch*, no. 1, 1996, pp. 26–27.

the long term instead of following the former practice of selling our franchise in certain technology niches, which has resulted in a lower standard of living in the 1990s in the United States.

Each foreign investor represents an opportunity and a challenge. Which side of the transaction are you on? Buyers will have to compete with foreigners who may have stronger currency, a longer-term outlook on cashing in on their investment, and/or a lower expected return on investments than U.S. buyers normally expect.

Why are the foreign investors so intent on buying American? The foreign-based firms are

- Inherently more prone to look to the U.S. market as the place to be and are not satisfied with having good market share in their country alone.
- Following strategic planning and looking for dominance or large market share in certain specific market niches in worldwide territories, especially those in major markets.
- Looking at the long-term investment returns rather than short-term earnings per share or early returns on investments. European and Asian investors look for long-term prosperity resulting from investments that offer initially low short-term profits and cash flow.
- Investing real cash for real business entities. Then they hold and grow the entire acquired company. This compares with the financial investors on Wall Street that buy with paper (junk bonds) and then strip down the company to a few base business units, trying to pay the early principal payments due with proceeds from divestitures of parts of the company just purchased.
- Buying technology.
- Buying market share in major developed markets rather than attempting to struggle in the tough position of taking market share from strong competitors.
- Increasing exports and imports to and from their native countries and generating foreign exchange in the process.
- Gaining new raw material supplies.
- Getting a break from time to time in the foreign exchange rate market and hedging currency exchange exposure by dealing in numerous currencies.

As the U.S. dollar weakens because of excessive government debt, government overspending, and trade imbalance, the values of a number of foreign currencies have strengthened against the U.S. dollar. This gives the foreign buyer a nontrading profit or bonus discount on the acquisition. Also, the foreign-based firms often can borrow funds in their countries well below the interest rates paid on debt instruments in the United States. Since income tax rates applicable to businesses are almost always higher abroad, the borrowing costs, after tax deductibility, are lower per investment dollar. Thus, the overall return is not as negatively impacted by the borrowing costs.

INDUSTRIES BEING TARGETED BY ACQUIRERS

Figure 1–1 shows the types of industries most favored by all acquirers of businesses globally during 1995, including those of U.S. buyers. The table includes all global cross-border acquisitions, minority investments, and joint ventures, which in 1995 totaled 5,952 transactions for $229.4 billion or about a $38 million average investment, compared to 5,312 transactions averaging $37.0 million each in 1994.

In number of transactions, the top target industries in dollars in 1995 were oil and gas (16.5 percent), chemical and pharmaceutical (10.9 percent), banking and finance (8.7 percent), food, drink, and tobacco (6.8 percent), utilities (8.2 percent), and electrical and electronics (6.0 percent). These were closely followed by media, leisure, and entertainment (5.6 percent), engineering products (4.8 percent), and business services (3.9 percent). The "all other" category not listed in detail in Figure 1–1 (28.7 percent) includes construction building products (3.9 percent), extractive industries (3.6 percent), vehicle manufacturing (3.0 percent), real estate (2.4 percent), hotels and catering (2.2 percent), transport (2.2 percent), paper and board (2.1 percent), wholesale distribution (2.0 percent), and others.

New rules are in effect from time to time that may restrict foreign-based companies seeking to acquire U.S. companies and vice versa. This is a changing scene; consult an expert before going forward with a foreign-based buyer.

FIGURE 1–1

Global Purchases of Businesses, 1995

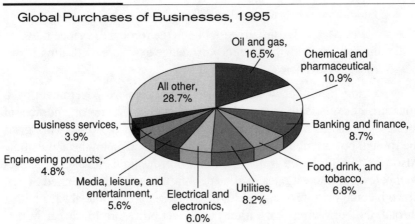

Source: KPMG Peat Marwick LLP, *Deal Watch*, no.1, 1996, "Number and Value of Cross-Border Deals by Industry," p. 30.

SUMMARY

This invisible war will have winners and losers with very visible results in the long term. U.S. business owners must go east and west to get and keep their share of the markets in the United States and outside its borders. Being happy with the status quo is not good enough! Competitors you recognize and some you do not are working on your market position right now. That is guaranteed. As a buyer, beware. As a seller, defend yourself aggressively or you may not have much to sell down the road.

Let us concentrate in this book on mergers and acquisitions in the U.S. market. The sound principles and practices in U.S. acquisitions, in the absence of intervention by government regulators, are the same all over the Free World. Surely, the competition for middle-market companies is becoming intense and will remain so. Small businesses, too, will partake in this insatiable hunger for growth by acquisitions, partnering, and venturing.

For accounting, income tax, and legal ramifications of mergers and acquisitions, see your accountant and income tax advisors. For ways to successfully buy, sell, or merge a business, read on.

CHAPTER 2

Your Business Culture and Its Effect on Acquisitions

I can say from my vantage point that more good business strategies have been destroyed by incompatible corporate cultures than by anything else. But, if I've learned anything over the past three-and-one-half years, it is that it's much easier to change the strategy than to change the culture.[1]

C. Robert Powell

BUSINESS CULTURE DOMINATES

The business culture of a company and its management represent the single biggest impact on whether a business will be successful in this era of the urge to merge. Surely, the buyer and seller will analyze each other for cultural deviations from their own norms or standards. Therefore, this foundation block called culture will be examined in this chapter before we go on. Subsequent chapters will cover acquisition strategies, procedures, negotiations, and completing transactions, each in some depth.

---

[1] C. Robert Powell's comment is included in Corporate Culture and Change Report No. 888 (highlights of a conference), Part 2B, p. 25, from The Conference Board, edited by Melissa A. Berman.

WHAT IS THIS THING CALLED CULTURE?

The human side of business is never more evident than during the process of investing funds in or with a third party with the object of owning all or part of the combined investment effort afterward. Whether joint venture, minority, equal, majority, or total ownership is the object, the individual personalities coming to the negotiating table will vastly affect the outcome of the proceedings. This always will be true, regardless of how convinced the financiers are of the validity of the pro forma projections of the joined businesses.

Influence While at Work Is Vast

As owner and/or manager of a business, you dramatically telegraph to employees, creditors, and interested third parties just how your culture and that of the company you represent fit in with the culture of others. Companies (although only legal entities, not real persons) exert major influences on the lives of all owners, managers, employees, and even customers and vendors. The culture of each person and that of the company mutually shape the future life of the others. Employees spend most of their available waking hours on the job, not at home with the family. Consider the typical workday for an average office or factory employee:

Activity	Time	Elapsed Hours
Wake up	6:30 A.M.	
Leave for work	7:30 A.M.	1
Leave work for home	5:30 P.M.	11
Arrive home	6:00 P.M.	11.5
Go to bed	11:00 P.M.	16.5
Sleep/rest	To 6:30 A.M.	24

Looking at those hours, you can see that much less time is spent awake and communicating at home than at work or with colleagues at or around the place of employment. Roughly, 58 percent more time is spent at or around work than at home during the week. The percentage will be even higher for those on overtime and in administrative and executive positions, where the clock is in less control. Allocation of time is always under the gun. Consider the quality of the time. Breakfast and dinner preparation time are hardly quality periods for most people. Then comes television viewing with its one-way street of information and junk, which is not well situated or even appropriate for communication among family members.

This allocation of time, imposed on each of us until retirement, creates an environment in which we are individually highly influenced by the culture of the workplace and the employees.

The Force Field on the Job Is Huge

Just as different teachers present the same scientific, language, and other course materials from different perspectives, so does a corporate environment have its own perspective. Individual contact with each employee presents a unique arena for dissemination of individual philosophies and dogmas in a way very different from those of other corporations and executives. The quality of each minute, the timing of those minutes, and the environment for receiving information influence the receiver of the data. Actions resulting from these contracts reflect one's culture.

The quality of sleep can be changed by mattresses, darkening the room, and even sleeping tablets. However, the forces of our time while in the office, factory, and marketplace with customers and vendors are considerable. How we act and think (our culture) are highly influenced by those forces. Consider this force field when going to work tomorrow! Think about it when you come home at night. How is your attitude and that of an associate or a marriage partner influencing the efficiency and progress of the workload and the attainment of personal, corporate, and professional objectives?

Culture Redefined

Someone who fights the system and the established culture may be a leader, be a follower, or be fired. Culture in this context is the composition of personal culture as perceived by the stakeholders and operating culture relating to all stakeholders, including employees, stockholders, customers, and creditors. However, this culture is not limited to the arts, intellectual capacities, and moral faculties. As defined in *Webster's Ninth New Collegiate Dictionary*, culture is "the integrated pattern of human knowledge, belief, and behavior that depends upon man's capacity for learning and transmitting knowledge to succeeding generations." This author's definition of culture is "the formal and informal ways one is perceived to consistently interact with people in social and business relationships over the long term with and in the absence of pressure." In business, this definition applies to each employee at all responsibility levels.

Culture Is a Collage

Top management cannot make the culture work. Everyone participates . . . knowingly or not, willingly or not. For example, if part of the desired corporate culture's goal is to offer high-quality products and services, each person impacts potential achievement of or failure to achieve that goal. Subcultures exist in all companies. Sometimes they are evident by department, other times by relationship or membership (as in the case of unions). The collage of these subcultures makes up the overall business culture.

Chemistry Must Be Right

How various stakeholders react (accept, adapt, reject, or tolerate someone's culture and that of his or her business) is key to whether a buyer or seller will succeed or fail in acquisitions. Financial negotiations are important and will influence success in buying or selling a business, but they are only one of the important issues. A buyer and seller each will analyze the person and the personality of that person sitting across the negotiating table. Surely, each will attempt to determine whether the "chemistry is right" between them. The process of evaluating culture is taking place. Is the business way of life compatible with each participant's way of life or sense of values?

CORPORATE CULTURE IDENTITIES

A definitive book on culture in business is *Corporate Cultures* by Terrence E. Deal and Allen A. Kennedy. In chapter 6 of that book, the authors identify four generic corporate cultures:

- **The tough-guy, macho culture.** Here is world of individualists who regularly take high risks and get quick feedback on whether their actions were right or wrong.
- **The work-hard/play-hard culture.** Fun and action are the rule here, and employees take few risks, all with quick feedback. To succeed, the culture encourages them to maintain a high level of relatively low-risk activity.

- **The bet-your-company culture.** This is a culture with big-stakes decisions, where years pass before employees know whether decisions have paid off. A high-risk, slow-feedback environment.
- **The process culture.** In this world of little or no feedback, employees find it hard to measure what they do; instead they concentrate on how it's done. We have another name for this culture when the processes get out of control—bureaucracy![2]

Those categories do indeed fit the majority of individual business managers, their businesses, and their management thinking. Which type are you? Are you the quick–trigger-finger person? That may be OK, unless you hold a loaded revolver pointed at your head. Which type do third parties think you are? Are those similar evaluations? Maybe not.

Nonetheless, the other party sitting at the acquisition table is appraising whether or not you fit in with their culture and their value system (that is, the value system they think they have in place). Actually, the real value system in place could well differ materially from the one they believe (hope) they have. If the two cultures do not match fairly closely, the transaction should probably not be completed unless both parties know in advance how and when culture adjustments will occur and what the impact will be on their people and, in turn, on their business.

Evaluate the Culture

A strategic plan should include an evaluation of the corporate culture today and the culture best suited for the long term in the industry niches selected for growth. Otherwise, survival may be the issue, rather than growth!

WHO CARES ABOUT CULTURE IN ACQUISITIONS? I LIKE MIX!

Harmony Beats Discord

The word *mix* is often used to define that mysterious mortar that can bind a company together and make it more cohesive because its managers have different philosophies, ideas, and operating methods for dealing with vari-

---

[2] Terrence E. Deal and Allen A. Kennedy, *Corporate Cultures* (© 1982 Addison-Wesley Publishing Company, Inc., Reading, Massachusetts, 1982), chapter 6, pp. 107–108. Reprinted by permission of Addison-Wesley Longman, Inc.

ous business and social issues. That is OK. However, they need to operate virtually as one in attaining the prime objective of the entity of which they are members. Perfect harmony exists where the prime objectives of the business and of each of its stakeholders are identical or at least compatible.

One Prime Objective, Please

A good definition of a prime objective is found in *Strategic Planning Workbook*, second edition, by Joseph C. Krallinger and Karsten G. Hellebust:

> A *prime objective* is a clearly defined, decisive, and attainable future for a business that is rooted in customer needs. A prime objective must embody a purpose that infuses all activities of a business. A single business must have a *single* objective at any one time—like a ship or plane, a business cannot travel in two directions at once.[3]

Can Cultural Differences Be OK?

A limit exists as to how different the overall culture of the total company can be if its individual business units are all different in culture and in prime objective. Will the discipline be there to somehow bring all these variables to some overall good? Perhaps so. Then again, perhaps not. Will managers adhere to the overall corporate plan? Will they go off on a tangent and make operating decisions based solely on the impact those decisions will have on the unit rather than on the consolidated group of units? Will they report timely on the business? Will they present financing and capital appropriations in time to allow rational decisions to be made in the best interest of the group? Or, are some managers going to remain loners, aloof and separated from the others who comprise the group of businesses all working to achieve the overall prime objective? Will each manager accept constructive criticism?

The answers to those questions will determine whether the management team stays together or splits apart. Are they concentrating on the customers, on the competition, or only on each other? Defer buying any businesses until satisfactory answers to those questions are known and can be tied to the prime business objective.

---

[3]Adapted from case example copyright © 1993 by Joseph C. Krallinger and Karsten G. Hellebust, *Strategic Planning Workbook*, 2d ed., reprinted by permission of John Wiley & Sons, Inc.

WHAT ARE THE MAIN CULTURAL ISSUES TO LOOK FOR?

When evaluating your own personal and business culture or another's, look for whether you see

- A leader or a follower.
- A creator, administrator, or caretaker. Each is different. Each is essential in particular situations.
- A detailer or a big-picture person. A numbers-driven versus business- or operations-driven person.
- A problem solver or a problem maker.
- A people person or a hermit.
- A competitive or noncompetitive person.
- A high, average, or low risk taker. Someone able to take failure and come back strong.
- A financial person. An administrator. A technically oriented person. A salesperson.
- The mentality to be efficient or inefficient.
- A negative thinker or a positive thinker.
- A possessor of good work ethics.
- Honesty or deceit.
- Ability to tolerate and implement change. Some amount of change always results after the acquisition date.
- A loner or a team player.
- Market-driven or technology-driven objectives.
- An individual decider or a consensus player.
- A delegator.
- A doer or a talker.
- A moral or immoral person.
- A person with a bent for action.
- Confidence or arrogance.
- Knowledge of the operations of the business and of the markets.
- A possessor of plain common sense.
- Just a daydreamer.

SUMMARY

You will get what you "incent." This is a law, not a theory! It works 100 percent of the time in all areas of life and business. Does the reward system for employees and sellers attract and reward people to fit in with and follow the business culture and attain its overall prime objective, and to retain the best people in key roles?

Invest time to save time. Spend a lot of time on the issue of culture in the business, in the social circles, and in the home. No single piece of advice is more important. You can buy assets or shares of stock in a business. You cannot buy people. People compose the overall culture of a business. That culture is virtually the most important asset or liability of any business. Be convinced your evaluation of these matters allows you (buyer or seller) to proceed with negotiating the final transaction with the proper people. It is better to miss doing a deal than to complete a bad one. The job of melding two similar cultures together is tough enough; the job of doing it successfully with two disparate cultures is even more difficult. Make sure you know the real culture of each party to the proposed transaction. Changing a culture is virtually impossible and certainly costly.

Having reviewed the basic fiber of a corporation at the level of its culture and its impact on acquisitions, we can propose some ways to strategically plan for acquisitions.

CHAPTER 3

Strategic Plans
Affect Acquisitions

Of course, I have a plan! I just don't know where it is and what portions of it we are following at this moment.

The average business owner

THE ACQUISITION PROCESS

Planning Is the Key

The acquisition process starts with planning the process and ends with planning how to make the acquisition a success after the closing. Actually, planning acquisitions never should end. If an acquisition is not successful, it will haunt the acquiring company for many years. The return on investment may be negative or low and impede the next acquisition. The remaining chapters of this book deal with the topics shown in Figure 3–1.

This book does not cover what company you should acquire. That matter is left to your strategic plan, and strategic planning is too broad to be given adequate treatment here. Several good reference texts are available, including *Strategic Planning Workbook*, second edition, by Joseph C. Krallinger and Karsten G. Hellebust (John Wiley & Sons).

This chapter touches on how strategic planning affects acquisitions and how to focus more clearly on the kinds of businesses to acquire and what influences success in the business of acquisitions.

F I G U R E 3–1

The Acquisition Process

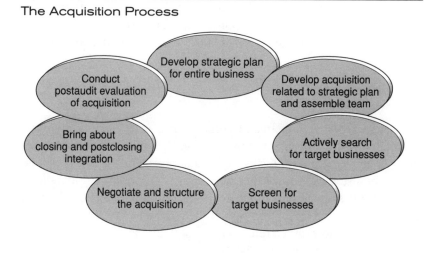

Owners and Managers Must Support a Plan

Strategic plans by definition should be those proposed and supported by owners and top management, who should certainly consider acquisitions as one avenue of growth and evolution. A good acquisition can be a real shot in the arm to rapidly gaining market share at the expense of a competitor, raising the barriers of entry to a competitor, buying the competitor's business, or obtaining new lines of business in new or related markets.

Buy versus Internal Growth

Is it better and less costly to develop your own new lines of products and services than to buy them? Great question. The answer to this question is not easy to grasp in advance. Top-notch leaders and managers will feel or sense the right answer more often than not. They have a great feel for the business. Mediocre leaders and poor managers will not find the right answers soon enough, if at all. They may lack sufficient experience, sound judgment, or good intuition.

Hopefully, all managers and employees want the acquisition process to be successful. Without commitment by top management, acquisitions will not happen, or if they do, they will not be successful. Buying the wrong business will set back achievement of the overall strategic plan. Further, the acquisition process is long and difficult. It is not something to race in and out of. At all costs, avoid the temptation to buy a business simply because the money is readily available. Buy only when the business fits strategically or when the opportunistic purchase of a business offers the potential rewards targeted for any business in the portfolio.

Publicly Traded Companies May Be Too Expensive

Acquisitions of publicly traded corporations, with their accompanying premium of 25 to 50 percent or more above the quoted market price of the target company, are not always the best strategy for the shareholders. In fact, several studies indicate that, as acquiring corporations buy other corporations, the shareholders of the acquiring corporation may well expect a decline in the quoted market price of their shares compared to the prices of their competitors' and a return on investment that will also be less than that projected by management before the acquisition.

Strength May Beget Strength; Weakness May Beget Weakness

Will you or your business leaders seek to acquire businesses managed by strong leaders? Too often a business leader will only acquire another business that has weak management, which is not an apparent threat. Is that a good idea? Is that what is needed to attain the overall strategic plan? Do your weak managers ever suggest buying a business known for having highly professional, truly competent managers? They should. They will not. That will adversely impact your business plan.

See Chapter 7 for additional data supporting the somewhat gruesome prediction that many, if not most, acquisitions are simply not good for the stockholders during the long term. So tell me one more time why this one will be better.

HOW STRATEGIC PLANS AFFECT ACQUISITIONS

For many foreign firms, the U.S. market is very attractive. Their currency may be at a premium exchange rate compared to the dollar and may offer a discount on the acquisition price. In the light of very few restrictions by regulatory bodies, it is frequently easier and certainly faster to buy market share than to build it from nothing. The strategic location of the United

States is attractive to many foreigners. It is a large consuming market. Also, abundant raw materials and reliable suppliers combined with a great capital market attract those from other countries.

A firm headquartered outside of the United States or any domestic business may want to penetrate the largest market in the world and accelerate growth by

- Acquiring a company in the same line of business.
- Hoping to obtain above-average management in place who will stay.
- Raising the barriers of market entry for other would-be competitors.
- Eliminating a competitor.
- Purchasing a product line or lines to complement current lines or eliminating total dependence on current narrow lines of products and services. This includes
  - Horizontal product-line extension to expand the currently offered lines into similar or related products and services, often with the same distribution. Examples would be adding (1) appliances to a hardware store, (2) electronic-sensing equipment to a mechanical or electromechanical measuring and sensing equipment line of products, or (3) generic products to brand-identified lines of merchandise.
  - Vertical expansion downward to become more basic in supply of materials or upward to seek more value added. Examples of downward integration include mining minerals if a business now only converts them to a more refined product, or manufacturing components if the business is now only assembling them. Examples of upward integration are the (1) reverse of the preceding actions and (2) opening retail bakery shops instead of only baking the items and selling them to wholesale distributors.
- Accessing new or better technology.
- Obtaining new markets and/or new customers.
- Purchasing manufacturing, distribution, sales, and administrative offices; buying other facilities and equipment to increase capacity; or using excess capacity of already-owned facilities.
- Obtaining marketing and/or production rights to increase coverage.

- Acquiring an unrelated business for economic cyclical mix or balance in a portfolio.
- Obtaining a consistently good-quality raw material supply.
- Investing otherwise idle and excess cash.

WHAT SHOULD THE STRATEGIC PLAN COVER?

The strategic plan should include

- The mission or prime objective of the corporation or its individual business units if the plan is covering that level of detail. An example of a valid prime objective could be to become (or remain) the leading provider of automotive chemicals of a noncommodity type. Another example would be to remain the largest provider of home health care products and services in the Southwest region. Still another example would be to become the leading manufacturer of electronic-sensing equipment for industrial applications.
- An evaluation of the present status in the industry niches in which the business operates. This includes
  - The current position of the business in the industry.
  - Current market influences.
  - The strong and weak points as they relate to personnel, experience and expertise, and reputation with customers for service and quality.
  - Facilities, equipment, and production capacity.
  - Distribution strengths.
  - Market shares and trends of those shares.
  - The technology levels of the business.
  - Unique product and service differentiation from the competition.
  - Analysis of each significant competitor.
  - Vendor relationships.
  - Financial condition.
- Projection of market dynamics for the business market niches for the next three to five years.
  - Customer needs.
  - Competitive pressures.
  - Regulatory restrictions.
  - Technological changes.

- Critical issues and priorities defined.
- Options for the business for the next three to five years.
- Operating strategies proposed. This includes
- Specific market niches to cover by customer type (even by name if appropriate) and geographic territories.
- Specific types of products and services. (Separate the base business from other product lines.)
- Quality levels.
- Methods of distribution.
- Rates of growth targeted for the base business and for each additional product line of size.
- The role, if any, for acquisitions, mergers, ventures, and partnerships. The strategic plan should always consider acquisitions as a possible growth avenue. They can fill in gaps in product and service coverage. Make the company a one-stop shop for an even broader base of customers. Acquisitions are not a panacea. The business may be changed from time to time as appropriate for its business cycle and that of the industry. Some companies wisely defer acquiring businesses during frenzied peak-pricing periods when buyers are bidding too high. Why pay 22 times net income if the price one year later might be down to half that amount?
- Financial objectives such as
- Target returns on investment.
- Real net income (without inflation).
- Cash flow growth of x percent over time.
- Dividends to shareholders.
- Defined financial stability including ratios such as working capital, debt to equity ratios, and targeted classification as an A-rated company.

Set Financial Return Minimums

Financial return targets and minimum acceptable returns should be included for each type of acquisition planned as well as the reasons for seeking acquisitions. These could include broadening the product lines and eliminating or reducing the power of a competitor, among other reasons.

Given no circumstances to do otherwise, these minimum rates of return or hurdle rates are those below which the acquisition would not be acceptable. Nevertheless, the planned rates of return can and will vary according to the purpose of the acquisition.

The lower and upper limits (either in dollars or in equivalent value of the buyer's shares of stock if used) to be paid for an acquisition should be stipulated. Financing should be in place or readily available within the time estimated to accomplish the mission of growth by external investment in acquisitions, venturing, or other means. Time lines to accomplish the acquisitions should be established. The personnel resources available or needed to find, negotiate, and complete the transactions should be provided for as well.

Establish Screening Parameters

Any acquisition should meet the screening tests set forth for the specific type. If the sole reason is to acquire market share, then the financial return on such investment may be acceptably lower than for an acquisition that is simply made for horizontal or vertical product line or service additions. Over the long term, it could be better to buy the competition than fight it. But that is not always the case. Buying one, but not every, significant competitor can also be a questionable decision. The remaining competitors will not freely give up market share without a struggle.

Buying substantial competitors may require approval of the U.S. government. Since it is unrealistic, and probably not financially rewarding, to buy every competitor of size, the would-be acquirer may have to continue to slug it out in the marketplace but do it smarter, better, and faster. Life is a series of trade-offs . . . so, too, are mergers and acquisitions.

WHERE STRATEGIES FAIL

How and When to Compete

Do not overemphasize where to compete. Markets change. Rather, delve into *how* and *when* to compete. Your how-to can include faster, more personal, and better service; direct sales versus independent sales representatives; consigned stock; and other issues. Spend considerable time analyzing the competitors' key people. They *are* the competition, not the corporations they are employed by. Analyze age, motivation, technical ability, culture, and influence of all key people in responsible positions at each competitor of size.

Buying May Not Be the Answer

Some buyers err because they mistakenly conclude it is easier to grow by buying a business than by starting one. They also may conclude that they can get the target business to grow faster than the seller did. Yet, competitors also have plans to grow in markets by taking market share from others including the target business. This "grass is always greener" theory of acquisitions led many U.S.-based buyers of businesses in the 1960s through the 1990s to eventually disgorge and sell off a number of acquisitions made even as early as three years after the acquisitions. Could that wrong acquisition have been prevented by more analysis and managing of the due-diligence process? Probably. Do not underestimate the value of taking time to really do due diligence before any corporate marriage.

Perhaps growth by hiring recognized industry niche leaders (key people) will be more logical and result in more solid growth at an inexpensive cost.

WHY SOME COMPANIES SUCCEED

How to Succeed

A good book on successful midsize corporations that contains the results of several years of research is *Winning Performance: How America's High-Growth Mid-Size Companies Succeed*, written by Donald K. Clifford, Jr., and Richard E. Cavanagh.[1] The authors define six principles of competition at the heart of the new tradition of winning entrepreneurs:

- Market-driven innovation underpins business success—and creates value to the customer.
- This value, not just low price alone, wins.
- Unrelated diversification is a mortal enemy of winning performance.
- Bureaucracy and business success are irreconcilable.

---

[1]Donald K. Clifford, Jr., and Richard E. Cavanagh, *The Winning Performance* (New York: Bantam Books, 1985), p. 7.

- The bottom line is much more than profit.
- The leaders somehow transform personal obsession with the business into enduring institutional values and energy.

Proper Fit Is Critical

Looking at those ingredients of success, you can see that acquisitions are and will be impacted by two possible competing forces: a buyer and a seller. The seller is selling a business that may or may not make a profit depending less on the past and more on the fit with the buying company, the people, and the cultures of both businesses and their customers. Innovation is not research and development. Innovation is not limited to high technology. Innovation can be as simple and as complex as giving the customers what they want, when they want it, and how they want it! What is so difficult about those requirements?

You Usually Get What You Pay For

Therefore, when you plan strategically and include acquisitions in those plans, give extra thought to, and perhaps pay more money for, the value-added feature of the people who are the innovators, the growth builders, the only absolutely mandatory factor in success. Ralph Shaw, president of Shaw Management Company, in a speech before the Business Leaders Forum in Seattle, Washington, said,

> Business success is far more than the science of managing scale and cutting costs. It's the art of leading people, nurturing them, challenging their creativity so they will figure out what customers really need and want. Successful companies realize that consumers know they get what they pay for. There are no free lunches in the competitive marketplace. That's where they often command premium prices in price-sensitive markets.

Mr. Shaw went on to explain the four general themes running through the culture of most winning companies:

- Earned respect—a sense that the enterprise is special in what it stands for, what it does, and how it does it, and demands and deserves uncommon effort and contribution from those who work there.
- Evangelical zeal—an honest enthusiasm that spills over on those with whom the enterprise does business, from employees and

prospective employees through customers, suppliers, distributors, and even competitors.

- Habit of dealing people in—the tradition of communicating just about everything to everybody in the organization and enfranchising them as partners in the crusade. Strategies, plans, ambitions, and problems are not the secret of the palace guard. They are known and appreciated throughout the company.
- A view of profit and wealth-creation as an inevitable by-product of doing things well.

Money is a useful yardstick for measuring quantitative performance and profit and an obligation to investors. However, even though most of the successful CEOs interviewed by Clifford and Cavanagh and those we have supported came from backgrounds of modest means, making money as an end in itself ranks low.

Fix Your Business First

If entrepreneurs are destined to failure in a current business, they should not plan on any acquisitions; they will surely accelerate the demise of the current enterprise. Fix the present business; then think about acquiring other businesses. The same advice goes for selling a business. Fix it to raise the price. On the other hand, if a business is reasonably healthy and has good planning, adequate finances, and solid management in place, it can more easily acquire or merge with other businesses successfully. Again, a seller will also receive more for a business that is not ill.

PRODUCTS AND MARKETS—FOCUS BY MATRIX

Focus Beats Opportunism

A buyer of businesses can do well from time to time without clear focus by being opportunistic and buying a good business when it becomes available at the right price, even though the timing is not perfect. Nevertheless, focus helps managers organize their thoughts and communicate their individual ideas, and it binds them to the overall targets and goal of the company. Further, defining the most logical markets and products in advance helps intermediaries and others more effectively target businesses for the buyer.

Synergy Is Good, but Hard to Acquire

Synergy (compatible or complementary business characteristics) can be obtained sometimes, but not always, by mergers and acquisitions. Synergy sometimes is misjudged as to its real potential value. It is often less realized in the real world. It may be fiction, not fact. Also, buying operating companies instead of trying to start a new product line without a sales organization or manufacturing facilities in place is difficult and takes considerable effort and time.

The key to correctly deciding which way to go is knowing all significant market niche facts and being able to evaluate the risks and financial rewards of going one route versus another.

Know What You Want

Knowing the characteristics you like, dislike, want, and need makes the acquisition process much more effective and cuts the waste of time and money. Do you want

- A business and people with a culture compatible with yours?
- Management to remain and continue to operate and manage the business according to their style and methods?
- To attract and retain good managers presently employed in the businesses you buy?
- To buy market share?
- Low, medium, or high technology?
- A natural business fit with your current business?
- A freestanding business unrelated to your industry niches?
- To reduce cyclical swings in volume?
- Low-risk investments if the returns on investments are adequate? Is any investment ever low-risk?
- A mix of different levels of risk with accompanying higher reward expectations?
- To be the low-cost producer?
- High-, medium-, or low-quality goods and services?
- Commodities?
- High, low, or average gross profit margins?
- High cash flow? High discretionary cash flow? *Discretionary* connotes that the cash generated need not be reinvested in the business for stable operations or normal growth.

- Property, plant, or equipment?
- Capital-intensive businesses?
- To partner or venture with someone already in the market you seek?
- International market entries?
- To own all, a majority, or a minority of a business?
- To create long-term value or short-term profits?
- To meet or exceed minimum financial hurdle rates of returns for the particular acquisition investment regardless of the reasons (market share gain, for example)?
- Freestanding, unrelated businesses rather than add-on product lines or related businesses?
- To avoid regulated businesses?
- To avoid union labor?

These issues must be decided before an acquisition program is implemented. Without a sharp focus, too much time will be wasted in the effort and the results will most likely be unacceptable.

Matrix Focus Helps

The use of a matrix can facilitate developing or targeting new markets, products, and services, or clearing the way to sell or cease doing business in a particular market niche with a specific product or service line. Table 3–1 shows a mythical company producing products only for the automotive industry. The managers very effectively put their thoughts about the business on one sheet of paper. Note how new markets (not just automotive) and new products were added as candidates to consider in future plans (for the next three years). Some products will not be manufactured. Instead, they will be simply bought and resold, which requires less capital than buying a business and often has fewer risks, yet acceptable rewards. Cross-licensing to manufacture or sell could also be valid alternatives.

The matrix can also be used to display product lines to be discontinued. Some products age, no longer fit the rest of the lines, or have lost their customer appeal. Product-line weeding in a business garden is a periodic necessity.

Each product and market segment in Table 3–1 needs to be reviewed separately before a firm decision can be correctly made as to where to place it and how to mark its characteristics. If the chart is prepared in colors, the

TABLE 3–1

Present and New Products and Services
Present and New Markets

| | Present Markets[1] | | | | | |
Present Products	OEM Cars	After Mkt. Cars	OEM Truck	After Mkt. Truck	Retail Chains	Prof. Mechanics
Brake linings	3 G	2 G	2 G	2 G	1 G	
Windshield wipers[2]	2 G	2 G	1 G	1 G		
Shock absorbers		1 G		1 G		
Tire chemicals		1 G		1 G	1 G	1 G
Cleaning oils		1 G		1G		1 G
Engine additives		1 G		1 G		
Mufflers[2]	1 G	1 G	1 G	1 G	1 G	
Carburetor cleaner		2 G		2 G	1 G	1 G
New Products						
Specialty cleaners		1 Y		1 Y		
Bug killers					1 G	
Smog inhibitors		1 G				
Golf cart brakes and parts						
Exhaust repair materials						
Wheel weights [2]	1 G		1 G	1 G	1 G	1 Y
Tire valves[2]		1 G		1 G		
Suspension systems[2]		1 G				
Filters[2]		1 G		1 G	1 G	
Specialty bonding chemicals		1 G		1 G	1 G	
Other—list						

[1]Company's market share shows

  1 = Minor market share

  2 = Average market share

  3 = High market share

Future growth of market niche:

  R = (red) for high

  Y = (yellow) for medium

  G = (green) for low profit margins due to competitive pressures

[2]Items bought from vendors and resold as purchased (buy/sell).

		New Markets				
Co-ops	Industrial	Electronic	Electrical	Mail Order	Tele mrkt.	Hardware
	1 Y			1 Y		
				1 G	1 G	
1 G	1 Y					
1 G				1 G	1 G	
1 G	1 G	1 Y	1 Y	1 G		
	1 Y			1 G		
	1 G					
2 G	1 Y	1 Y		1 Y		
	1 R	1 Y	1 Y	1 R	1 R	1 Y
1 Y	1 G				1 Y	1 Y
1 G	1 Y			1 Y	1 Y	1 Y
	1 Y			1 Y	1 Y	
	1 Y			1 Y	1 Y	
1 Y	1 Y			1 Y	1 Y	
1 G	1 G			1 G	1 G	
1 G	1 G			1 G	1 G	
1 Y	1 G			1 G	1 Y	
1 G						1 G

areas of most interest may be those with red colors showing high market growth and low market share unless the competition is too severe. If the market niche shows low growth (green) and low market penetration (marked as 1 in the table), it might be best to avoid it due to probable low profit margins due to competitive pressures.

Avoid False Starts

False starts can be minimized or avoided if all managers agree to the types of businesses to be bought or invested in. Of course, having the money available should speed up acquisition success. All parties will say they have the funds, but sellers and intermediaries know that is not always true. A consistent track record of good acquisitions will be the best proof to third parties, including sellers, that the acquirers are for real, know what they are doing, and are doing it well.

Size Should Not Dictate Size . . . But It Will

An interesting phenomenon is that managers for a particular business unit, subsidiary, or total corporation will not normally look for acquisitions larger in revenues or assets than their own operation. They fear they will not survive the acquisition in the long term because the targeted large business may and should have good management who appear as a threat to managers of the acquiring company.

Think about it. It may well be a real problem in your business today. Do not let it be, or good candidates for acquisition will be missed. It takes approximately the same amount of time to do a large acquisition as it does to do a small one. The rewards are not statistically related to large or small acquisitions. A good rate of return on investment varies more by the quality of management and the characteristics of the market niches, which include the quality of the competition and the elasticity of price based on supply and demand. Do not be limited by size per se.

An Example of M&A Specifications

The following illustrates one way to inform management, directors, interested third parties, and intermediaries of the types of businesses sought. You need to revise it to make the facts fit your circumstances.

CHARACTERISTICS OF BUSINESSES SOUGHT

Sample List for Internal Use
and to Inform Third Parties

Use your own specifications since the following is for illustrative purposes only. The odds of finding a good target business get much better if the areas of interest are well defined by buyers. Words like "Looking for an acquisition in manufacturing with a price of $20 to $100 million" will simply be deadly. Besides, it demonstrates that the buyer really has not invested time in the planning process to set sail for a specific harbor. That buyer's ship will never reach port.

Current businesses owned and targeted to expand by acquisitions (specify herein the targeted revenue volume for each business segment) are:

- Automotive aftermarket components for trucks and autos and distributed by jobbers, by distributors, and directly to large chain stores and co-ops. Sales to original equipment manufacturers are not desired.
- Machinery and equipment manufacturing for process and packaging industries, including controls and sensing devices, but excluding food and confectionery equipment.
- Health care services for home health care delivery, testing and analysis laboratories, and doctors' offices. Production of high technology medical instruments is not wanted.
- Manufacturing and/or distribution of specialty chemicals, not of a commodity type, with primary emphasis on industrial and hardware uses. Automotive specialty chemical niche is not of interest.
- Strong brand-name identification for all products or strong ties to the national accounts with their brand ID.
- If second-level management is strong and will stay, no need for the top-level managers to remain beyond the second year.

Freestanding businesses of interest, not included above, if revenues exceed x million up to y million. Minority interest is OK if leading to majority within five years:

- No unfriendly takeovers.
- Management above average and remaining for at least three years.

- Manufacturers of noncommodity products with gross profit margins of at least 35 percentage points.
- High market share in narrowly defined niche markets (prefer being in the top two or three market positions).
- High-quality image for products and services as perceived by the customers.
- No customer representing over 20 percent of revenues.
- Good cash flow generators with low to medium need to reinvest in property, plant, and equipment (not a capital-intensive business).
- No turnaround business.
- Consistent and profitable track record for the past four years.
- Nonunion work force preference.
- Preference for East Coast or Midwestern location of headquarters.
- Mining and agriculture not sought.
- No business in or dominated by operations in lesser-developed countries.
- No high technology products such as those in computer chips, biotechnology, aerospace, and similar fields.
- Sales to governments acceptable if not dominant.
- International sales a plus if weighted to Europe and Australia/Asia.

FIGURE 3–2

Sample Data Form for Use by Intermediaries and Others to Submit for Business for Sale

Business Activity:

_____

_____

_____

_____

Revenues by major product/service line

_____

_____

_____

_____

Patents and proprietary areas

_____

_____

_____

_____

New products introduced within the past five years, showing products and last year's dollars of sales

_____

_____

_____

_____

_____

Marketing and Sales:
Profiles of major customers, types, and names

_____

_____

_____

_____

Major markets served—niches and geographic concentration

_____

_____

_____

_____

Method of distribution

	Percent by	$ amount
Direct sales (in-house)	_____	_____
Distributors	_____	_____

Sales representatives   _____   _____
Other   _____   _____

Strategies for the markets

_____

_____

_____

_____

Competition:

Names of top five competitors and their market shares

_____

_____

_____

_____

Market share of company for major markets

_____

_____

_____

_____

Ownership and People:

Major stockholders and percentages of company they own

_____

_____

_____

_____

Names and years of service in company and in industry for key people

_____

_____

_____

_____

Evaluation of key people and their likelihood to remain with business

_____

_____

_____

_____

Total number of employees, union status, and labor relations history

_____

_____

_____

_____

Facilities:
Major plant and office locations

_____

_____

_____

_____

Capacity utilization

_____

_____

_____

_____

Major Vendors List:

_____

_____

_____

_____

Financial Highlights:
Balance sheet—attach current one and last year's
Cash flow analyses for last three years—attach

Anticipated capital needs for next three years:

_____

_____

_____

_____

Financial Highlights

	Sales	Gross Profits	Pretax Income
Three Prior Years			
_____	_____	_____	_____
_____	_____	_____	_____
_____	_____	_____	_____
Next Three Years			
_____	_____	_____	_____
_____	_____	_____	_____
_____	_____	_____	_____

SUMMARY

Acquisitions should be planned to increase their chance of success. Such planning should be in writing and included in the company's strategic plan. All significant parameters should be agreed upon in advance. These include minimum financial returns, screening parameters, and agreement on the general industry niches being targeted.

Certain strategies will fail. Perhaps the company should expand by growing internally in its present markets and new markets with its present product line and/or new products which can be developed internally. Also hiring industry niche key personnel may be a far cheaper way to grow with less risk than that involved in buying a business.

Success in acquisitions is more achievable if the target businesses fit those of the buyer as to business concepts, markets and operating principles, and culturally in terms of assignment of responsibilities and motivation of its people. Do not acquire another business until you fix your own.

Once you decide to acquire, determine your specifications for target businesses in as much detail as possible. Presenting your acquisition concepts clearly and concisely will greatly improve chances of success in locating good businesses and in ultimately completing the transaction.

CHAPTER 4

Venturing, Cross-Licensing, and Partnering

WHY BUY A BUSINESS WHEN YOU CAN SHARE ONE?

Buying Is Only One Way to Grow

Building, growing, or diversifying a business by internal development and investment is one way to go. Buying someone else's business is another—it is covered in the remaining chapters of this book. Nevertheless, buying 100 percent of a business is not the only way to grow or diversify externally.

Merging, Venturing, and Renting Are Growth Vehicles

The other way to grow externally is to obtain the resources developed by one or more third parties. In this manner, one can then more easily enter a new market, obtain rights to new products, buy or rent a window to the technology of others, fund a start-up business, or merge certain skills and assets to broaden the horizon of the business in question. Broadly, this can be accomplished by merging partly or totally with another entity, joint venturing, partnering, licensing, renting, buying, or joint investing in a new or existing project. Some parties do not want or need to purchase the legal entity owning such tangible or intangible assets or being in such markets. Some countries do not permit a foreigner to own all or a majority of a business within its borders. In those situations, some forms of joint arrangements are profitably used.

Alternative Vehicles May Need Less Capital

The attraction of going this route, instead of acquiring the third party directly, is that it normally requires less capital to get started, adds products or services to the line of business already on hand, probably speeds the entry into a market, and may increase the chances of success in the planned growth area.

Be Creative in the Structure

The ways to accomplish this external growth for a business are unlimited. There is little sense in defining them, since definitions will not make a profit. Too much defining may limit the thinking of the parties who need to create the right form of transaction to accomplish each party's objective. Since needs vary by company and by business within a company, do not stick yourself in a box with four sides and a lid and get trapped in the process. The means to attain the external growth are mechanics. Those mechanical form puzzles can be handily solved by the accountants and the attorneys.

Time Frame to Attain the Business Objective Can Dictate Growth Vehicle

Think about accomplishing the business objective . . . old and/or new products and services with growth in old and/or new markets. That is fairly straightforward and simple. How to do it is more complex, yet still as simple as finding out what another party has, wants, and needs from its perspective. The mechanics to solve the puzzle may be called a joint venture, a partnership (general or limited), an alliance, a cross-license, a license, a royalty, a right to use certain assets (technology, for example), or just a project. One or more parties may commit to manage the agreed-upon arrangement, and one or more may be active in it. For the purposes of this chapter, the term *joint arrangement* is used to cover the entire gamut of contractual commitments that might be used in whole or in part to mechanically solve the issue of how to legally evidence the arrangement.

WHAT IS THE JOINT ARRANGEMENT
TREND IN BUSINESS?

Large and some smaller businesses on virtually each continent in the world are racing the clock to seek joint arrangements in their own countries and in others of any size, importance, and capability. Size connotes market opportunity, and capability connotes manufacturing, marketing, sales, and research and development capabilities. Some corporations publicly refer to this trend as globalization. Regardless of the correct term, the trend is increasing. The accelerated use of joint arrangements, even by major corporations, is due to political events outside of their control, to the competitive scene in worldwide markets, and to the relatively high cost of establishing a fully integrated business on foreign soil.

POLITICAL AND FOREIGN PRESSURES
ON U.S. BUSINESSES

Look Abroad to Grow as Well
as in Your Home Market

European businesses have been ganging up on those domiciled in the United States for years. Those countries are heading fairly rapidly into a new type of cartel to limit outside competition while enhancing insiders' positions. Investment in Europe is also a result of seeing that growth in the U.S. market alone may not be good enough. Europe presently remains the largest general consumer market outside of the United States. On the other hand, its countries' businesses will always remain among our fiercest competitors. Asian markets are also developing rapidly and companies from those countries are now and will be tough competitors as well as attractive customers for decades in the future.

And, of course, the countries in the eastern bloc of Europe began their breakout of the Soviet Union's red control box in 1989. Since then they started to receive funds from the U.S. government for nothing, or close to nothing, so they can export to the United States and put some of the U.S. work force out of work! The U.S. government has generously done that before. Our charitable lend–lease and giveaway programs helped rebuild our worst enemies after each major war or political uprising. Strange politics. The object has been to get the particular country up on its feet and allow it to become more independent by national and international trade stimulation. Usually, the giver ends up being had by the very country being helped, at least in some industries. Think about shoes, soft goods, steel, automobiles, electronics, motors, photographic equipment, tools, and even toys. And this is called progress? Small companies all over the world should be seeking international sales via acquisitions, joint venturing, partnering, or cross-licensing for production and/or selling. Competition does make partners out of former enemies.

Get with the Language

Some U.S. businesses (usually small to midsize) are sending one or two people to Europe and Asia once or twice a year armed with a catalog of products and good intentions, but little else. Sometimes they do not even speak the languages of the countries they visit. Our U.S. schools and businesses fail to provide the training and incentives for these representatives to become more acceptable to the customers in the field.

Get Real on What Investing in Growth Costs

How can a small company possibly expect to properly service the customers thousands of miles from its talent base of operations? Real funds must be allocated to the overseas markets to penetrate them. Increased attendance at international trade shows and seminars is needed to educate U.S. business owners about the markets abroad. Contracts with outside consultants should be considered to help construct a realistic plan for international manufacturing and sales.

No longer does the sun never set only on the U.S. flag. Other countries' flags too are being raised up on flag poles all around the world. After World War II, the United States went international in investing in manufacturing and sales facilities throughout much of the free world. Then, believing it was the only show in town, the United States rested. Meanwhile, growing out of the rubble of wars, insurrections, and lesser-developed country gardens are the roses we now know in Europe, Asia, some countries in the Middle East and in South America, and soon Africa. Some of those foreign firms are giants in their own right. The largest banks in the world are now foreign-owned with a few exceptions. Surely, U.S. business must get on the bandwagon or miss the parade.

WHAT IS SOUGHT?

What are companies looking for when they seek out one of the many forms of joint arrangements instead of continuing to go it alone?

- Lower manufacturing costs. Such businesses seek the solution in lesser-developed countries with lower net wage rates. Net wage rates include manufacturing efficiency for acceptable-quality products and services.
- Broader markets and new or expanded ones for their present products.
- Firepower of investment funds, personnel, contacts, established customer base, and so on to grow in particular markets.
- Technology necessary for long-term survival in a market niche.
- Ability to continue operating profitably in selected markets due to inadequate capital, people, technology, or marketing expertise in those niches.
- Speed in getting going.
- Reputation of company or person.
- Technology.
- Technical service.
- Government relations.

Will You Limit Targets?

The important issue is whether the search should include only acquisitions and/or one of the many forms of joint arrangements. Clearly, all methods and forms should be reviewed in depth before selecting the next one for the business. Capital resources and speed in getting the project started must be balanced with control issues. A joint arrangement other than an acquisition is an area to explore.

FORM AND LIFE OF THE JOINT ARRANGEMENT

Formats Vary

The legal document binding the parties in a joint arrangement will vary by the type of agreement. A partnership agreement differs from a license or sales representation contract in form and period covered. A well-informed and highly qualified attorney will tailor the correct form.

Time Frames Vary

As to the life of such an arrangement, it might last less than a year, indefinitely, or any time in between. Again, the parties to the agreement know how long it should last. Certainly, the time limit and termination method should be agreed upon in advance. Usually, the contracts provide for renewal periods, often with automatic renewal unless one party notifies the other in writing in advance of the termination date.

Other Issues to Resolve

The other issues usually covered in jointly owned businesses are

- Marketing:
- Overall strategies.
- Marketing plans, including market niches, territories, pricing, and policies.
- Annual operating budgets; planned leases; annual capital needs for property, plant, and equipment; and other major expenditure budgets.
- Policies for contemplated sales not within the established marketing plans or policies.
- Other operating areas:
- Meeting dates to report on management issues and issues for stockholders.
- Election and termination of principal officers and directors of the joint arrangement, if appropriate.
- Day-to-day management and supervision.
- Hiring, promotion, and termination policies and procedures for all employees.
- Policies, practices, and contracting with vendors for purchasing all raw materials and supplies.
- Preparation and filing of all financial and operating reports for stockholders, taxation, and regulatory purposes.
- Bookkeeping, accounting, and other services for payroll, purchasing, billing, and collection of accounts receivable.
- Preparation of annual budget and long-term business and strategic plans.

- Declaration and payment of dividends and other distributions.
- Use of and any fees for patents, trademarks, trade names, and know-how.
- Acquisition of other businesses, product lines, or joint arrangements with third parties.
- Acquisition, sale, or disposal of major capital equipment, business segments, or major assets.
- Debts, major contractual commitments for any purchase or sale, controls over the issuance of guarantees, and transactions involving shares of capital stock.
- Future capital contributions or loans to the business by the parties and their impact on the ownership or sharing of the profits and losses.
- Sale or liquidation and termination of the business.

HOW CAN THESE JOINT ARRANGEMENTS WORK?

Depending on the type of arrangement, the arrangement and applicable contributions and compensation could include:

Joint Arrangements

Type*	Compensation
Sales representation	Commission
Distribution	Commission or outright buy/sell
Franchise	Up-front payment plus royalty based on sales and possible agreement to buy materials and supplies from franchisor
License to manufacture and/or sell (may involve cross-license with each having rights to other's technology, products, etc.)	Usually up-front payment plus royalty-type fees based on sales with annual minimums
Jointly own business and partnerships	Both contribute funds and/or services, product technology, distribution, manufacturing management, etc.
Rental agreement for facilities or management or a tolling production arrangement	Fixed rent charge or straight fee for services rendered or products produced
Agree to fund project with rights to project results or products	Sharing of expenses, or equal or unequal contribution of funds

*May be granted exclusive or nonexclusive territories.

SELECTING THE OTHER PARTY

Selecting the right joint arrangement partner is critical, just like selecting a marriage partner. A partner must, as you must,

- Have culture and business objectives that are similar or compatible to yours.
- Be capable.
- Be honest and honorable.
- Be predictable.
- Have proper credentials and an impeccable business reputation necessary for the business planned.
- Have proper business contacts—customers, vendors, and financial contracts.
- Have good and ethical contacts with government officials at local, state, and national levels.
- Be committed to the venture.
- Have adequate facilities, if essential.
- Live up to fully supporting the arrangement.

Constant Vigil Is Needed

Venturing, partnering, investing, and strategic alliances, whichever name fits, require constant attention. They offer dependency and loss of a certain amount of control, but do provide the speed to get the job done. Egos may become a problem. Decide in advance who will be in charge of administration and operations on a day-to-day basis. The customers should not have to decide that for you. A prime large competitor would normally not be one to join in such an arrangement since the odds favor eventual divorce and probable severe entanglements in the marketplace.

Some Deals Are Not Meant to Be

Inner strength and wisdom are required to say no to a bad merger, acquisition, or partnership as well as to avoid rushing into the wrong one. Similarly, it takes time to make the right joint arrangement with the best parties for all. Selecting the wrong partner in this joint arrangement is very dangerous, depending on how vulnerable you are at the outset or eventually. Some have lost market share. Some have had their technology, know-how, designs, or other technical information and plans stolen, misused, or abused by the other party. A foreign or domestic distributor or manufacturer may become your competitor after the market is developed by you or by them. Then you may be back on the street looking for the right partner or you may have to concede the territory to the partner/competitor. The champagne no longer flows for the celebration of signing the joint arrangement. Now the lawyers are flying around threatening lawsuits for everyone. The old adage applies sometimes: One partner is one too many. Well, there is good news and bad news. The good news/bad news is the joint arrangement may have started out great and ended less than great.

Resolve Not to Shoot Yourself in the Foot

Partners seem to have a way of always looking for a self-destruct mechanism. Is one living up to the bargain? Is one doing all the work and having to share part of the cash flow? Does one always come up with the good ideas, methods, and opportunities? Look at the love–hate relationship of some large and small sales representatives or distributors for quite a number of manufacturing companies. The constant strain is whether one is too dependent on the other and thus risks too much for comfort.

Surely, a joint arrangement should not be entered into without competent, experienced business and legal advice. Learn from those who have been there. Thoroughly investigate the proposed partner or other entity with whom you plan to have a joint arrangement before signing any agreement. That is the same advice you would give to a son or daughter planning to marry. Proceed with controlled enthusiastic caution!

PREVENTIVE MEDICINE

- Spend the time to investigate the other party or parties before signing the agreement. Determine whether the culture of the parties and their businesses blend or clash with yours. Are the long- and short-term operational and investment objectives of the parties in harmony and compatible?
- Document all material issues and agreements at the outset and all during the arrangement.
- Provide a fair and equitable way out for each party. Nothing is forever.

- Include confidentiality and noncompeting provisions where appropriate.
- Apply in advance of negotiations for all relevant patents and trademarks in those countries where needed.
- Specify the appropriate parties and legal system to arbitrate or judge future misunderstandings or abuses.
- Be cautious about all trade secrets, formulas, know-how, sales and market information, and customer data.
- Specify the geographic territories, the products and services covered, and the operating policies and procedures to be in effect.

REFERENCE BOOKS

Good reference books for ideas about specific structure, selection of partners, negotiating and understanding the legal process, and agreements covering joint ventures and corporate alliances are

- Johnson, Hazel J. *Bank Mergers, Acquisitions, and Strategic Alliances.* Burr Ridge, IL: Irwin Professional Publishing, 1995.
- Reed, Stanley Foster, and Alexanda Reed Lajoux, with case histories by Michael Marsalese. *The Art of M&A: A Merger/ Acquisition/Buyout Guide,* 2d ed. Burr Ridge, IL: Irwin Professional Publishing, 1995.
- Aquila, August J.; Allan D. Koltin, and Marc L. Rosenberg. *CPA Firm Merger Strategies That Work.* Burr Ridge, IL: Irwin Professional Publishing, 1994.
- Lynch, Robert Porter. *The Practical Guide to Joint Ventures & Corporate Alliances.* New York: John Wiley & Sons, 1989.

SUMMARY

Why buy a business when you can share one?

Good question, and it begs an answer before the buyer decides on the method of entering the very next market niche or before the appropriation is approved to develop the next facility, fund the next research and development project for new products, or buy the next business. All too often, the business owner does not even think about the creative ways to get to the marketplace other than buying a way in. While acquisitions are valid and often the correct way to go, they are not the only way. Surely, buying a business is not always the least-expensive or lowest-risk means of accomplishing the prime objective of the company.

Give due consideration to joint arrangements, which have almost unlimited forms by which two or more parties can come together, using the individual strengths of each other to wield strength in the marketplace of real power. Political, economic, and market pressures are accelerating globally. These pressures point many businesses toward joint arrangements in research, technology acquisition, manufacturing, distribution, and technical and repair services. Think about them. Talk about them. Do not allow the competitors to complete the best joint arrangements in your market niches.

CHAPTER 5

Selling Your Business

The entrepreneur is aging, either in years or because of competitive pressures, and is slowly coming to the realization that the baby nurtured for so many years should be sold. That owner may experience anguish prior to and for some time after the sale! It is not easy to pull out completely or even slow down via a check or capital stock received for the sale and an employment agreement with a buyer. The owner probably never had an employment agreement before. Employment agreement—just another legality to worry about. Just more restrictions to retard free-will–driven growth. Why have such a legal agreement now? Just run the business the way the new buyer wants it to run.

How does the owner face those loyal employees who stuck with the business when it was on the way up and/or down? It is a tough situation that can only be appreciated when you go through it. Well, many go through this wringer each and every year. Of course, some owners are not unhappy if the business is growing and profitable and the employees are benefiting. It is much easier psychologically to sell when the business is on the upbeat. Perhaps the owner no longer is challenged. The business may be easy to manage at this time. Alternatively, the business may not be so healthy and the owner needs help financially to keep it alive or needs more people power and market thrust to grow it. Whatever the reason, many owners sell out each year. Why does the concept of selling keep coming into an owner's head? A buyer should try to find out why. That would be a substantive accomplishment and key to structuring a good deal for both sides (buyer and seller).

HOW MANY BUSINESSES ARE SOLD ANNUALLY?

No one really can be certain just how many publicly held and privately owned businesses headquartered in the United States are sold each year in total. Further, some divisions of corporations and their product lines are sold without selling the entire corporate legal entity. Chapter 1 refers to official announcements of over 3,500 acquisitions in 1995, up about 170 percent compared to 1990. Those transactions averaged approximately $100 million each.

Best Guess

A range of 10,000 to 15,000 businesses and product lines of all sizes are probably sold each year. That guess is based on reported purchases of U.S. businesses by U.S. publicly held corporations and foreign-based companies, which probably represent about 25 percent of all acquisitions. One major firm of intermediaries with over 350 professionals has stated that over 35,000 businesses changed hands in a recent year. Perhaps, perhaps not. But whatever the number, it is large.

Small to Midsize

The vast majority of entities sold each year are small to midsize firms with between $1 million and $100 million in revenues. Prices probably averaged one to three times sales dollars. That multiple varies greatly with the type of business. Service businesses have different multiples than manufacturing businesses. To acquire businesses in this large, growing, competitive arena, the combatants need to understand what makes the other person tick. How does he think? What drives her? What are the person's sensitivities? Review these issues from the seller's perspective. You must understand them to be a successful acquirer.

WHY SELL YOUR BUSINESS?

Any one of a number of valid reasons may warrant the sale of a business or product line. Common reasons include

- Owner's personal situation may make selling desirable or necessary.
  - Owners who sell privately held businesses are often between 55 and 70 years of age and do not have a closely related family member who wants to or could readily become the successor/leader.
  - Some owners are tiring of the financial risk exposure caused by personal guarantees of business loans for working capital, facilities, and equipment needs. They want to "cash in." They are ready to convert the capital appreciation sweat equity to real, tangible capital realized in cash or a cash equivalent. They want to see richness in their personal lives through cash in the bank.
  - The owner may want to enjoy more tangible financial security and perhaps enjoy life a lot more.
  - There comes a time when owners wish to join friends who have already sold their businesses.
  - A new infusion of capital is often needed for working capital purposes or to keep the facilities, the equipment, and/or the research and development in state-of-the-art condition. The owner may be reluctant to load the business with debt or go on the line as a guarantor again.
  - The owners may not be mentally prepared to continue the battle of the marketplace due to competition or the litigious nature of the business. Perhaps the outlook for the business is uncertain at best.
  - The health of the owner or family pressures may be inhibiting effective business actions.
  - Estate planning may make a sale timely. Dividing cash proceeds from the sale of a business is much easier than dividing capital stock with attendant questions about controlling interests and the managing of the enterprise by one member of a family versus another.
  - The owner may want to start a new and different business.
- Competitive situation.
  - The historical competitors may be gaining market share at the expense of the business. This may be caused by pricing, quality differentiation, better service, and so forth.
  - New competitors may be entering the same markets on a global or regional scale armed with more than adequate resources to blow the owner out of the niche.

– Key employees may be leaving to go with the competition, to retire, or to change career directions.

– Newer technology may be a threat, and the owner cannot or will not invest to develop products and services with equal or better technology as perceived by the customers.

■ Pending income or estate tax law changes can present owners with better times to sell than other times.

■ Inability to attract and retain the right key people in the company influences the time to sell the business. Possibly a key manager just left for a super job at a competitor.

■ Desire to combine with a corporation with the financial and operational strength to speed the profitable growth of the business may encourage the sale.

■ Changes in the owner's strategic direction for investments due to any of the listed items or others are important.

■ The owner hopes to go into retirement with something to do at least part-time. For example, an employment agreement, negotiated as part of the sale, could offer relief but also responsibilities and meaningful work.

WHEN SHOULD YOU SELL YOUR BUSINESS?

Listen to Yourself

Always listen to yourself above all. However, when a reputable buyer asks to buy your business, you should listen. When that buyer's corporate culture is compatible with that of your business, you should consider selling. Be sure the buyer will treat each of your employees fairly. Then, when that buyer insists on paying you an unusually high price in cash or cash-equivalent securities, sell it! Make the buyer's day! Do not hold out for an excessive price. Pigs go to the slaughterhouse. A deal must be fair for all parties or it will someday fail regardless of price.

The Right Time to Sell

Mitigating circumstances may dictate otherwise, but there is a time to sell virtually every business. Finding the right buyer with a great offer at a later time when you may be more receptive may not be possible. Just as in telling a joke, timing is everything. For example, Japanese buyers have been purchasing many niche businesses at what are considered very high prices. The target businesses fit their long-term strategies. Real estate, certain machinery producers, electronic specialty firms, and a number of other specific business niches are just a few examples of areas where the sales prices at times were multiples of those normally accepted values offered by others.

Those buyers have been targeting niche market shares or prime locations or else they have other, as yet unknown, reasons to go beyond normal boundaries in pricing. Since the sale some buyers learned why the formerly reluctant seller sold. The price was just crazy. Why fight it? Let them have it! However, make sure no hitches exist or are built into the transaction structure. Then go for cash or short-term cash-equivalent securities, not junk bonds or promises that may end up in court before you can collect.

Consider the Usual Reasons to Sell

Here are four frequent motives to sell:

- The price ranges from super to OK.
- If you are ready to leave the business completely, you should sell. If not, think about it some more. You will lose substantial control after the sale, even if you have an employment contract.
- If the potential to grow your business is not good, you should consider selling. Otherwise, the real value of the enterprise will probably trend down. That is not to say that another owner cannot do better. You cannot or will not do better.
- You fit one of the categories cited earlier in this chapter under the topic "Why Sell Your Business?"

TO WHOM SHOULD YOU SELL YOUR BUSINESS?

Resolve the Question

The anxiety level of owners who sell their businesses is normally and understandably very high. That anxiety is sometimes a threat to getting a good price for the business. Sometimes the owner vacillates between selling and not selling for one or more years. Eventually the word gets out. This delay mode causes more confusion than is necessary or desirable. Try to resolve the issue of sale long before bringing in potential buyers. If a rumor gets out, even if unfounded, it will harm the value of the business. Employees and customers may depart.

Start the Sales Process Correctly

Once the decision is made to sell, find buyers who can and will complete the transaction quickly and discreetly! You must decide early on when to involve key managers in the selling process. If you inform them properly and involve them in the process, they may be very helpful in maximizing value to you and themselves. Try to convince them that you are committed to looking out for their long-term benefits and career success. If convinced, they will recover quickly from the shock of the sale, and their energies will return to enhancing the business. Try to find a buyer that will deliver on those issues and that also wants to preserve the management team and status quo of the employees.

Screen the Buyers

Naturally, everyone has different likes and dislikes, but clearly money talks and talkers walk . . . away from acquisitions. The best buyer may not be the highest bidder, but such a bidder is very appealing to most owners, unless the personal characteristics are unacceptable. Selling only a part of the business or taking in a partner may be attractive, since you sell only as much as you wish. The seller has much to offer, a fact that is not always appreciated by the seller. Buyers may want the patents, the copyrights, the trademarks, the technology, the black-box know-how, the managers within the business, the technical skills of the key people, and/or the market position of certain products and services.

Buyer's Credentials

The buyers who should be considered by sellers are

■ The highest bidder. Auctions are not always the right approach. Much damage can result from that process. However, putting that issue aside and presuming you sell in a professional way, the highest bid is usually the winner, excluding contingencies on competing bids.

■ The buyer most closely attuned to and aligned with the culture of your business and that of the customers.

■ A competitor. But be extremely careful how you approach the competitor. They may only want to look into your internal operation and walk away with more competitive intelligence and one or more of your best people. Then, too, the competitor may spread the word that you are selling. Your customers may well jump to the competition if they lose confidence in you, resulting in a fast loss of orders for your business.

Nevertheless, a competitor will want to lessen competition, and one way is buy it out of the marketplace. If that is, in fact, the buyer's motivation, the seller can command a premium price. That price probably will exceed any other buyer's bid. The competitor has more to gain in the future and can afford to pay more now.

- Companies that are not presently competitors but may want to enter the industry niche of the selling company. It is faster and sometimes cheaper to buy into the niche than to start from ground zero.

- Strategic investors and/or partners (foreign or domestic). Spend time trying to find who is targeting your industry niche. They may prefer to buy only part of your ownership initially or even on a long-term basis.

- A venture capital or financial investor, who might be suited for the purchase if armed with adequate direct funds or the ability to borrow on the strength of the financial statements with a leveraged buyout (LBO).

- Your employees, who may represent an excellent buying group through either an employee stock ownership plan (ESOP) or a management buyout (MBO).

SELLING TAKES POSITIONING

Divesting a business is mainly a negative issue. It rarely allows for enthusiasm to grow among the key people in the seller's company.

This may call for bringing in a third party to organize the sale effort and to place management in a better position to continue to manage and not start to look to their own good alone. The best situation would be for the outsider to weld the team together by demonstrating how the target buyer(s) can be even better owners for them as they continue to grow along desired career paths in the future. Clearly, a probable conflict situation is created within the company. Polarization of the owner away from the key people is not good during the sale and should be a prime enemy to combat at all times during negotiations.

Subsequent chapters of this book cover the structure of merger and acquisition agreements, which can be readily tailored to a particular buyer's needs and the seller's needs. One chapter covers the ways buyers evaluate sellers. Valuation of the business is too complex for many owners to do without professional assistance. Valuing a business is covered in Chapter 8 in this book.

WHAT SHOULD BE INCLUDED IN THE SELLER'S INFORMATION PROSPECTUS?

Each buyer and each seller is unique. In general, the seller should spend considerable time, with outside assistance if needed, organizing data about the business in a concise, but complete prospectus. Generally, the most desirable information to include is

- History of the business, including its founders and its evolution to today's ownership, size, and stature.
- Prime objective, also called the company's mission.

The prime objective has been described in one of the best books on strategic business planning and budgeting, *Strategic Planning Workbook*, second edition, as "a clearly defined, decisive, and attainable future for a business that is rooted in customer needs. A prime objective must embody a purpose that infuses all activities of a business."[1]

- The strategy plan to attain the prime objective and the tactics adopted to get there.
- The specific market segments and market share of those segments served, including profiles of major customers, geographical coverage, and product and service lines of business. Every business will have a base business on which the foundation of the company is firmly attached, unless the company is in transition. This base business should be described in depth. Other product lines or businesses should be covered as well.

Buyers will look in this section of the prospectus or in data provided for three of the six most vital issues in your business . . . **market share, market share, and market share.**

- The key personnel who will remain in the business, plus their ages and years of service in the company and in the industry. Buyers will look in this section of the prospectus or in data available for the other three of the six most vital issues in your business . . . **people, people, and people.**
- Revenues and gross profit dollars for major product and service lines of business for the past five years. Also list units sold for those lines for the same period.

---

[1] Adapted from case example copyright © 1993 by Joseph C. Krallinger and Karsten G. Hellebust, *Strategic Planning Workbook*, 2d ed., reprinted by permission of John Wiley & Sons, Inc.

- Revenues by major customers for the past five years.
- The technology stage of the main products.
- The company's underlying strengths and weaknesses.
- The basic marketing plan to be implemented in the planning period, including growth factors anticipated.
- The main competitors now and expected in the near to midterm future. This data describing competitors could be presented in summary form as shown in Table 5–1.
- The 5 to 10 major vendors and suppliers of raw materials.
- A description of the tangible and intangible assets included in the balance sheet and a recent appraisal of them if deemed appropriate.
- Historical financial statements including balance sheets, income statements, and analyses of cash flows for not less than five years with explanations for significant variations and changes.

Many buyers screen out potential sellers if gross profit and pretax income margins are lower than established hurdle rates. Reasons should be given if the selling company's profit margins are on the low side or are above average.

The cost of goods sold should be shown by the natural components of direct labor, direct materials, direct overhead costs, and the indirect cost components. Include percentages since all buyers want to know them.

Another useful schedule is one showing quarterly or monthly sales which may display seasonal or cyclical trending. Comparison of operating results with published industry statistics is also helpful.

- A schedule of the organization's key personnel chart similar to the one in Table 5–2, which lists key people by name and their staffs by number.
- List of current accounts receivable showing length of time outstanding and list of the largest customers for the past five years.
- Charts or tables of units and dollar sales and profits by product line.
- A forecast of basic financial highlights for at least the next three years by major business segments in the form of balance sheets, income statements, and analyses of cash flows.
- The historical financial statements, supplemented with a set of pro forma financial statements, if required to appropriately and accurately reflect the financial condition and results of operations.

The pro forma statements should show adjustments for unusual and nonrecurring transactions, especially those relating to owner's salaries,

TABLE 5-1

Competitive Profile of Krallinger Inc.

Background: An independent company founded in 1976 in Philadelphia. None of the owners are employed in the company. Key managers have been in place for eight years. Sales efforts are mainly Southwestern United States and Canada. New thrust noticed into Midwest U.S. and South America. All design and development is in-house. Growing in sales at double digits in each of past two years. According to Dun & Bradstreet and 10K reports, it is in excellent financial condition. Employs over 125 people.

Competitive Products	Company Sales	U.S. Market Share	Manufacturing Facilities	Distribution Strengths	Perceived Strategy
Indust. chem.	$10,000,000	39%	New plant in San Diego with 80,000 sq. ft.	Warehouses in Canada and Chicago. Uses two sales reps. Internal sales force totals eight.	Above-average quality, high growth in new products, and great service. Seems to be going after our Midwest customers. Prices are standard.
Aero. chem.	1,500,000	25%			
House chem.	500,000	N.A.			
Other	700,000	N.A.			
Total	$12,700,000				

Note: Sales figures derived from annual sales representatives poll held last May at marketing meeting. The numbers appear to be reliable as to dollars and share percentages.

TABLE 5-2

Key Personnel

Stockholders (Name them if limited in number)
Board of Directors (Name them)
Henry Competent, President

Chief financial officer: John Perrie (41/12) (39/9)	Vice president manufacturing: Horst Wilde (49/20)	Vice president marketing and sales: Meg Silmne
10 People	**103 People**	**15 People**
Controller—1	Direct mfg.—70	Direct sales—8
Cost accountant—2	Indirect mfg.—16	Sales agents—2
Tax director—1	Engineering &	Marketing and
Internal audit—2	quality control—6	advertising—1
Billing and payables—2	Purchasing—2	Order entry—2
Cash management and payroll—1	Receiving—1	Secretaries—2
	Data processing—4	
Secretary—1	Shipping—2	
	Secretaries—2	

Note: Numbers in parentheses are age and years of service in this industry. Numbers following positions are employee counts.

benefits, and expenses. Often, a large portion of such expenses will not be incurred under new ownership. A sample of such pro forma adjustments to the income statement is included in Chapter 8.

■ Inventory turns by product line or at least by raw materials, work in process, and finished goods.

■ List of major facilities, machinery, and equipment with an indication of age and physical condition.

■ Description of debt and bank credit lines.

■ Data on major contracts, commitments, and contingencies, including employees, vendors, and customers.

■ State and federal income tax returns. These should be available for the past five years, but not included in a prospectus. If the company has income tax fraud (occasionally by way of understated inventories or otherwise), the best action is for the seller to clean it up before the business is sold. Consult a competent tax advisor. Do not sell that type of tax exposure to a third party. Certainly do not buy that type of legal liability.

■ Visual presentation of a concise financial strategy planning worksheet. Such data is excellent, if included. The example in Figure 5–1 has been abstracted from *Strategic Planning Workbook.*[2]

HOW IS CONFIDENTIAL INFORMATION PROTECTED?

In all cases, a seller should not release confidential data to intermediaries, buyers, or other third parties, unless those parties sign a confidentiality agreement. Such a letter of agreement is meant to protect the seller from having sensitive and confidential information about the business's operations and financial condition to be seen by or given to competitors or unscrupulous parties who might use the data in a potentially damaging way. Sample confidentiality agreements are included in Appendix B of this book. Consult your attorney for the proper agreement to fit your particular circumstances and needs.

SUMMARY

There Is a Time to Sell a Business . . . Every Business

Age, the struggle, disappointments, and financial exposure push the business to the selling block. The business of selling a business can be mentally difficult for the owner. Employee loyalty and a family-type atmosphere may break apart when the new owner and new boss come in the door. Further, the seller has to eventually walk out of a business built on the foundation blocks that the owner installed so many years ago. Will the foundation of the company . . . its culture . . . change? What will the owner do in the future?

When to Sell

Many businesses are sold every year. Some are sold wisely and some are not. Some are packaged for sale, while others are just accidentally or intentionally put on the block without much thought and lacking an adequate supporting prospectus.

---

[2]Adapted from case example copyright © 1993 by Joseph C. Krallinger and Karsten G. Hellebust, *Strategic Planning Workbook*, 2d ed., reprinted by permission of John Wiley & Sons, Inc.

FIGURE 5-1

Financial Planning Worksheet

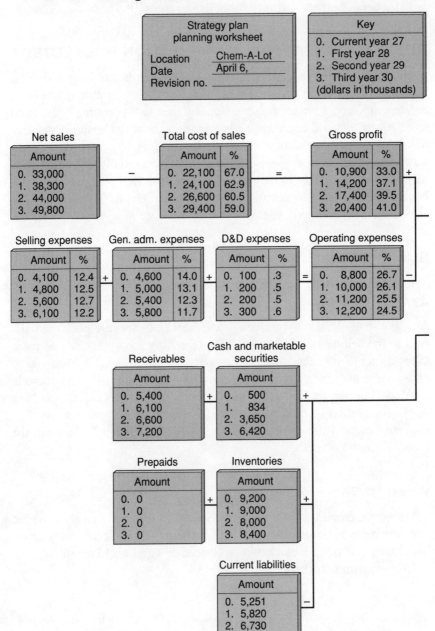

Submitted by

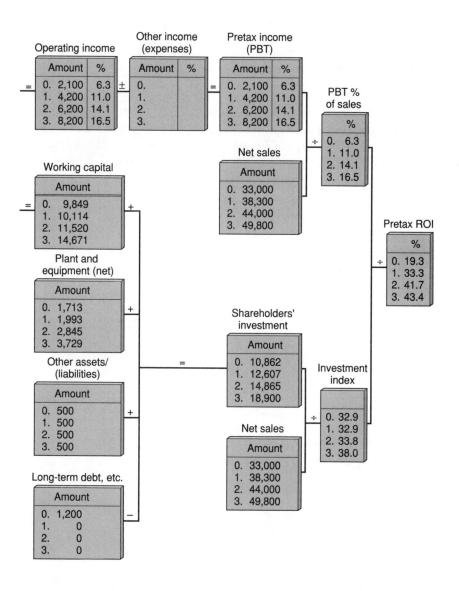

There is not always a clear answer to the question of when a business should be sold. Certainly a seller should not wait until the business experiences a leveling or decline in sales or profits. Even profit percentages going down with absolute dollar profits level or up is still a negative. It portrays a business niche in trouble.

The best time to sell is when the business cash flow and profits are peaking at an all-time high and are ready to drop, and a very willing buyer comes along. That is not normally the best time to buy. Yet a fair deal for the buyer and the seller can and should be transacted.

Selecting the Best Buyer

Selecting the best buyer requires evaluating the buyer's culture, reputation, financial resources, and plans. Presenting the buyer with an informative list or booklet of necessary information and data about the business is required to maximize the value of the business and to focus the buyer on the issues of consequence, presented in a good light for the seller, but also fairly and honestly.

Sell at the right time and the right price to the right buyer! It is not that difficult. You can manage that.

CHAPTER 6

Ways and Costs of Locating Businesses

BUYERS NEED VOLUME TO FIND THE RIGHT SELLER

Figure 6–1 depicts the effort needed to close on one acquisition. It is based on many years of experience and the experiences of many professionals in the field.

Volume Is Vital

Look at 100 candidates to find the right seller! Now, wait a minute! That is what every acquisition expert always tells me. What is the truth?

That is the truth—that is, unless a buyer already knows the particular company to buy or only wants to acquire a business in a very narrow product or service niche having few players. In that case, there may be fewer than 100 companies in the entire market niche. So try to buy a good, established business in that niche, but the odds are high against being successful in closing on one.

In all other situations where the market niche has many players, a buyer will need to put the search in overdrive and put patience in park. Good sellers are hard to find. Bank on it. The best companies are not for sale or will not readily admit to being available. They may be sold, but they are not openly on the market. These businesses do not have to be sold.

FIGURE 6–1

Deal Stream Statistics

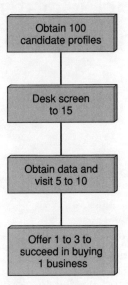

Screening Is Vital

A buyer should be prepared to do a desk audit of many businesses to find the right one. The trick is to keep the potential deal stream of candidates coming. Sure, go after specific sellers with a rifle, but also comb the entire territory with a shotgun.

Standard Industrial Classification (SIC) Screen

SIC code numbers and descriptions published by the U.S. Department of Commerce are included in Appendix E. Take time to review these. You will come away from that review with at least one more idea to pursue. Try to select specific classifications to help zero in on preferred business niches. That can speed up the process of locating a business of interest.

Get as many people as possible looking for the perfect candidate. If fortunate enough to receive many leads, the buyer cannot visit each candidate.

Manage Screening by Assignment

The buyer must have at least one very qualified and responsible person do the initial screening. This person need not be the dealmaker. This step is immensely important. Done correctly, much critical time is saved. Done incorrectly, many good opportunities are lost. Often the initial data received tend to sketchy, stilted, and sometimes misleading. Data are only as good as their source. A well-qualified and experienced person will be able to discern the good from the bad either intuitively or with a few incisive questions to the proper party.

Patience Is Vital

Be patient! Acquisitions are not meant to be accomplished in a week, a month, or even a year! You can buy a dog in the kennel on impulse and walk out the door. If you buy a business too quickly, you may have bought a "dog," but it will not bark, it undoubtedly will not be housebroken, but it will beg . . . for your cash flow for years. That type of dog may well eat a lot of food (cash) and return little, except on the living room carpet. The best people in the acquired company may walk out the door, leaving the buyer and the creditors stuck with a shell business. Such an acquisition almost certainly will not be a good investment!

BUYER'S APPROACH TO SUCCESS . . . STEP 1–DEFINE YOUR NEEDS

Do-It-Yourself Is Questionable

The do-it-yourself method is not recommended in locating candidates for mergers and acquisitions, except in those situations where you are only looking to buy or sell within an industry niche containing a very small number of businesses matching your criteria. Further, the sensitivities of selling a business are such that it is usually best to have an intermediary open up the conversation between the parties to avoid embarrassing the seller.

Do Not Buy Dogs

Companies known to be available for sale are usually dogs. These low-growth, low–profit-margin businesses are not the leaders in their market niches. Think twice about buying them and trying to turn them around.

That is an acceptable strategy in some, but not the majority of, cases. What areas should be defined in advance of starting the acquisition process? Here are the questions critical to success:

- Is there interest in turnarounds? A turnaround is a business with operating losses, negative cash flow, or marginal profits. Does the buyer have the management on board to accomplish turning the business around? Do not rely on the present management in the business to do it. They have had their chance and did not do it to date. Yes, they may have lacked the funds needed to accomplish the turnaround or have other excuses. Be careful; the missed turnaround may be a real miss and turn into a real mess.

- Do you prefer a business located in a particular geographic area for manufacturing, distribution, or service? Are shipping costs a factor? Will key people stay there or transfer there and remain?

- What customer profiles are desirable in a target business?

- What are the demographics? (Explain.)

- Who are the customers or what types of customers are desired?

- What gross profit margins are desired? What pretax margins are desired?

- What profit margins should the customers of the target business have? This is indicative of the attractiveness of the industry from a supplier's profitability view.

- Should you own or lease the fixed assets (real estate, machinery and equipment, and other capital items)?

- Do you want to acquire only manufacturing or distribution capacity?

- Is brand-name identification desired?

- Will you exclude tolling operations from acquisitions? These are job shops that have little or no technology of their own, but charge for converting the materials into a higher level of finished product.

- Are commodities not desired? How about value-added products?

- What are the minimum and maximum sizes of target businesses?

- What reputation in the industry would a target firm's products and services have? This can be checked with vendors, customers, a market study, and employees. The reputation of the acquiring or merging company will be affected by that of the target business.

- What market share and market share trends are desired? Does the buyer want a business that has share equal to or exceeding the nearest one, two, or three competitors alone or in total?

BUYER'S APPROACH TO SUCCESS . . .
STEP 2–GET HELP!

Do not try to buy or sell your business without seriously considering outside assistance. Going alone into the worldwide arena to find the best acquisition candidates is better left to the large corporations having the personnel resources and the established network within the industry. Yet, even the largest corporations often use third-party assistance to acquire or merge with other businesses. They also have the staff to accomplish that job. Depending on the seller's business size and business specialty, sellers should look for foreign-based buyers. That requires third-party assistance.

Finding good buyers is easier than finding good sellers. So, especially when searching for a good seller, enlist the services of professionals. The main sources in the United States to assist in selling or buying a business are

- You.
- Directors, officers (perhaps an officer directly responsible for the function), and employees of your company.
- An accountant for help in preparing historical, projected, and pro forma statements and analyses for either the buyer or seller. Pro forma financial statements are those prepared from historical book records, but adjusted for unusual, nonrecurring, or other additions and deductions. Financial projections may also require pro forma adjustments. Typically these show how a new owner might consolidate departments or divisions, change certain income and expense items, refinance the business, and so forth. Pro forma adjustments help the buyer and seller agree on what the financial statements would look like if the buyer owned the business and operated it in a more normal fashion.
- An attorney for advice based on experience and to assemble the acquisition agreement itself with its many exhibits and the documentation for the net assets or capital stock being sold and to aid in filing documents with stockholders and regulatory

agencies. Competent income tax and estate tax advisors are also required.

- Friends and business associates.
- Advertisements in *The Wall Street Journal*, regional and local television, and radio and news media.
- Trade associations, their journals, and the trade shows.
- Marketing and specialized industry consultants.
- Intermediaries, sometimes referred to as business brokers or finders.

Finding the right buyer or seller is not easy. It often is a tedious process taking up to a year or even longer. The best buyers are better known than the best sellers.

QUALIFICATIONS OF AN ACQUISITIONS (M&A) OFFICER

Title and Stature

Anyone in charge of acquisitions should be an officer of the corporation. The title will add stature in negotiating with sellers. Pecking orders still exist. A seller does not want to deal with a fledgling who is only digging up prospects, has no decision-making responsibilities, and may not be trustworthy with confidential information. Also, first impressions are lasting. The title may get the buyer's representative in the door. The challenge is to get beyond this introduction.

Common Sense, Brains, and Personality

The first person from the buyer's company who meets the owner should be selected carefully. An interesting person with a good personality who exudes integrity, a positive attitude, and good intellect is perfect. Do not send a "persona" without an individual character. Personas look and act alike. They have no identifying traits and characteristics that will intrigue, stimulate, and captivate the interest level of the seller. These are the types who begin by focusing on the financial numbers, talk totally about the financial aspects of the business, and end with numbers. These faceless personas forget to sell themselves and the buyer's company. They fail to really try to understand the seller's business as an operating entity with real people in it. They look like general ledgers with horn-rimmed glasses!

One thing the buyer likes to talk about is the business. Give the buyer every opening to do just that. Get to the numbers later. If a good rapport develops, the buyer will eventually shove financial numbers across the table for discussion. Then the numbers will relate to the preceding discussion or will look strange. If the numbers do not appear to tie in with the owner's preceding discussion of the business, look out. It could be a problem business.

Qualities of the M&A Leader

Each seller is different and has varying wants and needs. Therefore, the best person to find, negotiate, and close acquisitions would be a person who is

- Creative.
- A self-starter.
- Good with people.
- A possessor of common sense.
- Tactful.
- Inherently bright.
- Highly motivated.
- Able to perform alone.
- Positive and enthusiastic.
- Resourceful.
- Multidimensional.
- Professional.
- Responsive—acts quickly and completely.
- Willing to travel frequently and on short notice.
- Not too eager to do a deal just because the funds are available.
- Entrepreneurial—understands how entrepreneurs think as well as, what motivates and drives them.
- Intuitive.
- Able to second-guess the historical and projected financial numbers.
- Decisive.
- Intent on action.

- Self-confident.
- An independent thinker and doer.
- Able to develop excellent rapport with intermediaries.

The acquisitions and new-business-development leader must possess an untiring, dogged determination to get good deals done in spite of corporate bureaucracy, lawyers, and other barriers to success. The final touch this leader of acquisitions and new business development should possess is the ability to visualize the target business within the buyer's organization several years after the proposed investment. Some individuals have that ability and some do not. It is difficult to teach it. It is an innate sense worth a lot of money to the company who has such an M&A leader.

Credentials of the M&A Leader

The educational and job experience background can vary. One way to present them to a recruiter is given in Table 6–1.

TABLE 6–1

Acquisitions Applicant Credentials

Technical Attributes	Must Have	Prefer
Undergraduate degree	X	
Accounting/finance education		X
Strong financial background	X	
CPA certificate		X
Five years in industry	X	
Excellent analytical skills	X	
Above-average negotiation skills	X	
Extensive acquisition experience in diverse industries		X
Some acquisition experience	X	
Some knowledge of market analysis including ability to monitor markets, industries, and business trends	X	
Active membership in professional and trade associations		X
Middle-class background		X
Experience in family-owned business		X

WHO ARE INTERMEDIARIES?

Contacts and Time Pay Off

Intermediaries are third parties who spend all or much of their time calling on thousands of business owners every day. They help buy or sell a business for a fee. Some are very experienced in particular business niches, whereas others are generalists with broad industry background. Choosing the right advisor is key to efficient and well-executed acquisitions and sales. As in life, there are good and bad intermediaries.

Finding Intermediaries

How to find the right intermediary, also referred to as business broker and finder, is normally a matter of talking with other acquirers who have been helped by them. A number of books are published annually listing hundreds of intermediaries' names, locations, and any specialties. Interview them, ask for referrals, and determine if they appear to know anything about your industry niche of interest. If you are uncomfortable with the responses, go elsewhere for help.

Try all of the possible contacts at the same time in looking for a business to buy. Determine which will maintain secrecy best and be capable of selling a business. Often by chance, as a result of years of calls and letters, an owner will listen to offers if approached properly. Then, too, larger corporations occasionally sell divisions or certain product lines of their consolidated businesses. Intermediaries are often called at that time.

Types of Intermediaries

Intermediaries include consultants working part- or full-time in the acquisitions searches. They offer their services as

- Specialists working alone or loosely associated with others.
- Companies, departments of companies, or divisions of companies specializing wholly or partly in acquisitions. These firms may employ acquisition consultants, accountants, lawyers, and some marketing research people.
- Financial institutions such as investment banking firms and banks. Investment bankers offer suggestions on target businesses to acquire. They also have the capability and experience to help you

structure and finance the transaction. Commercial and private banking firms also are good sources for leads in acquisitions and generally will want to finance part or all of the transaction, depending on relative size. They expect a finder's fee for locating the right business.

- Accountants and lawyers. Accounting firms have the connections and experience to be of real service in finding acquisitions. Some have special departments solely functioning as intermediaries for a fee. Others perform the finder's function as an extra service to their clients in the hope that they do not lose them to competitors. A number of the larger public accounting firms have international presence in many countries for buyers and sellers looking for internationally based third parties. Attorneys often specialize in certain areas of law. Those in the corporate arena and those with estate-planning expertise can be valuable sources for leads.

References Are Vital

These professional intermediaries spend part or all of their time in acquisition searches. A word of caution: Not all intermediaries are as competent or as professional as you may need. They will all talk great and sound better than peanut butter and jelly. Ask them for details of their track record. How many businesses have they personally bought or sold in the past five years? Request at least three personal references and the names of two or more owners of businesses that they helped buy or sell for clients.

Remember, the person working on the assignment is more important than the name of the firm that person represents. Each intermediary brings different talents, contacts, and other resources to the table. Each advisor, personally or through contacts, should be able to present and deliver alternatives to you. These could include possible public and private financing, merger as well as buyout prospects, partners, possible employee stock ownership plans, and, finally, public and privately held buyers or sellers, as the case may warrant.

WHAT CAN INTERMEDIARIES DO FOR YOU?

In addition to locating buyers and sellers, you may prefer to have an intermediary also

- Assist in the evaluation and pricing of the business and prepare the financial information and other material in the prospectus or booklet describing the operation. Sometimes previously written-off assets or unrecorded ones come to light and should be included in discussions with buyers or included in pro forma adjusted financial statements.
- Negotiate the purchase price.
- Compare the sales price to similar transactions.
- Bring important issues about the business to your attention.
- Do none of the above.

Above all, as a buyer or seller, do not simply engage an intermediary by the name of the company he or she is employed by. Interview the actual person(s) assigned to your quest. Results are highly people-driven. Success often hangs on who is your representative. The fee will not change so get your money's worth.

WHAT DO INTERMEDIARIES NEED TO HELP?

Detail the Target

A detailed description of the buyer's or seller's needs and objectives should be available to the intermediaries to allow them to focus and remember more clearly. They have more than one client and can have trouble focusing in on a particular buyer's or seller's situation after the first meeting. The buyer and seller want to make the purchase or sale period as short as possible. How much attention is demanded and received depends on the track record of and the relationship with the intermediary.

Teamwork Is Essential

Work closely with the intermediaries. Insist they make on-site visits to all major locations on a confidential basis. They will become more knowledgeable about the business. They may suggest possible changes in site appearance. They may offer suggestions on who should represent the buyer at that particular site during buyer visits. And they will learn more about the wants and needs of the buyer or seller. Remember, a seller may want a king's ransom but may need shoes and socks and not own a castle. The particular specifications of the buyer and seller need discussion and analysis.

WHAT DO INTERMEDIARIES COST?

Fees Vary

Some banks, accounting firms, and law practices do not charge a fee for their services since they consider their introduction to be part of their service package. These professionals hope to be retained for professional needs. Others do charge fees. Virtually everyone else expects and deserves a fee. If the fee itself makes the purchase uneconomical, then you should not want to buy the business in the first place. Usually, buyers pay the fees due to intermediaries, but sellers may have agreed to do so.

Avoid incurring two fees (double fees). If two different intermediaries become involved, they will commonly, but not always, split a single fee on the basis of their efforts.

Retainer Fees May Apply

Some intermediaries request a retainer. Such fees are not customary. A buyer can contract to pay retainers on a monthly basis for one or more months. A retainer calls for the intermediary to allocate and spend a minimum of a stipulated number of hours a month searching for buyers or sellers. Retainer fee amounts vary and are quite negotiable, depending on what functions will be performed. For a seller, the fee can provide that a selling document is prepared by the intermediary. This avoids having someone in the seller's company get involved in a superconfidential matter. The law firm or CPA firm could also prepare a sales document or prospectus to retain confidentiality.

Usually, these retainer agreements provide that either the buyer or seller will pay a success fee if an acceptable buyer or seller is found and the transaction is completed. Success is defined as the intermediary introducing you to a party who ultimately completes a transaction with you for the business. Retainer fees are almost always deducted from the success fee of the intermediary.

Standard Fee Structure

Merger and acquisition fee structures are flexible but often will parallel the following fee computation referred to as the Lehman formula:

- 5 percent of the first $1 million purchase price.
- 4 percent of the second million.

- 3 percent of the third million.
- 2 percent of the fourth million.
- 1 percent of the fifth and subsequent millions up to and including $20 million.
- $1/_2$ to 1 percent of the balance, or agreement to some other fee for very large companies in the $50 million price range and upwards.

Some firms start the first million rate at 6 percent and use 2 percent of the fifth million dollars up to and including $20 million or so. Others ask for different rates of compensation as finders. Generally, you can expect fees that are not computed according to the given formula to average about $2^1/_2$ percent of the purchase price up to $20 million and $1/_2$ to 1 percent for larger transactions.

Computing Fees May Be Difficult

The computation of finder's fees deserves some attention. Frequently, the acquisition agreement will provide for earnout payments or other contingent and noncontingent payments by the buyer over time periods of up to five years and even longer. If so, the fee agreement should probably provide for discounting the future payments to a present value today. Alternately, acknowledge that the fees will be due to the intermediary when those contingent or deferred purchase price payments are finally made.

Other cases may call for royalty-type incentive payments to be paid to the seller for long periods of years. How will these be recognized between the intermediary and the other two parties to the acquisition? A definite understanding should be agreed to before proceeding with the acquisition.

Also, if net assets are purchased, are these adequately described in the agreement with the intermediary? Will liabilities such as debt be deducted from the price on which the fee is based? What if capital stock of the buyer is exchanged for capital stock? Will the intermediary agree with the valuation of the shares of stock, especially between privately held corporations with no publicly established and recognized value?

These fee-based issues should be covered in the fee agreement signed before the acquisition process goes beyond the initial inquiry stage. If a buyer tries to be noncompetitive on paying fees, the buyer will not get referrals first or at all from reputable intermediaries.

EXCLUSIVITY MAY BE GRANTED . . . AVOID TWO FEES

Sometimes the agreement with an intermediary will call for the exclusive right to sell the business for a period of time from three months to a year. Most intermediaries want such commitment, but few are lucky enough or good enough to receive it.

However, all contracts with intermediaries contain a provision that if a buyer signs their contract and they introduce the seller of a target company that the buyer purchases within one to two years after the introduction, then the buyer will be obligated to pay their finder's fee.

It is very important to keep accurate and timely records of who sent possible acquisitions candidates and to whom a fee would be due if the transaction were consummated. Otherwise, the buyer or seller may sign multiple fee agreements on the same target business and may fall into a legally binding trap of having to pay more than one intermediary and one fee.

Tell the intermediary why a buyer or seller, as the case may be, is rejected. Avoid signing a fee agreement with two different intermediaries for the same seller. That will probably cost two fees. This happens, but never should. Carefully document your search and contact base as to origin, dates, persons involved, and so forth.

BUYERS PRESENT YOUR NEEDS COMPLETELY . . . CONSIDER A SPECIAL M&A BROCHURE

As a buyer, prepare a brochure on the buyer's business and acquisition needs. An advertising agency can frequently assist in designing a great brochure just to be used for M&A. After all, the future of the buyer's company may rest on how successful the M&A program will be. In such a brochure explain why the buyer's company and people will be good for the seller and the intermediary. Include why the buyer's company is different and better for a seller than the thousands of others out there. The buyer must be convincing that the funds or securities to do the deal are available. Buyers must be convincing that they are prepared to move quickly and discreetly.

THE MIDDLE MARKET SIZE

The exact number of businesses with sales between $10 and $100 million (one definition of the middle market) is not known. An educated estimate derived from a number of database scannings indicates that the population of businesses in the United States is roughly 4 million corporations, 10 to 12 million sole proprietorships, 1 to 2 million partnerships, and many other informally organized businesses.

Based on the data available and using rules of thumb for average sales per employee, the author's best guess of the number of firms in the middle market is a range of 75,000 to 100,000. Whatever the real number is, an adequate inventory exists for buyers to locate, convince the owners to sell, and close deals.

NORMAL ACQUISITION TIMING

Seems Like a Lifetime to Buy Good Ones

Typically, it will take a buyer one year to find a good business of size—say, one with revenues of $10 million or more. Good luck, hard work, and the right connections with the sellers or their intermediaries will make the difference. Bad businesses will come to buyers much faster. Who needs a bad deal?

Small Is Not Always Beautiful

It takes the same amount of time to find, negotiate, and buy a little company as it does to buy a large one. Sometimes buyers should avoid the smaller ones and concentrate on one of good size with good management. Above all, buyers should not let money available for acquisitions burn a hole in their pockets and force the spending too soon. The buyer will tend to overpay or buy the wrong company. Both are big mistakes—pretty much unforgivable sins.

Patience Must Abound

Patience is a real virtue in the acquisitions arena. Only one out of 100 candidates will be for sale, be worth buying, and be sold at the right price for both buyer and seller . . . a good deal for both sides.

No Rules Exist

No firm rules or standards exist in the merger and acquisition field as to the time taken to find, contact, investigate, negotiate, and close a deal. Nevertheless, you should expect it to take no less than 2 months and as much as 12 months to start and complete a single acquisition. Although

TABLE 6-2

Acquisition Time Line

Procedural Steps	Time Line
Locate a good candidate	January 1
Initial visit	January 15
Second visit with operating personnel	January 31
Letter of intent and negotiations	February 20
Detailed due-diligence/purchase investigation	February 25 to March 31
Legal drafts by both sides, including exhibits to purchase agreement	April 15
Financing arrangements, as applicable	March 15 to April 15
Closing	April 15 to April 30

the actual time required to transact an acquisition will vary from company to company, a buyer can count on at least two months to over six months for complex deals.

Typical Time Lines Exist to Do a Deal

Assume a buyer strategically decided to acquire a business and has identified a seller. A fairly typical acquisition time line is given in Table 6–2.

RECOMMENDED APPROACH TO COMMUNICATE WITH INTERMEDIARIES

Specifics Accelerate the Process

To increase the buyer's efficiency when searching for acquisitions through intermediaries or otherwise, consider preparing the following type of informational data relating to areas of acquisitions. Being as specific as possible helps others and the buyer to better identify the types of target businesses of interest. Then, too, preparing the following information forces the seller to concentrate on the characteristics best suited for the buyer. There are subtle and not-so-subtle qualitative characteristics and quantifiable data that make a big difference in the attractiveness of certain target businesses. The following is a sample only. Prepare the lists more fitting to the particulars of a given situation.

Sample List—Acquisition Interest Areas

Specific characteristics of target businesses vary. The following list is simply designed to illustrate how to describe targets for a mythical company:

1. For currently owned businesses we are looking for businesses with strong brand-name identification. If the target has strong, well-qualified second-level management who will stay for at least three years, then no need exists for top-level managers to remain beyond the first year.

2. Our current businesses owned and targeted to expand by acquisitions having revenue volumes over $100 thousand and up to $100 million are

   a. Automotive aftermarket components for trucks and autos with distribution by jobbers and large chain stores. Sales to original equipment manufacturers are not desired.

   b. Machinery and equipment manufacturers for process and packaging industries, including controls and sensing devices, but excluding food and confectionery equipment.

   c. Health care services for home health care delivery, analysis laboratories, and doctors' offices. Production of high technology medical instruments is not wanted.

   d. Specialty noncommodity chemicals (manufacturing and/or distribution), with primary emphasis on industrial and hardware uses. Automotive niche is not of interest.

3. Freestanding or core businesses of interest are not included above and must have revenues in the range of $10 million to $100 million. Minority interest at the outset is OK if it leads to majority ownership within five years. The basic characteristics required for freestanding businesses or for an acceptable transaction are

   a. No unfriendly takeovers.

   b. Management with above-average abilities who will remain for at least three years.

   c. Manufacturers of products with gross profit margins of at least 35 percent.

   d. High market share in narrowly defined niche markets (prefer being in the top two or three in market share).

e. High-quality image for products and services as perceived by the customers.

f. No customer to represent over 25 percent of revenues.

g. Good cash flow generators with low to medium need to reinvest in property, plant, and equipment.

h. No capital-intensive businesses.

i. No turnaround business.

j. Consistent and profitable track record for the past four years.

k. Nonunion work force strongly preferred.

l. U.S. location of headquarters.

m. Mining and drilling of any type and agriculture not sought.

n. No business in or dominated by operations in less-developed countries.

o. No high technology products such as those in computer chips, biotechnology, and similar fields.

p. Sales to governments acceptable if not dominant.

q. International sales a plus if weighted to Europe and Australia/Asia.

One form for intermediaries to organize data for buyers follows

FIGURE 6-2

Sample Data Form for Intermediaries
to Submit for Business for Sale

Business Activity:

_____

_____

_____

Revenues by major product/service line

_____

_____

_____

_____

Patents and proprietary areas

_____

_____

_____

_____

New products introduced within the past five years

_____

_____

_____

_____

Marketing and Sales:
Profiles of major customers, types, and names

_____

_____

_____

_____

Major markets served—niches and geographic concentration

_____

_____

_____

_____

Method of distribution

	Percent by	**Percentage of Total**
Direct sales force	_____	_____
Distributors	_____	_____

Sales representatives   _____   _____
Other   _____   _____

Strategies for the markets

_____

_____

_____

Competition:
Names of top five and their market shares

_____

_____

_____

Market share of company for major markets

_____

_____

_____

Ownership and People:
Major stockholders and percentage of company owned

_____

_____

_____

Names and years of service in company and in industry for key people

_____

_____

_____

Evaluation of key people and their likelihood to remain with business

_____

_____

_____

_____

Total number of employees, union status

_____

_____

_____

_____

Facilities:
Major plant and office locations

_____

_____

_____

_____

Capacity utilization and condition of facilities

_____

_____

_____

_____

Major Vendors List:

_____

_____

_____

_____

Financial Highlights:
Balance sheet—attach for latest year and interim period
Cash flow analyses for last three years—attach

Anticipated capital needs for next three years:

_____

_____

_____

_____

Financial Highlights

Three Prior Years	Sales	Gross Profits	Pretax Income
_____	_____	_____	_____
_____	_____	_____	_____
_____	_____	_____	_____

_____

_____

_____

Next Prior Years	Sales	Gross Profits	Pretax Income
_____	_____	_____	_____
_____	_____	_____	_____
_____	_____	_____	_____

_____

_____

_____

_____

THE BEST WAY TO SCREEN ANY ACQUISITION CANDIDATE

Since a buyer cannot possibly visit every candidate for sale, the screening process is very critical to a successful acquisition program. How can that best be achieved?

- Get to the detailed numbers later. For now, screen each candidate based on whether the business has an attractive business niche. Why? What is the probability that the attractiveness will improve in the next three or more years?

- Next, review the nature of the target business and the competitors known to be strong in that market niche. Will the business be integrated into a presently owned business and be complementary? Will it be a freestanding business after the acquisition? Is it large enough to be freestanding?

- Are the profit margins adequate based on the past five years' operations? This is subject to a much more thorough review later if the target passes your other screening steps.

- Are the key managers going to stay after the acquisition? Do you want them to? Who is the driving force of the business? Is that person leaving? If so, the buyer may want to stop and find another business instead.

- Finally, if the answers to the general screening criteria are acceptable, set up a field trip to the headquarters for on-site interviews of the owner and key people.

The most important phase of acquisitions is to find the target business. The next chapter outlines the second most important phase of acquisitions—the due-diligence process or purchase investigation.

CHAPTER 7

Due Diligence—The Purchase Investigation

It's so easy to get burned when buying a small firm.

Barbara Marsh, The Wall Street Journal

WHAT IS THE *FATAL FLAW*?

Well, Barbara, you are so right, but it is just as easy to get burned buying any other size of firm. Getting burned will occur if a *Fatal Flaw* exists and it is not discovered, addressed, and corrected. A *Fatal Flaw* is any significant operating problem or market condition facing the target company or its product lines that, if not solved or properly addressed, will cause measurable harm to the business.

Internal *Fatal Flaws*

These should normally be easier to solve since they are more controllable than external flaws. These include

- Loss or impending loss of key personnel.
- Major pending or recent loss of one or more major customers.
- Financial crisis about to hit. This could include, but is not limited to
- Internal fraud.
- Uncollectible accounts receivable.

- Very slow moving or obsolete inventories of size.
- Major unplanned cost increases in inventories that cannot be passed on to customers.
- Need to replace expensive production equipment.
- Underinsured fire, theft, fidelity bonding, general and professional liability, and workmen's compensation liability losses.
- Understated liabilities, including product warranties, unfunded pensions, insurance claims, underfunded environmental remediation costs, and litigation.
- Unfunded calls for large amounts of cash from any creditor.
- Shareholder suits.

External *Fatal Flaws*

A number of problems for a business may exist or be about to exist in the marketplace. Some can be easily determined. Others are not as readily discoverable, understandable, or solvable depending on your knowledge base and the nature of the *Fatal Flaw*. In general, these include

- Technological changes in the marketplace impacting future sales demand and/or production methods.
- Changes in consumer/customer buying habits and related sensitivity issues.
- Foreign and domestic changes in competition. These may be increased due to differentials in tariffs, exchange rates, labor rates, taxes, and so forth.
- Unionization trends.
- Government regulations.
- Environmental concerns.
- Income, general business, and export/import taxation here and abroad.

Other crises and how to discover them in advance of buying a business are listed within the Due-Diligence Program in Appendix D.

WHY ARE *FATAL FLAWS* MISSED?

Falling in Love Too Soon—Alias Convert to a Believer Slowly

The heat of the hunt, the pressure of the deal, and the environment of negotiating on someone else's turf all present buyers with untold challenges. No wonder so many acquisitions do not live up to expectations. Horror stories abound even when the sellers did not misrepresent anything and answered all questions honestly. The buyers may not have asked the right questions. Possibly, the buyers were unfamiliar with the manufacturing processes, product costs, distribution system, competitive scene, fast-moving technological changes, or personnel problems. Some buyers are unable to decipher which answers received from sellers are incorrect and why. Some buyers do not know the important questions to ask. Some do not have a capable team (whether internal staff or consultants) to really do an adequate job of analyzing the target company.

Some *Fatal Flaws* Are Hard to Find

The due-diligence procedures can be likened to taking out an insurance policy on the transaction. The investigation does not guarantee buying a business without built-in surprises, nor does it guarantee obtaining a fair return on the investment. It will be only as effective as the buyer and the seller allow it to be.

WHAT THE BUYER LOOKS FOR

Fatal Flaws Kill

As a buyer, look for the *Fatal Flaw!* Where do you look? Search everywhere within and outside of the target company for factors that could and/or do materially influence the business.

Although a fairly typical due-diligence program is included in this book as Appendix D, here is a list of important matters a buyer should examine.

1. Reasons the seller wants to sell:
   - Personal wealth protection.
   - Need for outside capital to fuel growth or survival.
   - Burnout or frustration.

- Business no longer challenging.
- Estate planning.
- Health.
- Combination of several or all of these issues.

- Regardless of whether the buyer is or is not able to determine why the seller is selling, a prime concern should be whether the business is too mature. Are the products in the latter stages of growth? Are they in a stage or period of decline as to customer acceptance of their level of technology or usefulness?

Perhaps the owners are no longer interested in taking action to revitalize the business due to their age, lack of successors, or financial risks. Maybe the owners have lost their zeal for battle with the competition. Again, the owners may no longer look toward growth as a challenge, fun, and a goal. Growth might be an impractical target given loss of personal motivation. Owner family members might be bickering over how to operate the business or whether to sell it, or may decide to sell for a host of other reasons.

2. Character and capabilities of the people at all levels.

3. Appraisals of every officer and manager and the people directly reporting to them, by function, in order to assess the strengths and weaknesses of each functional operating and staff department. Were any key people promised ownership or other benefits that may cause them to leave if not received?

4. Level of decision making.

- Is it at the top by a monarch, by committee, or at the lowest practical responsibility levels (which builds good managers and employees at all levels)? Will the monarch remain? Is that person necessary?

5. Reputation of the company and its leaders in the industry.

6. **Market share, market share, market share.**

7. Complementary or supplementary methods of distribution and common complementary customers.

8. **Cash flow, cash flow, cash flow.**

- Cash flow generated and available to fund growth or be redeployed (free cash flow), if consistent and predictable, is an excellent and rare trait. To understand the individual elements of cash flow for each of the past five years is to thoroughly understand the cash-generating and cash-usage drivers of the business. These cash-flow drivers will affect the economic quality of the target company for years after the sale.

9. Low-cost producer.

10. Quality products and services equal to or exceeding buyer's standards.

 — The products and services may also be complementary horizontally (as with a one-stop shop having broad product and service lines) or complementary vertically (as in a business with value-added integration).

11. Ability to utilize or add to manufacturing capacity.

12. Proprietary technology, patented or not, and know-how.

13. Potential to reach the profitability targets the buyer has as a goal.

14. The company's track record of introducing new products timely and with good technology.

15. The current-year sales dollars that represent products introduced three to five years ago.

16. The number of customers representing 50 to 65 percent of the sales of the company for the past three years.

 — A good balance of diverse customers and a solid track record of repeat sales are good signs. Sales dominated by a few customers is dangerous. One or more customers may stop ordering. Also, some customers may not order products produced by the buyer for competitive or other reasons.

17. Territories representing the majority of revenues. Are those statistics good or bad? Does the seller dominate or control any major markets geographically? Does the seller's dispersion complement the buyer's?

18. The company's financial statistics compared to the industry's, to competitors', or to the buyer's own expectations.

19. Income tax fraud or other unrecorded tax liabilities and contingencies.

 — Generally, the buyer should walk away from situations in which the seller is or was prone to commit tax fraud or other questionable business practices. Buying assets rather than the capital stock of the corporation will shield the buyers from all or much of the otherwise adverse potential income tax liabilities of the seller.

20. Understated or unrecorded liabilities and contingencies including taxes, employees' costs, and contractual commitments.

21. Insurance costs for product liability and employee health care.

22. Litigation history and probability for future litigation.

These are not the only things the buyer is looking for, but they represent the initial issues that can make or break a deal.

HOW GOOD IS THE BUSINESS?

Buyers must view every acquisition candidate as having *at least one **Fatal Flaw***. The object of accomplishing a due-diligence purchase investigation is to determine the potentially ***Fatal Flaws*** and their possible impact on the acquisition or expected investment returns.

People Are the Anchor of Any Good Business

The business is only as good as its people. Good people in key positions will add considerable value. Buyers must spend more time in interviewing key people than in evaluating any other facet of the business. These key people employed within the target company know the strong and weak points of the business and represent them in the flesh. The points referred to exclude market weaknesses over which the people have little or no control.

Market Share Must Be Determined

Naturally, market share is vital. If there is too little market share in a specific niche, you can write off the business. What should the share of market be? Not an easy question, but some general rules of thumb follow. These are not from textbooks but were learned from observing many businesses over the past 40 years.

■ Assume the top three or four competitors in specific major market niches all more or less equally share 65 percent or more of those markets. The remaining market shares belong to the other companies, the largest of which has a 5 percent market share. The buyer of that business or any other with even less market share will have a real problem competing over time since the domination is too severe by the larger–market-share firms. Companies do not willingly give up market position very quickly, if at all. Taking market share will almost always cost a lot of money and take a lot of time. It is a usual goal, but one not often attained.

- Assume one company dominates the market with 50 percent or more of the market share. Unless the business you are targeting to acquire has something in the order of 20 percent share or better, consider passing on the acquisition. Or, determine how the target company will continue to exist profitably and/or grow profitably producing the cash flow levels needed to make the acquisition a good one.

Market Share Is Vital to Higher Profits

With market share comes tremendous power to beat the competition by being the low-cost producer (resulting in higher gross profit and higher operating income margins), offering better quality or improved service, and/or having more funds to reinvest in innovation, design, redesign, and research and development. Low market share held by a target acquisition requires special and considered attention. Study before you buy! It is extremely difficult to determine precise market shares—in fact, it is virtually impossible to be precise. Nevertheless, a fairly narrow range of market share can be estimated with much attention to details available in the market arena. Vendors, employees, available information from publicly held companies in the form of their annual and quarterly reports to the SEC, information obtained by professional market research firms, and a number of database reports can also be helpful. Manage the transaction. Take time. Be thorough. **Do not fall in love too soon!**

WHAT THE SELLER LOOKS FOR

The seller has a distinct interest in knowing a lot about the buyer or surviving company in a merger. The seller may be entitled to receive deferred purchase price payments, compensation, royalties, or other valuables over a period of years. Whether the seller can remain associated with, stay friendly, or rely at all on the buyer is important. Areas of interest include

- The historical evolution of the buyer.
- The reputation of the owners and their key managers.

- The synergy of the business fit with that of the buyer.
- The acquisition track record of the buyer.
- Interview some former owners of businesses acquired and determine their satisfaction level, and so on.
- Find out how many businesses have been sold by the buyer. Does the buyer have a reputation of trading in companies versus building them for the long term?
- Buyer's key people—quality and culture.
- The seller should interview current key people in the buyer's organization in responsible line and staff positions to sense their relative autonomy, their level of comfort, and the demands placed on them on a day-to-day basis by the buyer's top management or owners. Determine how control is exercised in operations via reporting and other standard operating procedures.
- Technical, financial, and managerial assistance available from the buyer.
- The business culture of the buyer compared with the seller's business and personal culture and that of the management and employees.
- Acceptability of compensation and bonus plans.
- Corporate charges or interest on funds assessed and deducted from the seller's prebonus profits for bonus calculations. Will such charges affect an earnout whereby part of the proceeds of the sale are contingent on future earnings or cash flow?
- The staffing of buyer's operations with union employees.

SPECIAL CAUTION FOR SELLERS OF FAMILY-OWNED BUSINESSES

If the selling owners are family members who clearly lack a competent successor to the chief executive officer (CEO) post, they have these options:

- Let the business continue on as is. If they do this, they might have to sell or dispose of it later . . . before it gradually or precipitously liquidates itself.
- Install a younger family member to replace the CEO who is aging. This step might or might not be a good solution for the long term, depending on the abilities of the candidate.

- Recruit an unrelated person to succeed the CEO. Employing an unknown outsider can be a high-risk move. Promoting an insider (someone who has at least worked for the company) might be acceptable, but it may accelerate the demise of the business or simply delay the inevitable decline of the business, unless that person is truly capable.
- Sell the business to the employees, to specific buyers, or to the general public.

Each option has risk associated with the decision. The correct choice is not always obvious to the seller. Knowing the seller's reasons for selling is critical to the buyer.

WHAT BUYERS DO NOT NEED

The areas to avoid or certainly to be careful about before leaping into an acquisition as a buyer are

- Low-growth, low–market-share businesses in markets that are not expanding.
- These businesses are beautifully situated to be eliminated from the market or at least reduced to permanent, very low profitability. They should not be bought or else should be bought for nominal sums. A buyer will have to invest much more than is reasonably predictable to keep the business alive and competitive over time. Although the opportunity may exist to buy a number of them cheaply in a highly fractured market, a buyer should consolidate their operations and have a mass sufficiently large to make a dent in the marketplace.
- Average- to high-growth markets are not as dangerous if the target business has average to high market share. This is especially true if selling prices in the market niche generate good profit margins.
- Dilution of earnings over the long term if a public company is the buyer.
  Dilution of earnings per share occurs when a buyer exchanges shares of stock for the seller's company or the seller's assets, and the net income from the seller's operations after the acquisition is less per share in proportion to the shares received than that of the

buyer's operations. If the acquisition will eventually result in increased net income per share, then the initial dilution may be very acceptable. The latter (a long-term approach) is commendable if the economics eventually pay off and the stockholders are in agreement. Preparing the stock market investors to expect such short-term decline with a plan for long-term increases in earnings and cash flow is a good idea.

- Unreasonably high growth forecasts on which the purchase price is based.
- The sellers or key managers "going to the beach" after the sale, unless planned.

  Regardless of how cheaply the buyer may think the acquisition was, if the key people leave the business or stop working effectively after the sale, the price may prove to be too high.

- A rush into completing the settlement and paying for the business before the purchase investigation is completed.

  Run, do not walk, away from deals that are being too hurried by either party or its advisors. A good deal can survive time pressures. Extend time lines so you can be comfortable with completing all pertinent and meaningful details. On the other hand, do not hold up the other party with minutia and truly meaningless issues.

- Lack of an acceptable exit on the way in.

  This means that the buyer should be able to realistically estimate downside risk before the acquisition. What are the odds against success? What are the ways to sell the investment in the near term and long term? Are there sufficient entry barriers for others who may think about coming into the market?

WHERE TO GET DATA ON THE SELLER

Numerous sources exist to locate information about the seller and similar companies. The most common ones are

- Companies themselves (if publicly held) via their annual and interim-period reports to stockholders.
- Competitors.
- Vendors.

- Customers.
- Distributors and manufacturers' representatives and sales agents.
- Trade industry association meetings, periodicals, reports, and trade shows. See *Encyclopedia of Associations* (Detroit: Gale Research, annual) and *National Trade and Professional Associations of the United States* (Washington, D.C.: Columbia Books, annual).
- Government reports or those filed with the government, such as annual reports and interim reports filed on Forms 10K and 10Q with the Securities and Exchange Commission. Also, *Business Statistics*, the *Census of Manufacturers and Census of Mineral Industries*, and other informative reports can be obtained from regional U.S. Government Printing Offices.
- Third-party specialists in particular market and operating niches.
- Marketing firms.
- *Encyclopedia of Associations* (which lists various associations by type, their publications, and other valuable data) and *Manufacturing USA* listing many industrial companies. Both are published by Gale Research in Detroit, Michigan.
- Research reports published by various investment brokerage firms.
- Standard & Poor's and Dun & Bradstreet, Inc., reports.
- Value Line materials and reports.
- Your local library, which may have some of these items and also local news media information about local businesses.
- The computer Internet with its many search tools.

HOW TO SCREEN OUT THE BAD ONES FAST

First Get Quantity

Buyers who are able to obtain a quantity of potential candidates are either lucky or very good at acquisitions. Finding a complementary business to acquire usually takes less time due to the focus than attemping to locate and acquire a business in an unspecified industry niche. Nevertheless, many prospects will be needed to acquire one good business.

Then Get Quality Screening

To be totally certain that a business is not the right one, the buyer should make a field trip to the major location. Too many times this trip is a wasted one. Few buyers have the time to spend on the road and in the air looking at each one of the population of available companies to find the right one.

Other than possessing superbly accurate intuition, which is very helpful if you are so gifted, the buyer should consider the following guidelines in the screening process. The assumption is that the buyer has obtained as much data as possible on the candidate from the intermediary or other sources of the lead and has signed a confidentiality agreement.

- Review the nature of the business and the industry it operates in. Are the product and service lines the type a buyer really wants? Does the buyer inherently or because of experience understand the market niches? Are they attractive? Is this a highly regulated industry and business? Are there too many sales to governments or to industries that are not of interest?
- Is this a turnaround situation? Is the buyer interested in trying to turn it around? Does the buyer have the time and the experienced people to do it?
- Why does the owner want to sell?
- Is management likely to be competent based on its track record of the past five years? Will the key people stay on for at least three years?
- Is the business technology-driven or market-driven?
- Is this a high-, medium-, or low-technology business?
- Who are the major players (competitors) in the market niches now? Who are they likely to be soon? Is the buyer comfortable with that type of competitive arena?
- Is pricing of the products likely to be commodity-driven (involving low gross profit margins)?
- Do sales and profit growth in the past five years indicate this to be the kind of business wanted?
- Do the gross profit margins meet minimum rates of return on investment?

After Screening, Visit the Seller

Given comfort as to these screening issues, a buyer and seller can proceed to the next level of negotiations and information gathering. This now involves a meeting at the seller's offices or at a mutually agreed upon confidential site. Sometimes additional financial and/or operational information will be sent by the seller to the buyer to further allow the buyer to come up to speed on the seller's operations and track record and maximize the efficiency of the purchase investigation procedures.

The seller must be prepared to clearly display and explain the cash flow attributes of the business to the buyer. Future cash flow of the business will permit the buyer to pay for the company and reinvest in it for its growth. How to best display this most important attribute is shown in the next section.

CASH FLOW IS NOT JUST SOMETHING, IT IS EVERYTHING

Ask any banker what single financial statement is the most important one to closely analyze before granting a large loan, and the answer will be the cash flow statement.

Break-Even Points Are Key Indicators

Another way to present the cash flow sensitivities of the business is to prepare a break-even chart. Such a chart is usually prepared on the accrual basis of accounting rather than the cash basis of accounting. Either one can be used with accounts receivable, inventories, accounts payable, and various accrued expenses being the largest factors that are treated differently in cash versus accrual financial statements. The following examples are ways to present such very important data to yourself, to your stockholders, or to any interested third party.

Standard Cash Flow

A typical cash flow statement is presented in Table 7–1. The cash flow should be available for the past five years and projected for the next five years. (First year projections should be made by month or quarter.) Buyers will look for how much cash has been needed or will be required for working capital and for capital expenditures. They will be interested in how much cash was borrowed and how many borrowings were paid off during

TABLE 7–1

Statement of Cash Flow

Net income	$100,000
Depreciation and amortization	10,000
Cash generated by operations	110,000
Additions (deductions) in cash resulting from changes in	
Accounts receivable	1,000
Inventories	−500
Prepaid expenses	0
Accounts payable	100
Other accruals	0
Discretionary cash flow	110,600
Other receipts (disbursements)	
Sale of assets	0
Capital expenditures	−5,000
Purchase (sale) of long-term investments	0
Net cash flow from operations	105,600
Financing and nonoperating cash flow	
Borrowing (loan repayments)	−2,000
Other—dividends	−500
Miscellaneous	1,000
Net cash flow	104,100
Cash beginning of period	12,000
Cash end of period	$116,100

the periods. Daily or at least monthly data must be looked at to see if loans are needed to fund interim periods. Finally, free cash available for dividends will be viewed as the acid test of the type of cash generator the seller is selling.

Standard Break-Even Analysis

Now look at a break-even analysis. Break-even charts are typically used to display the relationship among the operating revenues, costs, expenses, and net income after taxes. The charts are based on best guesses or approximations of the variability of various costs and expenses under different revenue streams. The techniques employed classify the costs and expenses as to whether they are fixed, semivariable, or directly variable with revenues (volume in units and/or dollars). The break-even point is that in which your revenues will approximate your costs and expenses resulting in no profit or loss. These are always approximations since certain costs and expenses are frequently partially variable and cannot be precisely estimated in advance.

In the example shown in Table 7–2, the assumption is that the cash and accrual basis of accounting will not materially change the resulting picture of the fixed and variable nature of the costs incurred by the business. For a more detailed discussion of break-even analysis, see *Strategic Planning Workbook* by Krallinger and Hellebust.

TABLE 7–2

Break-Even Point

Sales	$39,500,000
Variable costs:	
Materials	8,505,000
Manufacturing	12,407,000
Design and development	155,000
Selling	2,166,000
General and administration	1,051,000
Total variable	24,284,000
Contribution margin (38.5% of revenues)	15,216,000
Fixed costs:	
Manufacturing	3,618,000
Selling	2,829,000
General and administration	4,099,000
Design and development	0
Total fixed	10,546,000
Operating income	$ 4,670,000
Break-even point (Fixed costs ÷ contribution margin = $10,546,000 / 38.5%)	$27,392,000

Source: Adapted from case example copyright © 1993 by Joseph C. Krallinger and Karsten G. Hellebust, *Strategic Planning Workbook*, 2nd ed., reprinted by permission of John Wiley & Sons, Inc.

Calculating Break-Even Points

The break-even point is calculated by dividing the fixed costs by the contribution margin rate to give the dollars of revenues needed at the estimated level of fixed costs and margins to break even in profitability. See Table 7–2 for an example of how to determine the contribution rate.

Computing True Break-Even Points Requires Good Costing

The cost accounting concepts underlying break-even analyses are very important. If they are used to analyze the manufacturing or service operations of a target company, much about the sensitivities of the corporation's operations will be learned. A buyer must understand the fixed costs of a business at different operating volume levels before projecting the future profitability of that business. Whether a graph or a table is used to display the data is not important. That is a communication technique. The cash will flow differently at various volumes of operations; getting a handle on those flows at those levels is critical. The break-even analysis is a major method used to learn the numbers driving the business.

The data from Table 7–2 can also be displayed in chart form (Figure 7–1).

FIGURE 7–1

Chem-a-Lot Break-Even Analysis

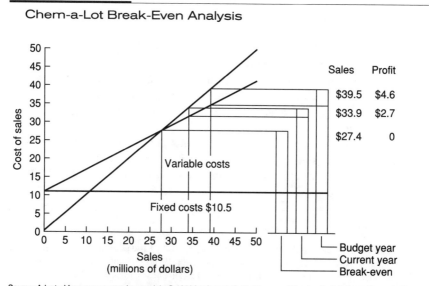

Source: Adapted from case example copyright © 1993 by Joseph C. Krallinger and Karsten G. Hellebust, *Strategic Planning Workbook*, 2d ed., reprinted by permission of John Wiley & Sons, Inc.

ACQUISITIONS—A RECORD OF SOME WINS AND SOME LOSSES

Let's examine the track record of acquisitions. Does the record reflect good or bad results? The statistics show a mixed bag of some successes and a number of bad deals for the investors and even for the sellers in certain cases. A bad deal for this purpose is defined as an acquisition that failed to ultimately reward the buyer's stockholders with acceptable returns on the funds paid or securities exchanged.

Acquisitions Often Cause Price Pain

One of the most extensive studies of corporate acquisitions was completed by Claudio Loderer of the Institut für Finanzmanagement der Universität Bern, Switzerland, and Kenneth Martin of the College of Business Administration and Economics, New Mexico State University, in a paper entitled "Corporate Acquisitions by Listed Firms: The Experience of a Comprehensive Sample" printed in *Financial Management* (Winter 1990). Their extensive research involving over 10,000 acquisitions, mergers, tender offers, and so on offers a solid base upon which one can draw conclusions. Their evidence coincides with the extensive and current field experience of the author of this book. Here are some of their findings:

> It appears that acquiring firms pay too much for large targets. Managers could be so fascinated by these acquisitions for the publicity they attract and for the challenge involved in closing these deals that their judgment could be impaired. (page 25)
>
> Large firms, for instance, seem to pay too much for their targets, and large bids seem to be overpriced on average. These effects are strong enough that, in the aggregate, corporate acquisitions appear to reduce shareholders' wealth. (page 32)
>
> On average, acquisition announcements depress stock values by $2.7 million. As a result, investors with the misfortune of holding portfolios of acquiring firms would have incurred a total wealth decrease of $13 billion between 1966–1984. (page 27)[1]

---

[1]Claudio Loderer and Kenneth Martin, "Corporate Acquisitions by Listed Firms: The Experience of a Comprehensive Sample," *Financial Management*, vol. 19, no. 4 (Winter 1990), published by the Financial Management Association, Tampa, FL (telephone 813-974-2084).

Manage the Transaction—Paying Too Much Is Bad Medicine for Pain

That heading is quite a summary of what the author of this book has believed in and has seen occurring all over the world. Acquirers are too eager to give away the store to grow by acquisitions rather than by internal growth. Sellers are only too eager to please the buyers by raising the price or having the price raised via the auction process. The latter process traps the buyers into giving away all or much of the underlying value difference they originally saw before the auction. This difference is the spread between the price of the target company on the public market or original target price by the seller and its perceived value. The understatement of the value gets corrected or even overcorrected through the bidding by aggressive buyers.

Other studies of consequence are contained in a book *Mergers, Sell-offs, and Economic Efficiency*. This valuable book uses, as a rich database, the Federal Trade Commission's line of business information on the financial performances of 471 U.S. corporations over the years 1975–77, linked to information on some 6,000 mergers and takeovers for the period 1950–76, and then uses 1974–81 divisional sell-off data. History does repeat its mistakes. The pattern discovered in the research over the years continues to prove that a *Fatal Flaw* seems prevalent in acquisitions and mergers. Here are some of the points raised in this book:

> Making a corporate acquisition is risky. After the fact, some acquisitions turn out well, some badly. There are things one can do to identify problems before a commitment is made, but often the pressures of time, competition, or acquired entity reticence prevent a thorough examination. Even when a careful pre-merger inspection is undertaken, some problems are so subtle that they elude detection. In many cases, they are not visible even to the incumbent management, and when they are perceived, there may be disagreement within the organization over their significance. Those who take a relatively pessimistic view of latent or newly emerging problems are not likely to be paraded before the visitors from a prospective acquirer. Would-be sellers naturally present their best face. (page 133)
>
> In at least ten of the acquisitions selected for our case study research, detectable latent problems unnoticed or unheeded by the buyer grew eventually to be a source of considerable distress. In eight of the acquisitions, including seven of the latent problem cases, subsequent bad luck, most commonly associated with macroeconomic events of the turbulent 1970s, contributed to disappointment and the ultimate decision to divest. Thus, if

one sought the simplest and most sweeping explanation of why our sample mergers ended in divorce, the answer would be: reality often falls short of anticipations. (page 135)

After merger, the acquired entities sooner or later divided into two groups—the sell-offs and the survivors. Our estimate of the sell-off fraction remains uncertain; a compromise between the solidly based extreme values suggests that roughly a third of all acquisitions were eventually divested, with an average lag of nearly ten years. For the divested entities, the story from an efficiency perspective is overwhelmingly one of failure. Operating income fell, turning negative on average in the year preceding divestiture. The reasons for this decline are not rooted simply in industry-specific problems. The fall was nearly as severe in relation to four-digit industry averages as in absolute terms. Our case studies illuminate the reasons. The targets were often acquired at or near a profit peak, and some subsequent disappointment was virtually inevitable. Bad luck struck frequently. But the fault was not only in the stars. The acquired entities often coped poorly with adversity because the new and more complex organizational structures imposed upon them slowed corrective responses and sapped motivation. Crises aggravated the organizational mismatch between parent and subsidiary and impaired constructive problem-solving. Although it is impossible to prove the counterfactual, the evidence points strongly toward a conclusion that the loss of control was worse under merger than it would have been in the simpler organizational structure of an independent entity. And in a smaller set of cases, organizational complexity and incentive breakdowns actively precipitated new problems, rather than merely impeding the solution of exogenously generated problems. (pages 192–93)

These findings indicate that the average acquisition, if not downright unprofitable, was not highly profitable. (page 207)[2]

These are powerful findings and represent worthwhile reading for those in business who manage, merge, and acquire and for the students who will manage, merge, and acquire.

Increase the Odds to Buy Right

To increase the odds in favor of buying the right company, the buyer needs to uncover the main reasons other acquisitions have failed within the buyer's company and the general reasons for failures by others. History can and does repeat itself, even in the acquisition game. Look for the *Fatal Flaw.*

---

[2]David J. Ravenscraft and F. M. Scherer, *Mergers, Sell-offs, and Economic Efficiency* (Washington, D.C.: The Brookings Institution, 1987).

WHY DO ACQUISITIONS FAIL OR DRAG DOWN THE BUYER'S BUSINESSES?

A sound way to avoid disaster in buying businesses is to review why so many acquisitions fail or do not achieve the goals set by the buyer. This happens, in spite of how well thought out the acquisitions seemed to have been.

Causes of Failure

Certain causes for failures in acquisitions apply to all sizes of businesses purchased, while others are more related to the sizes of the buyer's and seller's companies.

General Causes of Failure

- Overpaying is the worst and most frequent mistake made by buyers.
- This statement presumes that future growth in value of the target business will not overcome the initial overpricing. Optimism abounds in projecting revenues, profits, and cash flow. Too often, the buyer is even more optimistic than the seller about the growth prospects of the business and the industry. The latter situation is particularly in evidence when the target company is in a similar business or the same business niche. The buyer assumes too quickly and too often that he or she knows that business and is confident of being able to grow it profitably. But individual businesses have very individualistic characteristics, some good and some bad.
- The author's experience shows that related businesses after being acquired fare less well than planned compared to acquired businesses unrelated to those of the buyer. More time is spent on understanding the unrelated business, and independent experts are often hired to second-guess revenue projections, costs, and cash flow.
- Buying the wrong business is another major mistake.
- It may not fit well enough to produce the synergies expected in gaining market share at the expense of competitors, reducing production costs per unit, or increasing distribution strengths, among other issues. The buyer's managers may not know and understand the seller's business and market niches.

- The funding needed for additional working capital, property, plant and equipment, or research and development to attain the projected growth is too often underestimated.
- This is surprisingly true for a number of acquisitions of businesses related to the main business of the buyer. Why? Because that buyer may assume that all is known about the industry niche, the particular customers of the seller's business, or industry trends. Such a buyer falls too quickly in love with the seller's business (perhaps even with the seller). These buyers stop questioning and start buying before all important and relevant facts become known.
- The buyer's standard operating and reporting procedures are imposed on the seller's employees, are not understood, are not implemented fully, and may not apply.
- Are the buyer's proposed procedural changes necessary? Are they really important? Will the target business be better because of the changes?
- Some buyers insist on placing one or more of their own key people into top management positions of the acquired business.
- Lack of concern for the human factor in acquisitions is a sure way to fail quickly. You can buy or acquire assets, but you cannot buy people. You only rent people for varying periods of time. Treat employees with respect, deal with them honestly, and be aware of their wants and needs. If the buyer plans to place some people in the target company, the seller should be told before the company is purchased. Do not plan surprises. Plenty of surprises arise as it is!
- The buyer changes or standardizes the previously successful incentive compensation plan of the seller's company.
- Industry conditions and special circumstances of the seller's business may cause the buyer's standard incentive plans to become a negative influence. Unless the target business is to be completely merged into the buyer's operations, proceed with much caution before changing pay scales and incentives. They are supersensitive issues!
- The seller's product and service pricing policies are quickly changed by the buyer without sound basis or good communications within the company.
- The buyer stops the purchase investigation too soon.

- Perhaps valuable data are not found that would, if known, have changed the purchase price, caused a change in the other terms of the acquisition, or resulted in canceling the acquisition. Once again, falling in love too soon can be deadly!
- The financial statements and/or books and records of the target company were materially misstated prior to acquisition.
- Yet, these records and statements were influential in establishing the purchase price. If the financial statements were certified by an independent certified public accountant, a buyer might recover some of the price or loss in value from the auditor or auditor's firm. Another possibility is to attempt to recover some or all of the loss of value or damages from the seller, perhaps from escrow funds.

Causes of Failure When Buying Mid- and Large-Size Businesses

- Centralization of operating responsibilities is a real issue in acquiring a mid- to large-size business.
- Key people rarely want to give up responsibilities. They are especially sensitive to how their roles will evolve in the new organization. Perhaps some were promised capital stock, increased responsibilities, and/or higher salaries. They will become disgruntled unless the buyer discovers these issues and deals promptly and effectively with them.
- The buyer replaces one or more managers in the target company with the acquiring company's managers.
- If the people replaced were leaders and if they were replaced by administrators who lack human resource skills, the acquisition may not meet expectations.

Causes of Failure When Buying Small Businesses

- Buying a small business takes virtually the same amount of time and effort as buying a larger company. Legal and audit costs, finder's fees, and purchase investigation costs are proportionately higher as a percentage of the purchase price.
- Small businesses have small numbers of key people in positions of authority reporting to the entrepreneur/owner.

- After the acquisition, if the seller "goes to the beach"—that is, takes the proceeds and quits working or works less than planned by the buyer—the buyer will experience difficulties with the acquisition. A key person at the second level of management may not exist or may leave the company too quickly following the sale.

■ Personalities and business culture of the managers of both buyer's and seller's companies are found to be incompatible.

■ The buyer does not focus on or understand what made the seller's company successful and changes the way it operates to its detriment.

■ The buyer centralizes (takes over) some or all of the major responsibilities previously assigned to the managers of the seller's business.

- Will the owner and other key managers of the seller be left to operate the business as before the sale? Or will the buyer begin to interfere or take over all of the managers' roles?

- So what specific procedures could a buyer employ to perform a purchase investigation and find those *Fatal Flaws?*

SAMPLE DUE-DILIGENCE PROGRAM
AND SUMMARY

Appendix D contains the overall scope and many detailed steps ordinarily included in business auditing many acquisition candidates. To use a single, standard series of steps and procedures in the due-diligence process (purchase investigation) is not practical or appropriate for every investigation. Readers of this book are encouraged to change that program and tailor it to the particular business under consideration and review.

Above all, do not rush the process. That is not to say that buyers should delay and take inordinate amounts of time in completing the due-diligence program. If buyers dally, they may lose the acquisition to someone who is more motivated and more efficient in completing the considerable effort called for in closing a deal. Likewise, the seller must not inhibit the buyer's investigation, or the buyer may walk out and leave the transaction to a less-acceptable buyer. There is a time to buy and sell. That time is not always predictable. That time should not be unduly influenced by overly long delays in the investigation process caused by either party.

CHAPTER 8

Valuing the Business or Product Line

I do not purchase regret at such a price.

Demosthenes

REAL VALUES ARE THOSE TO WHICH A WILLING BUYER AND WILLING SELLER AGREE

Although buying the wrong business may be the worst mistake a buyer can make, paying too much for a business is right up there in severity. It is unforgivable. Losing the deal for a small difference in price is also not a great practice. Let's face it, the value of a business is whatever a willing buyer will pay to a willing seller.

How Do You Manage Getting the Right Price?

The right price is the price a willing buyer will pay to a willing seller. But that price varies since the same business will be worth more to some buyers than others. Also, its worth to the same buyer may vary depending on timing and other circumstances.

Prices vary because of economic cycle timing, stock market speculation, profitability, and pricing variations of industry niches as well as buyers' reasons for the acquisitions and sellers' needs. A seller's market share, cash flow, business outlook, revenue and profit growth potential, and personnel do impact valuation greatly. *No single factor or formula is always the right one or the most critical one to use in valuation of each business.* Only the future will confirm the wisdom of the transaction price and terms.

CASH FLOW IS THE ANSWER TO VALUE

Produce cash flow! That is what every buyer wants the target business to do. Predictable, positive cash flow is certainly a key area to investigate and analyze before deciding on a value or range of values for a business.

Consistent, predictable cash flow is not just something; it, rather than earnings per share, is everything over the long term. Earnings per share (EPS) is just a calculation derived by dividing the net income of a company by the number of common stock shares outstanding. Did the calculator use last year's net income, the last 12 months' income ending last month, or estimated income for the current year? However computed, EPS cannot be consumed, spent, or paid as dividends until converted to cash. Accounts receivable and inventories may be overstated, plant and equipment may be obsolete, and liabilities may be understated, but cash can be instantly checked at virtually no cost. Over a period of three or more years, the cash flow analysis will reveal telltale signs of strength or weakness. It is a simple and highly effective tool to assist your evaluation of the underlying traits of any business in any industry.

Cash flow may well be the best single tool or measure to judge the value of the company including its past and its future values.

Unrealized Appreciation versus Realized Appreciation

An increase in the underlying fair market value of an enterprise is one definition of unrealized appreciation in that asset. It cannot be realized until the business is sold or merged. The appreciation then comes in the form of cash, cash equivalents, and/or securities in another entity. Realized appreciation comes in the form of dividends or distributions from the entity during the period of ownership. Finally, the balance of appreciation or depreciation is realized when the investment is "cashed in" (sold or merged with an entity whose securities are readily tradable for cash). The time required to ultimately cash-in affects the present value of the asset based on the time value of money. The longer it takes to exchange the asset for cash, the less the asset is worth today. Interest rates used to discount the future values of assets often range from 5 to 10 percent depending on the risk level perceived to holding that asset until it can be realized in cash, net of any taxes or attendant liabilities.

How to Determine Cash Value

The change in the real value of a company or in the value of a share of common stock is nice, but unrealized appreciation does not buy the bacon and eggs for the table. The problem is how to determine or predict the cash value of a business at the time of the acquisition or investment and thus justify the purchase price. A few clues exist to aid in that judgment.

Clue 1. Check the Operational and Financial Track Records

How has the target company done over the years, especially in the last five years, compared to the other companies in the same business niche? Is the trend improving or declining?

Clue 2. Evaluate the Track Record

Evaluation of the success or failure of the company mainly involves an evaluation of management who attained that track record.

Personal evaluations of the management are mandatory prior to buying in, even if the managers will not remain with the business. If the managers are average or below average, can a buyer change future attainments within the business to a range of average to above average? Can an acquirer do better with the same management or with some changes in management?

Clue 3. Determine Market Share

How does the company's market share, with its related impact on costs and pricing policies, compare to market shares of its significant competitors? Has its position changed materially in the past five years? If so, why?

Market share is one of the tremendous driving forces causing the cash to flow fast, slow, positively, or negatively. Understanding the particular markets in which the company operates or in which it intends to operate is crucial to evaluating the acquisition candidate.

Do not acquire a business if sufficient data about the market niche(s) in which it operates are not yet available or cannot be obtained. The deal can be held off a little longer. Now is the time to invest in data rather than investing in a company whose market share position may be precarious. This bears repeating. **Wait for the market share data.**

Clue 4. Review Target's Planning Efforts

The current and prior three- to-five-year planning effort should be discussed and reviewed in detail. This includes strategic plans, business plans, and budgets of the company.

How did the company do compared to the past plans? Do the current plans appear reasonable and attainable? Specific valuations of a case study business are presented at the end of this chapter to illustrate the most commonly accepted and used valuation methods. However, first the subjects of market share, cash flow, pro forma adjustments to historical financial numbers, less-quantifiable valuation items, and price trends are presented. Since the specific valuation methods presented at the end of this chapter are quite encompassing, other methods more on the order of textbook approaches are not included in those valuations. One such method values a business by formulas starting with those in Table 8–1.

The purchase price is then estimated, which, when coupled with financial projections, will result in no less than a 15 percent return. The problem with this approach is not the theory. The theory is very accept-

TABLE 8–1

Investment Return Hurdle

Risk Base	Rate*
Risk-free U.S. government long-term bonds	3.5%
Inflation rate expected	5.0
Risk associated with the industry, say, medium technology	1.0
Risk associated with the company, say, average track record, average market share, but high debt level, capital intensity, no RD intensity, average-age facilities with average management in place	4.5
Other risks, such as amount of international business and currency exchange risks	1.0
Total return hurdle rate for business	15.0%

*The rates of interest on invested funds are simply examples only and are not applicable to any specific case. Use those that are appropriate for you and the economic times, but do not rely only on this method. Other suggested valuation methods are discussed later in the chapter.

able. The problem is in applying it to a specific business. How does one quite specifically determine the industry risk? The company risk? Other risks? Surely, economists need to keep these approaches in mind, but they do not acquire businesses. The acquisition team needs to use the valuation methods listed later in this chapter. Let's now examine the most important answer to value . . . cash flow.

CASH FLOW DEFINED

Cash flow is defined as the cash receipts and cash disbursements of the enterprise in a given period or periods. Positive cash flow results when cash receipts exceed cash disbursements. Negative cash flow results when the reverse is true and cash expenditures exceed cash income.

Basically, accountants, bankers, and financiers also define cash flow in various stages. For example, net income after all income taxes (known by many as the bottom line) plus noncash charges (such as depreciation and amortization of intangibles and leasehold improvements) are usually titled *cash flow generated by operations.*

Any cash used for working capital or generated by working capital is then added to or deducted from cash flow generated by operations to subtotal to *discretionary cash flow.* The term *discretionary* is used in the context that funding working capital (cash, accounts receivable, and inventories, less payables and accrued liabilities) is required to keep the business going. Discretionary cash flow excludes those expenditures for long-term assets such as machinery, furniture, and buildings since they usually could be postponed to a future date if cash is not available. From that discretionary cash flow subtotal is added or deducted cash used to buy property, plant, and equipment or derived by selling such assets to now subtotal to *net cash flow from operations.* Finally, any payments of debt or cash obtained by borrowing, cash obtained from sale of capital stock or partnership interests, and cash used to buy back such shares and interests are added or deducted from *net cash flow from operations* to arrive at *net cash flow.* Table 8–2 shows a sample format for a typical cash flow statement.

MARKET SHARE IS THE KEY TO CASH FLOW

In real estate one thinks of the three most important factors affecting ultimate cash flow profit . . . **location, location, location!**

TABLE 8-2

Statement of Cash Flow

Net income	$100,000
Depreciation and amortization (noncash charges included in the income statement)	10,000
Cash generated by operations	110,000
Additions (deductions) in cash resulting from changes in	
Accounts receivable	1,000
Inventories	−500
Prepaid expenses	0
Accounts payable	100
Other accruals	0
Discretionary cash flow	110,600
Other receipts (disbursements)	
Sale of assets	0
Capital expenditures	−5,000
Purchase (sale) of long-term investments	0
Net cash flow from operations	105,600
Financing and nonoperating cash flow	
Borrowing (loan repayments)	−2,000
Other—dividends	−500
Miscellaneous	1,000
Net cash flow	104,100
Cash beginning of period	12,000
Cash end of period	$116,100

In just about every other business the three main factors determining the cash flow and viability of a business are . . . **market share, market share, market share!**

High Market Share Drives Positive Cash Flow

High market shares in most businesses allow products to be produced with good gross profit margins resulting from being the profitable low-cost producer, or having the best-quality products and services, or both. With the volume consistently and predictably high, many other operating decisions become easier to make correctly. Spending for new or better technology and investing in more efficient production equipment can be accomplished by reinvesting profits. The best people will be affordable and can be hired to further increase market share or raise the barriers of entry for present or future competitors.

Yes, market share is most important. Market share will cause the cash to flow over time in particular amounts quite sensitive to the share when compared to major competitors.

Market Share Is a Power Base

If the top two, three, or four competitors in a particular market niche control 65 to 75 percent of that niche's market share, watch out! Unless each of the competitors has a nearly equal share and the target company's share is close to that percentage, living in that market niche will be very uncomfortable. This is especially true if one of the competitors is much larger than the rest or dominates. Then the buyer may wish to exit stage left. Try another ballpark!

Well, maybe the buyer could acquire a business or partner to strengthen the position in that market niche. These market share percentages are rules of thumb based on the author's experience, not on textbooks. They work.

Violating these rules is OK, just dangerous! Enjoy your business career, go for high market share.

PRO FORMA ITEMS NEEDED
TO DETERMINE VALUES

In searching for values within a business, the historical earnings, cash flows, and balance sheets are important. Assuming a single set of books of record, those are what can and usually should be presented to start the valuation process. Some companies have two sets of books, especially those in certain foreign countries.

The Old "Income Tax Basis" Routine

A sizable number of companies claim to be "on the tax basis" of reporting. This is intended to indicate that profits are understated via aggressive expensing of assets, lowering reported inventories, and accelerating depreciation or expensing of plant and equipment. Maybe so. On the other hand, these companies may not be as inherently profitable as sellers want buyers to believe.

Also, buyers should be aware that income tax fraud is not something to ignore. What should buyers do if income tax fraud is discovered during a purchase investigation? Tell the seller to correct the matter before you proceed if you are contemplating acquisition of stock rather than assets. Acquiring stock presents you with owning the problem.

Seller, clean up your income tax act before selling. Seller, do not ever involve third parties in your income tax problems unless those problems are clearly proper and debatable issues rather than outright fraud.

Case for Pro Formas

A series of adjustments is frequently needed to fairly present the values of the enterprise from different perspectives. These are commonly referred to as pro forma adjustments. Special or nonrecurring income or costs may have been incurred during a period or periods requiring at least explanations or pro forma adjustments retroactively to more fairly present the operations and financial condition of the company for applicable periods. Historical financial statements should be adjusted to reflect the quantifiable items. Both the historical and the restated financial statements should be available to all parties to an acquisition. Such restated statements are often described as pro forma.

Nonquantifiable issues or items also may be and often are appropriately disclosed. Both types are described here. Some have income tax ramifications, so a competent tax advisor is recommended for all acquisitions, regardless of size. Universally, the buyer will discount those pro forma adjustments proposed by the seller, and the seller will attempt to puff up the pro forma adjustments, adding to income to obtain a higher sales price for the business. Negotiations and an experienced accountant can be very helpful to bring the parties into agreement on what, if any, pro forma adjustments are appropriate for the particular situation. An example of such a statement is shown in Table 8–3.

MORE QUANTIFIABLE VALUATION ITEMS

Attributes and assets that may or may not be recorded at fair values or reflected on the books and financial statements include

- Debt versus equity ratio. Divide the debt by the stockholders' equity to see the percentage level of debt. This is important for financing and for deciding whether the price is too high if debt levels are disproportionately high.
- Ability to be a low-cost producer, given certain quality levels.
- Salary and wage levels compared to competitors'.
- Ability of target customers to grow.
- Ability of target customers to buy at right price. Some industries and some companies have higher profit margins and are able to and will pay more for the best merchandise or services.
- Quality and availability of suitable raw materials at the right costs.
- Ability to substitute raw materials.
- The right key people in the target business who will stay, if properly motivated.
- Level of gross profits.
- Level of selling and administrative expenses compared to others in the niche.
- Cost of employee turnover.
- Income tax loss carryforwards and income tax credits.
- Intellectual property such as patents and royalty rights. These may represent value to be received or paid over many years. They may be affected by terms, exclusivity, assignability, price elasticity, profitability, industry trends, and so forth.
- An appraisal of the assets and liabilities.

LESS QUANTIFIABLE VALUATION ITEMS

Attributes or assets that are not recorded on the books and records of a target company might include

- Special market niche penetration of products and services that may add pull-through of buyer's products and services.
- Special customer base or concentration of customers.
- Special suppliers or concentration of suppliers.

TABLE 8–3

Seller Company Pro Forma Income Statement

(Dollars in Thousands)	Per Books	Adjustments	Adjusted
Revenues	$10,000	–$100 (A)	$10,000
Cost of revenues	6,000	< –300 (B)	5,600
Gross profit— $	$4,000	–400	4,400
— %	40%		44%
Operating expenses			
Selling			
Salaries, wages, and benefits	1,180	–100 (D)	1,080
Rent	150	–50 (E)	100
Supplies	20		20
Insurance	20	–5 (C)	15
Advertising	50		50
Travel and entertainment	250	–50 (F)	200
Utilities	20		20
Dues and subscriptions	20		20
Maintenance	15		15
Depreciation	25	–10 (A)	15
Other	50		50

- Countercyclical markets.
- Level of gross profits.
- Level of utilized capacity of the manufacturing, research, engineering, and selling and administrative facilities.
- New products under development.
- Condition and location of facilities, including real estate, plant, machinery, equipment, and offices.
- Union versus nonunion work force.
- Value of present or future patents, patent rights, trademarks, trade names, and cross-licensing agreements.
- Special technology, black-box know-how, and similar items.
- Good name in the industry.

Total selling	1,800	−215	1,585
% of revenues	18%		15.9%
General administration			
Salaries, wages, and benefits	900	−150 (D)	750
Rent	160	−160 (E)	0
Supplies	30		30
Insurance	140	−10 (C)	130
Travel and entertainment	120	−75 (F)	45
Utilities	40		40
Dues and subscriptions	10		10
Maintenance	20		20
Depreciation	40	−10 (A)	30
Contributions	40		40
Director fees	30	−30 (G)	0
General taxes	30		30
Professional fees	120		120
Other	20		20
Total general and administration	1,700	−435	1,265
% of revenues	17%		12.7%
Total operating expenses	3,500	−650	2,850
% of revenues	35%		28.5%
Total operating income	$500	$1,050	$1,550
% of revenues	5%		15.5%

(A) Reduce depreciation to straight-line method from accelerated methods recorded on books and tax return.

(B) LIFO cost of goods sold is higher than FIFO cost. Adjustment converts to normal costs at FIFO.

(C) To eliminate life insurance on owner and insurance on cars operated by family of owner.

(D) Reduce owner's salary by $50,000 and eliminate family members from payroll and fringe-benefit plans.

(E) Eliminate headquarters, sales, and administrative offices' rent. Building to be sold with business. Sales offices in other locations remain leased.

(F) Reduce trips and entertainment.

(G) Eliminate family members as directors.

(H) Other expenses in research and development, amortization of goodwill from acquisitions, new sales brochures, heavy advertising campaign last year, and lack of prior sales price increase are not included above. An average 8 percent sales price increase will be in effect on January 15 with the range of price changes going from −2 to 12 percent. These should result in a weighted average rise in sales of 5 percent without unit increases, but are not included in pro forma income statement.

GOODWILL HAS NO REAL VALUE FOR PRICING

Assets minus Liabilities Are Rarely the Correct Value

Some buyers and some sellers attempt to value each asset and each liability on the balance sheet and look at the net amount (net book value) as
the value of the business. This is not usually appropriate unless the buyer
is buying only the net assets and not the future earnings stream of the
business.

In most cases, neither the historical cost basis of assets, net of depreciation and amortization, nor the replacement cost appraisal of such
assets is indicative of the real value of those assets to be used in the future. The buyer expects to mainly profit from the future cash flow generated from the sale of the products and services, not from selling the actual
property, plant, and equipment used in the production of those products
and services.

Soft Assets Are Rarely of Value

When looking at the balance sheet of the seller, the buyer must decide
whether the business is being bought for its net assets or for its future
earnings stream, which comes about when people use those assets produc-
tively for profit unrelated to the original cost or more recent acquisition
cost of those assets.

Of all assets on financial statements, be most wary of goodwill or
any deferred "soft" asset such as deferred consulting, software and organization costs, and noncompetition costs not expensed. It would be better if
so-called goodwill was not recorded at all or was recorded as a deduction
from stockholders' equity. Goodwill is the name accountants who never
ran a business give to the excess of the purchase price over the value paid
for other identifiable net assets.

Too often, income tax regulations and generally accepted accounting
principles, rather than good business judgment, are used to value assets in
an acquisition. As a result, a series of so-called intangible assets is
recorded on the balance sheet, and even sophisticated shareholders and
otherwise astute investors start to believe these intangibles have a value
beyond the income tax return.

In general, do not bother to revalue the balance sheet for most acquisitions, except to placate the accountants and tax attorneys. Spend your
time on what the true costs of sales are and what the future earnings capa-

bilities of the business are to generate profits and cash flow over and be-yond the needs of the business itself. Otherwise, how will you get your money back out of the business, except upon resale? Will the buyer have to invest more funds to grow the business after the purchase is completed? Does that mean the buyer paid too much at the outset?

DO NOT PAY FOR THE BUSINESS TWICE!

You pay once when the acquisition is completed. Then you pay again by reinvesting in the business to make up for inadequate working capital, necessary repairs, fixed asset replacements, payment of excessive debt on the balance sheet at date of acquisition, and so forth.

PRICE TRENDS

The problem with any single valuation method is that it may not be appro-priate for the business. For example, price earnings ratios (P/Es) are aver-ages quoted for an industry or for a particular sale of a business. Tables 1–1 through 1–4 in Chapter 1 list the historic P/Es for many companies in-cluding the Standard and Poor's (S&P) 500 companies for many years. In the case of the S&P 500, P/Es vary from a low in 1982 of 11.1 to a high of 26.1 in 1991.

P/Es Rarely Indicate Value

Historic P/Es may not be related to any particular business. However, the P/Es do show the stock market speculative approach to valuing publicly held businesses of size. Is it at all logical to presume that the P/Es reflect true value of a continuing business as the P/Es halve or double during the years? Hard to believe.

Financiers, stockbrokers, and various investors drive the values up and down in strange ways. This book and this chapter present some lasting methods to get at value, which should serve the buyer and seller over the long term. Only chance and a fickle marketplace may allow the P/Es to ap-proximate the real value of a company over the long term.

The public stock market values companies on a very speculative basis. That is why the P/Es vary from time to time and from one corpora-tion to another. So how does a buyer or a seller begin to value a business?

HOW TO LOOK AT AN ACQUISITION
AND WAYS TO VALUE A BUSINESS

One of the very obvious ways to price a business is to see how much a buyer can afford to pay. That is the limit. That is also not the best or only way of valuation. Fortunately, much more practical and economical ways exist to get a handle on pricing. To start, we need to understand why a buyer may want to make the acquisition.

Price Depends on the Purpose
of the Acquisition

Pay more for

- Buying market share.
- Raising the barriers to entry for potential competitors.
- Reducing the power of competitors or eliminating a competitor.
- Adding complementary products and services to a current business for vertical or horizontal coverage.
- Opening a new market for already existing products.
- Buying a low-risk, high–market-share, high–profit-margin, and predictable business with good cash flow.
- Buying production capacity or products to fill currently owned, underutilized production capacity.

Purchase Price Influences Relate to the Nature of
the Target Company

Price varies due to internal aspects of a business, which include

- Publicly held corporation with quoted market prices for its shares versus privately owned acquiring company.
- Quality and experience of the people and their expected turnover rates.
- Risk levels.
- High, average, or low gross profit margins.
- Predictable and consistent profitability.
- Commodity versus some technological product differences.

- Capital intensity (amount of facilities, machinery, and equipment) of the business.
- Nature of the customers: dominant few, good mix, government, international, and others.
- Nature of major vendors.
- Off–balance sheet assets or hidden assets as well as liabilities and contingencies.
- Turnaround costs and expenses required to make the transition to consistent profitability.

Some Purchase Price Influences Relate to External Economy and Market Factors

The business value will be affected by

- Market share trends and the target company's share.
- Size and strengths of the competitors.
- Barriers to entry for new competitors.
- Mature or old product technology (life cycles) that may not sell well in changing markets with obsolescence risks.
- Future growth of markets for target products and services.
- Recession in progress or expected soon.
- Inflation rates in material or labor content of products and services and price elasticity for major lines.
- Impact of supply and demand on unit selling prices for major lines.
- Interest rate trends affecting the business and its customers.
- Overseas foreign exchange rates.
- Government regulations.

WHAT ARE THE FINANCIAL GOALS FOR INVESTMENT?

Should a buyer compute the present value of projected net income and cash flow over future periods and discount them to today's values using interest rate assumptions? Some investors say yes and some say no. In every case, those projections will be an estimate with all the vagaries of the marketplace, domestic and international business, political influences, and so on. You should discount the amounts, since you may want to compare alternative investments (given limited funds) or to compare the likelihood of getting your money back versus the risk inherent in waiting longer for certain investments to produce the cash flow than the time needed for others to do so. Income tax rates, foreign exchange, and repatriation regulations influence the answer as well. Two of the ways investors often judge an investment are the payback and the return on investment approaches.

PAYBACK APPROACH

How many years will it take to get the purchase price back when comparing the purchase price to the cash flow generated by operations? That is the simple payback period. Not that the buyer expects cash flow generated to equal net cash flow available for dividends. It will not. Working capital, fixed capital expenditures, debt repayments, and other items are first deducted or added, depending on the circumstances. See Table 8–2 for an example of a cash flow statement near the beginning of this chapter.

Rule of Thumb for Payback Period . . . Five or Six Years

Investors have different criteria when setting minimum payback periods. Nevertheless, a buyer's good rule of thumb calls for the purchase price not to exceed five or six years of cash flow generated by operations. If the payback period is seven or more years, the reasons for the acquisition may include buying a competitor or market share now to be of benefit over the long term. Other long-term purposes may also be driving forces rather than instant financial gain.

Why Not Accept Long Payback Periods?

Long payback periods directly influence the level of comfort in forecasting. Why are seven years an outside number for payback?

Once again, there are no hard and fast rules as to the maximum number acceptable to investors. However, most businesspeople are comfortable with projecting the financial operations of a business for at least three years. They feel the numbers. Even for five years, the feel is more fuzzy and less intuitive, but the same businesspeople generally can offer projections for that period with an acceptable degree of certitude—not 100 percent accuracy, but within a range of accuracy acceptable to an investor. Now, looking six or seven years from today, few of the same people will want to hazard a guess as to numbers and market conditions for the latter years in those forecasts. That lack of comfort, the concern about an unknowable future, begins to solidify into "I cannot estimate those latter years with any degree of certainty." Who can blame them?

Yet a business acquired today is expected to be around for a decade, two decades, or even well beyond the lifetime of the acquirer's negotiator.

Therefore, if the buyer senses a long payback period (defined as approximately seven or more years), and assuming the other factors regarding the purchase price are not indicating otherwise, the buyer will probably walk away from the acquisition. Technology may change. Competitors do and will change. Pricing and profitability are and will be affected by many pressures and influences. The economy may cycle in and out of one or more recessions or depressions. Who knows what else might occur during the next seven or more years?

RETURN ON INVESTMENT (ROI) APPROACH

Return on investment is typically presented as a percentage. It is the percentage of the investment earned as currently generated income or capital gains upon sale or disposal of the investment divided by the initial investment plus future required investments to keep the business going and growing, and less dividends or distributions from the entity until disposition of the business or investment in it.

Numerators Used in ROI Calculations

Investors use different numbers for the income *numerator* to calculate ROI:

- Operating income before interest income or interest expense and before income taxes.
- Income before income taxes.
- All dividends and distributions received plus unrealized appreciation or decline in the underlying business.

Denominators Used in ROI Calculations

Some investors use different denominators as the investment base to divide into the income:

- Stockholders' equity or net worth (capital stock, contributed capital, and retained earnings).
- Stockholders' equity or net worth (capital stock, contributed capital, and retained earnings) plus long- and short-term debt.

Acceptable ROI Targets

Usually, the ROI figures in financial publications are computed using net income after income taxes divided by stockholders' net worth (equity).

Typical ROIs for U.S. companies frequently fall within the range of 11 to 18 percent based on net income after taxes divided by the historical stockholders' equity. In fact, the median ROIs (return on stockholders' equity) for the Fortune 500 companies and many others in the United States for over a decade typically range around 15 percent with a lower and upper point of about 3 to 4 percentage points under or over the 15 percent median, depending on the economy and the industry niche.

If a buyer pays more for the company than stockholders' equity (*net book value* and *net worth* are other terms used interchangeably), the attainment of the same level of ROIs is more difficult, given no added features to the acquisition.

Venture Capitalists' Targets Are Higher

Normally venture capitalists shoot for at least a 25 percent minimum ROI. Venture capitalists strive for higher ROIs through leveraging their investment and/or by structuring good deals for themselves that may or may not have attendant risk proportionate to their investment base.

Establish Your Targeted Minimum ROI

Long-term U.S. government securities' annual returns on investment range from around 3.5 to 4.5 percent over the years for virtually no risk, depending on inflation rates. Common stock annual returns average about 12 percent over long time periods.

Corporate acquirers of businesses hope to exceed the passive investment returns by a comfortable margin. Usual return on stockholders' investments in corporations in the United States fall in the 11 to 18 percent range, with many above and many below that range. Establish your minimum ROI target and have it approved by the shareholders or at least the board of directors.

HOW PAYING MORE THAN NET BOOK VALUE CHANGES THE ECONOMICS

One of the main common comparisons for publicly held corporations is to state the net income after income taxes as a percentage of stockholders' equity or net worth. Equity and net worth are also synonymous names given to the difference between all assets and all liabilities. Another name is net book value. Each term is used for the same items, and they are represented by the common and preferred stock, additional paid-in capital, and the accumulated earnings of the corporation, less dividends and distributions made to the stockholders.

Paying More than Stockholders' Equity Needs Thought

Figure 8–1 shows what happens if the purchase price per share for an acquired company exceeds stockholders' equity on a per share basis. This is usually the case.

On average, the larger companies in the United States tend to have annual net income in the range of about 11 to 18 percent of stockholders' equity. Therefore, if a buyer pays more than the equity amount (more than net book value), the odds of earning more than the average earned by the company increase against attainment unless special programs are instituted or markets change.

Look at Figure 8–1 and assume the company has net income of $24 per share and a net book value of $100 per share (24 percent return on net book value). Further, assume the company's shares are trading in the marketplace at a premium of 50 percent over net book value. Then the stockholders' return at the quoted market price is 16 percent ($24 per share divided by $150 per share net book value). If a buyer wants to acquire the business, a premium over quoted market prices of 25 percent to much more is often required to induce the present owners to sell.

Investment Returns

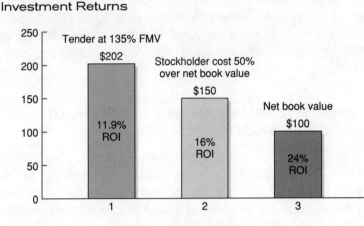

The average premiums over quoted fair market values before the deal transaction announcement in 1994 and 1995 were 41.9 percent and 44.7 percent, respectively, for those acquisitions announced. (See Chapter 1.)

The lowest average premium for the six-year period was 35.1 percent for 1991. If the premium is 35 percent over quoted market ($150 × 135% = $202.50), the return on that investment drops to 11.9 percent ($24 ÷ $202.50). Unless the buyer has programs or knows reasons for the net income to rise sharply, the return on the new investment, made by the buyer at a premium over net book value and over quoted fair market value, will almost certainly drop.

HOW USING LEVERAGE AFFECTS THE RATE OF RETURN ON AN INVESTMENT

The rates of return on an acquisition will vary for a specific investor depending on how the purchase price was obtained. If a buyer can pay for an acquisition without using any personal funds, that is the ultimate in leverage. Borrowed funds to finance the acquisition are referred to as leverage. Buyers leverage the net assets of the target company and the buyer's equity by borrowing on the underlying value of the target company's net assets if that value exceeds book value.

TABLE 8-4

Impact of Leverage on ROI

	Case A: Pay All Cash	Case B: Borrow 50%	Case C: Borrow 80%
Purchase price	$10,000,000	$10,000,000	$10,000,000
Equity paid in cash	10,000,000	5,000,000	2,000,000
Borrowings	0	5,000,000	8,000,000
Earnings before interest and taxes	2,000,000	2,000,000	2,000,000
Interest on borrowings at 14%	0	700,000	1,120,000
Income before taxes	$ 2,000,000	$ 1,300,000	$ 880,000
Less income taxes @ 40%	800,000	520,000	352,000
Net income after taxes	$ 1,200,000	$ 780,000	$ 528,000
Rate of return on investment—pretax	20%	26%	44%
Rate of return on investment—after tax	12%	15.6%	26.4%

Reducing Initial Investment by Financing Increases ROI

Since return on investment equals the income before or after taxes divided by the investment, reducing the initial investment increases the returns as illustrated in Table 8–4.

Assume

- Purchase price for the target business is $10 million.
- Income before taxes and before interest expense on funds borrowed for the acquisition is $2 million.
- Interest on purchase price borrowings is 14 percent.
- Federal and state income taxes total 40 percent of taxable income.

Conclusion of Some Buyers

Many investors are aggressive. If they have $10 million to invest, they may try to buy two or more companies or larger companies with the same base equity capital using leverage as the driving force for funds. Normally a higher return on the investor's capital occurs when investments are leveraged. This is caused by the added income earned by the larger business acquired exceeding the cost to borrow funds to buy the business, net of the interest expense deduction on the investor's income tax returns.

FINANCING THE TRANSACTION

The previous section presents the use of leverage on the return on investment. This section illustrates how the acquisition could have been financed as seen by a banker or other lender. Assume the purchase price is $10 million. How is the leverage possibly determined by the lenders? Cash flow should be the answer, but often the lenders look to the hard assets as a conservative lending approach. They do not want to own the business if the loan is not repaid. Rather, they will sell the business directly or liquidate its assets for cash.

Case Illustration of Leverage

The target company's balance sheet immediately before the acquisition is given in Table 8–5.

CASE STUDY: MACHINERY AND EQUIPMENT MANUFACTURER PURCHASED

This case study has been prepared to reflect the experiences of the author in valuing and negotiating the purchases of businesses and large product lines of all sizes (price range: $100 thousand to $175 million) in many industries.

This particular case example, including the description of the mythical owners, the business, and the financial numbers and statements, is not based on, nor is it meant to represent or portray, a real business. The case does include sufficient financial data created to make the valuation possible. The buyer also is assumed to have sufficient other important data concerning the operation itself upon which to judge the overall proposed transaction. The case should permit the reader to apply the same or similar valuation methods to real businesses being sold in today's and tomorrow's world.

The company has been a producer of machinery, equipment, and repair parts for the process oil, plastic, chemicals, and minerals industries for over 35 years and is known for high quality in the past, but with some old products needing future redesign and development to keep up with customers' current needs. Headquarters and plant are located in one city in

TABLE 8-5

Borrowing on Assets

Borrowable		Percent Leveragable	Amount
Current assets			
Cash	$ 1,000,000		
Accounts receivable	4,000,000	80%	$ 3,200,000
Inventory	2,400,000	50%	1,200,000
Prepaid expenses	500,000		
	7,900,000		
Fixed assets			
Machinery and equipment, net	3,000,000	30%	900,000
Real estate	3,400,000	70–75%	2,400,000
	6,400,000		$ 7,700,000
Total assets	14,300,000		
Less total liabilities	4,300,000		
Net equity (book value)	$10,000,000		

Sources of cash to finance the acquisition:	
Total borrowing	$7,700,000
Surplus cash in the business in excess of normal needs	500,000
Buyer's equity contribution	2,000,000
	$10,200,000

Uses of cash:	
Purchase price	$10,000,000
Closing costs (legal, accounting, broker, loan fees, appraisals, etc.)	200,000
	$10,200,000

Shortfall contingencies:

If we assume borrowing ability is limited to $6,700,000 instead of $7,700,000, the shortfall of $1,000,000 needs to be raised. Some of many options might be to

1. Have the seller take an interest-bearing note for $1,000,000 or more.
2. Pay the seller for a not-to-compete covenant for $1,000,000 and pay for it over the period of years covered by the agreement not to compete.
3. Sell the real estate for $1,000,000 over book value and lease it back, thus eliminating the $2,400,000 borrowing shown above.
4. Secure a loan convertible into target's capital stock or have warrants or options to obtain some shares later.
5. Create other options depending on sources of financing at the time.

the United States. Eighty-five percent of sales are shipped within the United States. Employees total 252 (for about $115,000 in sales for each employee).

Three major product lines are produced for markets, with different distribution systems for each. The company has been considering consolidating all into one in-house distribution approach with some outside sales representatives for smaller regions and special customers. The sales price of each piece of machinery averages about $24,000 but varies widely by product line. Gross profit varies by each product line.

In the past, as is somewhat typical of capital goods producers, sales have varied as the industries the company serves go into and out of business recessions. Historically, a four- to six-year business cycle existed from a peak in sales through a slowdown to another sales increase and peak. These trends are changing now and are less predictable, especially as customers consolidate by merger and acquisition, and as internationally based companies attack this company's traditional markets and vice versa. These trends were not obvious during the purchase investigation. Many times the trends will not be.

Using sales and cost information for many years will help detect fairly subtle trends in units shipped, pricing changes, loss of market share, and possible obsolescence. Use data for as many years as possible in analyzing the target. Most buyers do not but should do this. A minimum of five years is recommended for **unit and dollar** sales and related cost of sales **for each major product line.** Unit data can be a key to determining if the business has experienced real growth, net of inflation. Inflation can easily mask flat or declining sales trends. It takes a lot of time to obtain unit information, but it is worth taking the time. Some sellers say they do not have unit data. Yet unit data may be available in the records. Perhaps the seller never knew the importance of unit data.

The owners are 62 and 67 years old with no family members interested or qualified to manage the business. Age of the owners is relevant. At an advanced age most people will not be interested in continuing to reinvest in the business—their main or only asset base. They are more focused on estate planning and how they might spend their remaining years a bit more relaxedly and at peace with the world. Perhaps their lawyer, CPA, or other financial advisor recommended selling the business. Once an owner begins to think about selling, the concept rarely goes away. It intensifies.

As to this case, in recent years, capital investments by the owners were not really sufficient to keep ahead of the competition, but this was also not obvious during the purchase investigation. Such issues are rarely easy to discover at that time. Keep that in mind as you and your team begin to heighten interest in acquiring any business.

Experienced managers from other businesses owned by the buyer were assigned to the purchase investigation to cover marketing, manufacturing, technology, accounting, and taxation. A market research firm was retained to analyze the world markets, including the United States, to see if the buyer's and the target company's individual and somewhat different projections were reasonable for the next five years. The market research firm also studied other complementary businesses that might be acquired to strengthen the position of the target company.

From start to finish, it took two and one-half months to complete the purchase, including the signing of the purchase agreement. Times were planned carefully to keep a high touch contact ongoing among managers of both the buyer and seller during the negotiating and closing period. It was difficult to meet top management before the agreement was signed. The owners initially insisted on keeping their managers uninformed until the deal was completed. Many owners feel the same way. However, the buyer requested and was eventually permitted to hold a series of meetings with key managers of the target company before signing the purchase agreement.

Tables 8–6 through 8–9 show the financial statements applicable to this case upon which purchase price ranges are based. Those tables contain fairly typical financial data available from most sellers of businesses.

DETERMINING A PURCHASE PRICE

The following methods for computing fair values for a business cover pricing publicly and privately held corporations of every size. They do not cover those situations in which the liquidating value of the business is appropriate, where a quick sale is required for whatever the reason, or that include the sale of net assets where the inherent value is the value of those specific assets such as a sale of minerals or inventory prepared for shipment to the buyer. Those are special circumstances requiring special valuations that will be mainly dictated by the influences existing at the time of valuation.

The financial numbers upon which the methods are based are derived from those included in the case represented in Tables 8–6 through 8–9 inclusive. Price and value can be different. The buyer will pay the seller a stipulated price. Yet, the value of tax benefits related to the sale, the amount and timing of deferred payments, or the type of payment can

TABLE 8-6

Balance Sheet (000s Not Shown)

Year	Last Year	Nex
Cash	$ 500	$ 691
Receivables	5,573	6,300
Inventory	9,300	9,085
Current assets	15,373	16,076
Property, plant, and equipment	20,000	20,550
Less depreciation	(18,287)	(18,557)
Net property, plant, and equipment	1,713	1,993
Other assets	500	500
Total assets	$17,586	$18,569
Short-term loans	$700	$700
Accounts payable	3,650	3,694
Taxes payable and other accruals	1,001	1,568
Current liabilities	5,351	5,962
Long-term loans, etc.	1,200	0
Total liabilities	6,551	5,962
Stockholders' equity	$11,035	$12,607
Total liabilities and stockholders' equity	$17,586	$18,569

Source: Adapted from case example copyright © 1993 by Joseph C. Krallinger and Karsten G. Hellebust, *Strategic Planning Workbook*, 2d ed., reprinted by permission of John Wiley & Sons, Inc.

be taxed differently over time due to taxation laws in effect at the time, changes in tax rates, and variations in interest rates affecting the receipt of money (price) over a period of years.

Method 1. What Price Do the Owners Want?
Small to medium-size businesses are often owned by people who have a price in mind based on what they always dreamed of selling a company for, or what a friend sold a business for, or a multiple of profits in the best year ever achieved, or other reasons. That price is often unrelated to historical earnings.

Method 2. Guess a Price!
No need to comment, but sometimes it will be a good number!

TABLE 8-7

Comparison of Income Statements (000s Not Shown)

	1991	1992	1993	1994	1995	1996
Sales	$35,000	$36,200	$30,500	$28,600	$32,000	$39,500
Cost of sales	23,100	23,900	20,100	19,400	21,800	24,530
Gross profit (G.P.)	11,900	12,300	10,400	9,200	10,200	14,970
% G.P. of sales	34.0	34.0	34.1	32.2	31.9	37.9
% G.P. of 1991 G.P.	100.0	103.4	87.4	77.3	85.7	125.8
Operating expense (O.E.):						
Selling	4,600	4,775	4,071	3,650	4,100	4,995
General & administrative	4,600	4,775	4,129	3,650	4,100	5,305
Total operating expenses	9,200	9,550	8,200	7,300	8,200	10,300
% O.E. of sales	26.3	26.4	26.9	25.5	25.6	26.1
% O.E. of 1991 O.E.	100.0	103.8	89.1	79.3	89.1	111.9
Pretax income (P.T.I.)	2,700	2,750	2,200	1,900	2,000	4,670
% P.T.I. of sales	7.7	7.6	7.2	6.6	6.3	11.8
% P.T.I. of 1991 P.T.I.	100.0	101.9	81.5	70.4	74.1	172.9
Income taxes	1,212	1,234	988	853	898	1,744
Net income (N.I.)	$ 1,488	$ 1,516	$ 1,212	$ 1,047	$ 1,102	$ 2,926
% N.I. of sales	4.3	4.2	4.0	3.7	3.4	7.4
% N.I. 1991 N.I.	100.0	101.9	81.5	70.4	74.1	196.6

Note: Depreciation is $300 each year included in the numbers above.

Source: Adapted from case example copyright © 1993 by Joseph C. Krallinger and Karsten G. Hellebust, *Strategic Planning Workbook*, 2d ed., reprinted by permission of John Wiley & Sons, Inc.

TABLE 8-8

Statement of Cash Flow (000's Not Shown)

	1992	1993	1994	1995	1996
Net income (after taxes)	$1,516	$1,212	$1,047	$1,102	$2,926
Add—depreciation	300	300	300	300	300
Other items	0	0	0	0	0
Cash generated—operations	1,816	1,512	1,347	1,402	3,226
Increase (–), decrease in working capital	–300	1,425	475	–850	–1,875
Discretionary cash flow	1,516	2,937	1,822	552	1,351
Less capital expenditures	–300	–250	–320	–280	–299
Net cash generated or used (–)	1,216	2,687	1,502	272	1,052
Less dividends	–1,216	–2,687	–1,476	–250	–600
Net cash increase or decrease (–)	0	0	26	22	452
Cash, beginning of year	0	0	0	26	48
Cash, end of year	$ 0	$ 0	$ 26	$ 48	$ 500

Source: Adapted from case example copyright © 1993 by Joseph C. Krallinger and Karsten G. Hellebust, *Strategic Planning Workbook*, 2d ed., reprinted by permission of John Wiley & Sons, Inc.

TABLE 8-9

Break-Even Point

Revenues	$39,500,000
Variable costs:	
Direct material costs of sales	8,505,000
Direct labor and direct overhead	12,562,000
Direct selling expenses	2,166,000
Direct general and administrative expenses	1,051,000
Total variable costs and expenses	24,284,000
Contribution margin (38.5% of revenues)	15,216,000
Fixed costs	
Manufacturing	3,618,000
Selling	2,829,000
General and administrative	4,099,000
Total fixed costs	10,546,000
Operating income	$4,670,000
Break-even point (fixed costs ÷ contribution margin = $10,546,000 / 38.5%)	$27,392,000

Source: Adapted from case example copyright © 1993 by Joseph C. Krallinger and Karsten G. Hellebust, *Strategic Planning Workbook*, 2nd ed., reprinted by permission of John Wiley & Sons, Inc.

Method 3. Premium over Quoted Market Price for Publicly Traded Corporations

Over the years, certain rules of thumb are applicable to pricing publicly traded corporations. For example, in spite of normal price earnings ratios for the company and its competitors, shares of similar companies might be acquired by buyers at, say, 15 to 50 percent (sometimes higher). They averaged 41.9 percent in 1994 and 44.7 percent in 1995 over such quoted market prices.

It is indeed rare to be able to buy all of a publicly traded corporation's shares at the recent quoted market prices. Premiums are the norm. The premium depends on specific circumstances. Consult a financial advisor for advice appropriate for the circumstances.

Method 4. How Much and What Types of Debt and Other Securities Will the Cash Flow Support?

This is the wild and dangerous method frequently used by the leveraged buyout and junk bond investors who have no operating experience or expertise. How can anyone be certain the projections will be met or exceeded? This method is not recommended!

A number of lenders and investors will become sufficiently burned by overlending or overpaying and loading the business up with mountains of debt that will not be paid in full. Then this stupid method of valuing and paying for companies will diminish as it started to in the early 1990s when lenders began to have debt collection problems.

Method 5. Historical Price Earnings Multiple

	Net Income after Taxes	Factor	Total
1996	$2,926,000	5	$14,630,000
1995	1,102,000	4	4,408,000
1994	1,047,000	3	3,141,000
1993	1,212,000	2	2,424,000
1992	1,516,000	1	1,516,000
Totals		15	$26,119,000

Average yearly net income = $ 26,119,000 / 15 = $1,741,267
Price range = price earnings (P/E) ratio of, say 10 to 15 times the average net income which equals **$17,413,000 to $26,119,000.**

The number of years can be less or more than those shown. That is a matter of negotiation and is influenced by perceived risk. Financial newspapers do not usually present more than the P/Es for the year last ended (trailing earnings).

Method 6. Modified Historical Price Earnings Multiple

	Net Income after Taxes	Factor	Total
1997 (estimate)	$3,500,000	5	$17,500,000
1996	2,926,000	4	11,704,000
1995	1,102,000	3	3,306,000
1994	1,047,000	2	2,094,000
1993	1,212,000	1	1,212,000
Totals		15	$35,816,000

Average yearly net income = $35,816,000 / 15 = $2,387,700
Price range = price earnings ratio of, say, 10 to 15, times the average net imcome which equals **$23,877,000 to $35,815,000.**

This method adds the next year and deletes the earliest historical year, which would indicate a belief that the projected results of operations will be achieved in the coming year. If the seller refuses to use only the past for valuation, if the business is coming into a new growth period, and if you believe it, then there is merit in this approach.

Method 7. Last Completed Year's Net Income Multiplied by a Range

Net income after taxes for 1996   = **$2,926,000**
Price range of, say, 10 to 15 times net income = **$29,260,000 to $43,890,000**

This method is similar to that used in financial newspapers and magazines which show a P/E based on historical earnings of the year last ended.

Method 8. Historical Cash Flow Not Valued with Interest Factor = Cash Flow after Taxes and Adding Back Depreciation and Amortization without an Interest Factor

	Net Income after Taxes	Depreciation	Cash Flow
1996	$2,926,000	$300,000	$3,226,000
1995	1,102,000	300,000	1,402,000
1994	1,047,000	300,000	1,347,000
1993	1,212,000	300,000	1,512,000
1992	1,516,000	300,000	1,816,000
1991	1,488,000	300,000	1,788,000

Total for past 5 years = **$ 9,303,000**
Total for past 6 years = **$11,091,000**

The underlying theory of valuing a business based on cash flow is that an investor will not invest in a business that has risk, unless the investment can reasonably be recouped in less than six or seven years. Otherwise, the funds will be safer and produce adequate income if invested in government securities or less risk-oriented businesses.

Some sellers demand that buyers rely on future cash flow projections to price the business. This is dangerous. The buyer may end up paying twice for the business: once to buy the company, and again to finance the growth incorporated in the very same projections used to buy the business.

Method 9. Historical Cash Flow with Interest Factor = Present Value of Prior Earnings

	Historical Cash Flow	10% Interest Value, 1996	Present Value Cash Flow
1996	$3,226,000	–0–	$3,226,000
1995	1,402,000	1.10	1,542,200
1994	1,347,000	1.21	1,629,870
1993	1,512,000	1.33	2,010,960
1992	1,816,000	1.46	2,651,360
1991	1,788,000	1.61	2,878,680

This valuation method is similar to method 8 except for the interest factor. It is used by those buyers who rely heavily on cash flow and who will not invest in businesses with risk, unless the purchase price is recouped in under six or seven years. Sellers would want to persuade such buyers to use higher interest rates to roll the prior years' cash flow numbers to today's or use higher projected cash flow numbers.

At the end of 1996, the present value of the past five and six years' cash flow, had it been invested at 10 percent per year compounded, would have been

5 years ended 1996 = **$11,060,400**
6 years ended 1996 = **$13,939,100**

Therefore, you could assess the fair market value of the business from historical cash flow to be in the range of $11 to $14 million. The interest rate used normally would be that which could have been obtained on invested funds during the periods generated. Different experts use different rates at various times. Use one that makes sense to you. The number of years of cash flow used to determine values by this method is also very debatable. However, most buyers will not compute values with more than five or six years based on the risk factors associated with longer periods of time. Seven years normally connotes a stable, predictable business, whereas use of less than five years would indicate a higher degree of risk in the future of the business. On the other hand, many will argue for value to be based on the future, even though the future is nebulous.

Method 10. Projected Cash Flow to Be Received Discounted at Hurdle Rate Assuming $25 Million Acquisition Price

This method projects the cash flow of the business operations for a series of years (as many as you believe can reasonably be estimated accurately) and then assumes a resale of the business at the end of those years. All amounts are then discounted to the present using one of several rates of interest.

In this example, we use the buyer's hurdle rate of 17 percent (the rate below which the buyer would not invest in risk securities or businesses). If the discounted stream of cash flow realized exceeds the initial investment, the opportunity qualifies for consideration from a financial return standpoint.

How do you set hurdle rates? Investors settle on them based on investment risk, alternate investment opportunities, time needed to realize an adequate return, cost of capital (generally the lowest return usable), and/or shareholders' expected returns. Investors use different rates. Use the hurdle rate that makes sense to you. Assume the following dividends are received to the date of reselling the business at the end of 1995 for $60 million.

	Projected Cash Dividends	17% Hurdle Rate	Present Value Cash Flow
1997	$1,226,000	.86	$1,054,000
1998	1,400,000	.73	1,022,000
1999	2,000,000	.62	1,240,000
2000	2,500,000	.53	1,325,000
2001	3,100,000	.46	1,426,000
2002	3,900,000	.39	1,521,000
Total			$7,588,000

Present value on January 1, 1997, from sale of business on December 31, 2002, equals

Gross sales price	$60,000,000
Less acquisition price January 1, 1997	−25,000,000
Less amounts reinvested in business which increases the tax basis	−10,000,000
Taxable gain	$25,000,000
Capital gain taxes of, say, 35%	8,750,000
Sales price on December 31, 2002 of $60,000,000 less capital gains taxes of $8,750,000	$51,250,000
Present value January 1, 1997 discounted six years at 17% investment hurdle rate	$19,979,000
Present value of dividends received (see dividends received table)	7,588,000
Total cash projected, discounted to January 1, 1997, at hurdle rate	$27,567,000
Purchase price, January 1, 1997	25,000,000
Excess cash over purchase price	$ 2,567,000

Since the proceeds received in today's dollars (discounted by the investment rate of 17 percent) are projected to exceed the investment cost (by about 10 percent), the acquisition passes the financial constraints established to screen opportunities. The estimated internal rate of return (IRR) on the investment, which is the interest rate that will discount all cash flows to the exact purchase price, is 19.2 percent in this example.

IRRs are most commonly used to measure real estate investment returns; projected returns on property, plant, and equipment; and capital appropriation requests and evaluations of them. Nonetheless, the same theory is applicable to valuations of target businesses.

Method 11. Projected Cash Flow (Gross and Discounted)

The discounted cash flow (DCF) valuation method, a popular method today, takes into account the amount of cash that has been generated (historical) or may be expected to be generated by the business. See prior examples in this chapter of historical cash flow valuation methods for an explanation of why buyers often limit acquisition pricing to the computed value of less than six or seven years of cash flow.

Any projections included in the final valuations showing long periods exceeding your comfort level or those over six or seven years to recover the investment and produce an average rate of return increase the risk. Future results of operations may well vary materially from the historical results. If a longer period would be expected, many buyers decline to invest in the business with its unknown risk.

	Projected Cash Flow	Interest Rate	Present Value Cash Flow
1997	$3,400,000	.91	$3,094,000
1998	4,000,000	.83	3,320,000
1999	4,500,000	.75	3,375,000
2000	5,100,000	.68	3,468,000
2001	5,900,000	.62	3,658,000
2002	6,000,000	.56	3,360,000

In this example, the DCF for the five years ending 2001 using a 10 percent interest rate is $16,915,000 and for the six years ending 2002 is $20,275,000. Also, if a 15 percent interest rate is used to discount the future cash flows to today's values, the present value is $14,789,000 for the five years and $17,383,000 for the six years ending 2002. Some buyers use rates of return on equity that the buyer or seller experienced or that are similar to competitors' returns to calculate such present values.

Quite a difference exists between the projected cash flow method and the historical valuation method used in the preceding example. Which one should you use? Are you buying or selling? Who knows? The marketplace will set the pace. Then, too, this method is only one of many you should use in the process of valuation. You should use the most logical one for the circumstances. Remember, the projections are just that—projections, not reality. You are not calculating a known result. Precision is not the object since the basic numbers are unknown. Use of more than one valuation model will insulate you from selecting the wrong one and will afford a realistic range of values.

Also, some investors do not use any discount to compute cash flow values as of the present time. They simply look to the projected cash flows and see how many years it would take to pay the investment back without discounting the amounts. If it is over six years, they may not invest.

Method 12. Projected Return on Investment
People in different companies define rates of returns on investments differently. Some compare realized returns on investments (dividends) and unrealized appreciation or decline in the value of the investments to their original cost and subsequent investments at cost, less dividends and other distributions. This is referred to as the investment-at-cost method. This is a cost accounting approach.

Others compare the realized and unrealized amounts to the changing fair market value of the investment without regard to the cost basis of the investment. This method is an investment portfolio approach used for valuing and trading stocks and bonds in a personal or corporate portfolio.

It is the fair-market-value method. Then, too, some investors compare the described returns to their invested assets (return on assets). This latter method is not recommended in valuing businesses since the depreciation methods used by businesses are highly judgmental and vary within a corporation and from industry to industry.

The investment-at-cost method and the fair-market-value method are presented in Table 8–10. Assume the purchase price asked is $20 million at the beginning of year 1. Note how the returns vary. Each method is valid. Again, use of more than one or two methods to derive a range of values for a business is highly recommended.

The investment at cost in Table 8–10 reflects dividends each year exactly equal to reinvestments for working capital. ROI for the fair market value method equals fair market value at the end of a year plus dividends received during that year, less fair market value as of the beginning of the year, divided by fair market value as of the beginning of the year. The weighted averages of these figures could be used if materially different from month to month. ROI on the cost method in Table 8–10 equals the increase or decrease in the fair market value during the year plus dividends, divided by the cumulative cost basis (original cost basis of the investments made less dividends and distributions), at the beginning of the year. The weighted averages of these figures could be used if materially different from month to month.

Method 13. Stockholders' Equity Multiple

Some businesses are valued as a multiple of stockholders' equity or net worth. This is not the only method to use, but it is a valid one for a limited number of businesses. It is not usually appropriate for S corporations, which generally are not subject to U.S. federal income taxes. They are treated almost like a partnership, and the owners are taxed instead of the S corporation. As a result, the companies often distribute most or all of the profits earned each year to the stockholders, so they can pay taxes and enjoy the profits without subjecting them to taxation at the corporation level, thereby avoiding double taxation of the profits (once as income to the corporation and once as dividends to the owners).

Then, too, the real value of most businesses will be determined ultimately by future cash flow generated rather than by the cost of original cost-based net assets (net book value). The price range might be a multiple of one to two or more, or less, times the last stockholders' equity amount, depending on debt levels, working capital, property, plant and equipment needs, contingencies for pending litigation, and other matters. Assuming the stockholders' equity at the end of 1996 to be $11,035,000, then the value could be computed as

TABLE 8-10

ROIs—Investment-at-Cost Method versus Fair-Market-Value Method

	Year 1	Year 2	Year 3	Three Year Avg.
Net income	$ 2,200,000	$ 2,500,000	$ 2,800,000	$ 2,500,000
Price earnings ratio (P/E)	10	10	10	10
Fair market value = P/E × Net income	$22,000,000	$25,000,000	$28,000,000	$25,000,000
Investment at cost	$20,000,000	$20,000,000	$20,000,000	$20,000,000
Dividends	$ 300,000	$ 300,000	$ 300,000	$ 300,000
Net income return on investment				
Fair-market value method	11.0%	11.4%	11.2%	11.2%
Investment-at-cost method	11.0%	12.5%	14.0%	12.5%
Total return on investment				
Fair market value method	11.5%	15.0%	13.2%	13.3%
Investment-at-cost method	11.5%	16.5%	16.5%	14.8%

Multiplier of 1 to 2 = **$11,035,000 to $22,070,000**

Method 14. Multiples of Sales

For some businesses, especially those in service sectors, a multiple of revenues is sometimes a good method for ascertaining value. An example of the approach using the case study numbers for the past year follows. The base year can be different. It could also be an average for several years if volatility is a factor. Further, the next year's forecast could also be appropriate at times. Again, this is just one of several methods that should be considered. Rarely is one method the only one to use.

50% of 1996 revenues = 50% × $39,500,000 = **$19,750,000**
150% of 1996 sales =   **$59,250,000**

Method 15. Cost to Duplicate Operations

Cost to duplicate or replace operating assets in their present condition or in prime condition (two different values) usually is appropriate for a business with a history of operating losses or a business at or near the brink of bankruptcy. Appraise the assets and operations as to what it would cost to duplicate them in their present condition. But what is the value of a going business with a staff of employees? What, if any, is the value of the company's intangible assets over their useful lives? Such intangibles include patents, trademarks, trade names, licenses, know-how, and reputation.

In this case study, these costs were estimated to range between $22 and $24 million. Since those are difficult to value, *use of a number of valuation methods is highly recommended.*

Method 16. Liquidation Value

Any business has a value at a minimum of its liquidation value. This method of valuation presumes sale of the assets, payment of liabilities, and realization of a net remaining balance, if any, of cash. The liquidation presumes an orderly liquidation in a fairly short period—say, one year. Such value in this case might be derived as follows:

	Liquidation Value
Current assets	$15,373,000
Less reserves for obsolete inventories	−873,000
Property, plant, and equipment	2,051,000
Less liabilities	−6,551,000
Net realizable value	$10,000,000

A CAUTION

Do not pay twice for the same business! Buyers will pay for the fair market value of the business at the acquisition date. Those funds go to the seller and rarely to the business treasury. Yet the buyers may be required to infuse the business with substantial amounts of additional capital to keep it alive or make it grow. Too often, sellers want to be paid for the increase in value to be generated in future years by the buyer's substantial working capital infusion, guarantees of debt, marketing and distribution power and investment, or design and development capabilities. For a buyer or seller to ignore these is not realistic! Yet some buyers will pay the price . . . twice. Small wonder so many acquisitions hit the rocks! Table 8–11 reviews the summary of values computed on the case business.

In addition to the base price above, an earnout was added. The earnout equaled 50 percent of net income after taxes in excess of 20 percent return on the base price of $28 million for the first four years after purchase as long as the seller remains with the business for that period (golden handcuffs). The company's incentive bonus plan previously in effect is continued. This golden handcuffs approach simply means that the buyer tries to make it worth the seller's and key people's time and effort to remain in the employ of the business after the sale for the benefit of both buyer and seller—a good deal all the way around!

CONCLUSION ON VALUATION METHODS

There is no one single best method to value a business or a product line. Facts and circumstances are different for each seller and every buyer. Further, the buying arena changes from month to month and from year to year. Nevertheless, use of multiple methods such as those illustrated will keep a buyer in the ballpark in pricing.

Low bids are losers. High bids can be disastrous. The money will not return to the treasury of the buyer in a suitable period of time. Sometimes buyers should wait out a period if a buying frenzy still exists. Those frenzies die off, as do the investors who are causing the stir. Be your own self in valuing a business. If you are not comfortable, even for unknown reasons, with the value asked by the seller, stop! Go on to the next seller. There is more than one good company to buy for yourself or your company! Don't fall in love with any of them too soon!

TABLE 8–11

Summary of Different Value Ranges

Method 1	What price do the owners want? Answer: more than its worth!
Method 2	Guess a price! No need to comment. Insert your guess.
Method 3	Premium over quoted market price for publicly traded corporations. No price is included for this privately held business.
Method 4	How much and what types of debt and other securities will the cash flow support? This is not determinable until the bidders come in with their creative financing. This method is not recommended.
Method 5	Historical price earning multiple = $17,413,000 to $26,119,000.
Method 6	Modified historical price earnings multiple = $23,877,000 to $35,815,000.
Method 7	Last completed year's net income multiplied by a range = $29,260,000 to $43,890,000.
Method 8	Historical cash flow not valued with interest factor =$9,303,000 to $11,091,000.
Method 9	Historical cash flow with interest factor = $11,060,000 to $13,939,000.
Method 10	Projected cash flow to be received discounted at hurdle rate = $25,000,000 to $27,567,000.
Method 11	Projected cash flow (gross and discounted) = $16,915,000 to $20,275,000.
Method 12	Projected return on investment = Price should be less than $20,000,000 since the ROIs are too low (ranging from 11.5 to 16.5 percent) for either the cost method or the fair-market-value method at a $20,000,000 price.
Method 13	Stockholders' equity multiple of 1 to 2 times = $11,035,000 to $22,070,000.
Method 14	Multiple of one-half to one times sales = $19,750,000 to $59,250,000.
Method 15	Cost to duplicate operations = $22,000,000 to $24,000,000.
Method 16	Liquidation value $10,000,000

Cash at closing	$10,000,000
Four-year notes payable bearing interest at 9%	18,000,000
Base price before earnout	$28,000,000

CHAPTER 9

The Acquisition Team—Skills and Experience

SELECT TEAM MEMBERS BASED ON WHAT DUE DILIGENCE IS PLANNED

Common steps a buyer should accomplish and a seller should prepare for during the investigation phase of mergers and acquisitions (M&A) are listed in Appendix D. Each target company differs from others in size, complexity, shareholder control blocks, industry niches, and many other ways. Therefore, the due-diligence program will vary. The appointments for both sides of an M&A transaction should be tailored to the needs of the particular deal at hand.

Preparation Affects Price

If the seller is well prepared and responds to those areas being reviewed, the price may well go higher. If the seller is not prepared to address the issues completely, the sale may never occur or the price may be lower.

If the buyer has capable people assigned, the due diligence will be properly and adequately executed. Neither party should ignore the importance of being careful and diligent in appointing the right personnel for the tasks. Buyers do not always concentrate sufficiently on who should contribute to the M&A effort in spite of well developed plans to expand via M&A.

Virtually every company engaged in actively seeking growth has delegated the general M&A function to a specific person. That person will be expected to expend substantial time searching for candidates. The search process will involve communicating with many people within the company and many more on the outside. The nature of this person and job was detailed in Chapter 6.

Once a target company is located, who should comprise the M&A teams for the buyer and seller? Finding and negotiating M&A is covered elsewhere in this book. Let's look at the vital issue of who should be involved in planning to divest or acquire. Who should be the deal negotiator for a deal in progress? Who should do the due diligence? Who should supervise the entire efforts of the buyer and of the seller in some detail? The people may change depending on the target company and its business niches, technology levels, geographic coverage, and a number of other factors.

PERSONALITY AND SKILL ARE NEEDED

The personality traits of each person on the buyer's and seller's teams are very important to getting M&A transactions accomplished within an acceptable time frame. The higher the visibility, the more important the personality. Nevertheless, personality must take second place to inherent talent and general technical skills of those on both sides of the table. Otherwise, one side will lose in the negotiation process or in the due-diligence process.

Be Flexible in Assigning People

Different people may have distinct talents applicable for one transaction, but not for another. The market niches, distribution methods, technology levels, operating locations, languages spoken, and a host of other characteristics may be prominent and pertinent in one transaction, but not in another. Then too, some companies have highly centralized M&A functions whereas others are more decentralized and rely on the managers in the operating locations to accomplish M&A. Given that diversity, the M&A function is conducted differently in various companies. Nevertheless, the roles of those normally involved in M&A are described below. Change them to be compatible with your company's style of management and system of internal controls. Consider changing your normal M&A procedures on a deal-by-deal basis.

THE DEALMAKER'S ROLE

The dealmaker is the person responsible for seeing that an individual transaction is accomplished. Each transaction may have a different dealmaker depending on the nature of the particular target businesses. The level of competence and responsibility of the dealmaker on the other side of the table and the required expertise for the particular transaction under consideration also influence who should be assigned the dealmaker role.

Is the Dealmaker the Person Who Heads M&A?

The dealmaker does not necessarily handle M&A. That depends on the circumstances in a particular transaction. For megamergers, perhaps the two presidents get together to start the discussion phase and to control confidentiality. For small to midsize transactions, it depends on the instant transaction. Some people excel at finding and analyzing target businesses, but are not even close to being skilled at the negotiating phase.

Buyer and Seller Must Appoint Only One Dealmaker per Transaction

At all times, only one person should be in charge of the individual contemplated transaction on a day-to-day basis for each party. Everyone should know who that person is. Having just one dealmaker per party should prevent misinformation and negotiation errors by avoiding situations in which issues are prematurely agreed upon without the knowledge of other dealmakers or knowledge of their impact on other pending issues. Once a negotiable point is agreed upon, that point rarely ever makes another comeback.

The Dealmaker Must Control and Report on the Deal

The dealmaker must keep the overall transaction moving at an acceptable pace, making sure that prearranged functions are being carried out by each member of the M&A team and that the other party to the transaction is on schedule as well.

The dealmaker could be any responsible person from director to officer to employee. Some even use a third party as the dealmaker so their managers can stay focused on their daily jobs of operating the business. Do not permit responsibilities of the M&A team members to be unclear at any stage of the proposed deal. The dealmaker must report on the status of the transaction on a routine basis. Significant deal issues (those settled and those open), stage of the due diligence and its findings, and all other important matters should be reported in writing at least twice a month until the deal is consummated.

Dealmakers Should Insist on Who Prepares the First Draft Agreement

Always attempt to obtain the right to have the first draft of the proposed M&A agreement prepared by your attorneys. Sure, it costs more at the start, but will save you a lot in the long run. Time after time, inserting and deleting clauses from a draft agreement becomes a time-consuming, frustrating chores. To manage the deal well, control the M&A agreement right from the start.

THE ROLE OF DIRECTORS

Each director is elected by the shareholders to represent them in all matters of importance within the company. They have a fiscal and fiduciary responsibility to be involved. The directors should have a broad range of experience to assist management in guiding the business through an acquisition or merger as the buyer or seller in many ways.

Directors Must Question Realizability of Fair Market Value for Every Business Owned

Without question, directors of any company must periodically question whether a business should be sold or merged and at what value. Each shareholder should be able to rely on the directors to be aware of potential diminution in the value of the assets entrusted to their supervision.

Similarly, if the present fair market value of a business has hit or may soon hit its peak, the directors must question whether it is time to sell, spin off, or otherwise maximize the investment value and realizability of its value for the shareholders. It is not easy to sense a peak in value, but after all, directors must review how the president and other officers are managing the assets entrusted to them by the shareholders.

Think of the business as one share of stock in a publicly held corporation. Will that share's value continue to appreciate? Has it peaked? Should the board of directors seriously discuss selling the business?

Directors Do Not Usually Negotiate, but Could

Although the directors rarely are visible in negotiating for the sale or purchase of most businesses, they have the right and duty to be aware of where the deal stands before corporate commitments are finalized.

Be Careful of Guarantees and Contingencies

As an aside, in the heat of negotiations, one side may be pressured to grant a corporate or personal guarantee to back a given security or transaction. That guarantee may not appear to represent value given up or may not have to be recorded on the books, but it is a potential asset surrendered or liability assumable at a future date.

The dealmaker must be restrained in advance by the directors from giving away the store. Guarantees of debt instruments or other securities often will decrease the borrowing capacity and creditworthiness of that business or person granting such guarantee. Guarantees are a favorite place for lawyers and financiers to get away with too much in an almost subtle way.

The same issue is involved in the assumption of contingencies that may place a call on assets because of some paragraph buried in the bowels of the M&A agreement relating to earnouts, employment or consulting arrangements, and so forth.

Specific M&A Duties of Directors

Specific duties of the directors are listed in Table 9–1.

THE ROLE OF PRESIDENTS

Below the directors level, the two most important functions in a corporation are those of the chief executive officer (CEO) and chief operating officer (COO). These are often assigned to the president in small to midsize companies and will be so treated here.

The president is the number-one leader on the daily business scene and should be setting the direction and pace of the business with the blessing of the directors.

TABLE 9–1

Director's Responsibilities for Buying or Selling

Acquisition/Merger—Director's Functions as:	Buyer	Seller
Is the seller acceptable?	X	N/A
Is the buyer acceptable?	N/A	X
Is the target a good fit?	X	N/A
Should the target be a new core business?	X	N/A
Is the price, including contingencies, acceptable?	X	X
Are the terms of the agreement, including any corporate guarantees or debt, acceptable?	X	X
Should one of their own businesses be sold?	X	X
Is this the right time to sell or acquire?	X	X
Who should run the acquired/merged business?	X	X
How will the acquisition be financed?	X	N/A
Read the M&A agreement.	X	X

Keep the Presidents out of Deal Making Arguments

In general, the presidents of both the buying and selling companies must be available and involved, but only involved at appropriate times.

Presidents should not get involved in early disputes with the other side in the negotiating process. Never, ever get the presidents of both companies into debating deal issues unless others cannot resolve the issues. The last thing you want is the two top people in the respective companies ruining their future relationship by bickering and arguing over deal issues. They will need to work very closely together for years. That is too tough to do if they lose respect for one another before the deal is done. If one gets put into a corner on any particular issue, it takes a heck of a person to give in and not regret it. How would you react?

Specific M&A Duties of Presidents

Table 9–2 lists a number of duties for the president in M&A.

TABLE 9-2

President's Responsibilities for Buying or Selling

Acquisition/Merger—President's Functions as:	Buyer	Seller
Is the seller acceptable?	X	N/A
Is the buyer acceptable?	N/A	X
Is the target a good fit?	X	N/A
Should the target be a new core business?	X	N/A
Is the price acceptable?	X	X
Are the terms of the agreement, including any corporate guarantees or debt, acceptable?	X	X
Should one of their own businesses be sold?	X	X
Is this the right time to acquire or sell?	X	X
Who should run the acquired/merged business?	X	X
How will the acquisition be financed?	X	N/A
Positioning the company for sale.	N/A	X
Appointing key people to the seller's team.	N/A	X
Maximizing seller's values.	N/A	X
Appointing key people to the buyer's team.	X	N/A
Staying involved at the right level of contact.	X	X
Read the M&A agreement.	X	X

THE OPERATIONS EXPERT'S ROLE

No business should be acquired or sold without involving an operations expert far in advance of deal consummation.

This person (or, more likely, these persons) may already be on the payroll of the buyer, especially if the target business is in the same business or one similar to that of the buyer. The operations manager for the buyer should have the upper hand in trying to convince the buyer of how well everything is going within the plant and service area walls. The seller's resident expert may not disclose the operating problems encountered on a day-to-day basis. It will take a resourceful and sharp operations expert for the buyer to see through the cloak of protection covering the current manner of how the business is being operated at the cost-of-production level.

Do Not Hesitate to Ask for Help

Often, the target business niche or niches may be unfamiliar to the buyer's management. If so, the services of outsiders may be required to become comfortable with the target's operations and costing procedures for every activity from order entry through to shipping. Typically such outsiders may have been in the industry for years and are now retired or they may be from a consulting firm specializing in the target's niche businesses.

Do not go alone into a new arena. Someone is available to assist you through the difficult operations review. Invest now to save money later. Think of that assistance as part training and part insurance against a bad deal that will otherwise haunt you and the shareholders for years. There is nothing wrong with admitting your company's lack of expertise in a particular area now. Avoid the embarrassment of a mess later. Get help. This sage advice applies to every area of the target's business unless only assets are purchased.

The business niches of the target may include wholesaling, retailing, general manufacturing, natural resource production, high technology production, and so forth. That will dictate who should be assigned to the acquisition team to cover operations, including research, design, engineering, manufacturing, and service. This area of investigation requires a high level of ingenuity, great expertise in the industry, and a super feel for the abilities of key personnel within the target's operations departments.

The roles of design and research and development need to be assessed. Does the target verbalize fair amounts of research and development to build for growth, but actually spend its engineering on solving current customer needs and correcting internal manufacturing quality issues *(Fatal Flaw)*?

Cost Allocations and Costing Methods—Every Operations Expert Needs a Great Costing Expert

Not a single person on an acquisition team is more important than one who can quickly and accurately determine the following:

- The most applicable costing methods that should be used by the target given different volume assumptions and varying product mix in the sales. How should cost allocations be made? Why? Under what circumstances?

Usually at least 30 to 50 percent of all manufacturing costs assigned to a product are allocations rather than direct costs. These indirect costs are often assigned by applying them as overhead charges using a percentage based on direct costs such as direct labor. Relatively small changes or errors in direct costs can cause large differences in total product costs because of those overhead allocations. This area is tricky. The best talent available may not be good enough.

- The real costs of production and services rather than the costs stated by the target's management or as contained in the target's records.

- The cost efficiencies probable from downsizing the target or from integrating its operations, divisions, departments, and/or functions with those of the buyer, if appropriate.

- Any new or increased costs to be incurred after the acquisition to fill a need, attain an objective, expand the business, and so forth.

Why Is Cost Accounting (Cost Allocation) So Important?

Time after time experience teaches us that the real costs of sales are very difficult to ascertain. Revenue volume changes; different costing methods and dynamic vendor costs will dramatically affect the profitability of businesses. Every acceptable costing method will result in different operating costs assigned to individual products in a line of products and services.

Who is the right person to accomplish the costing analysis? That all depends. The buyer must have that talent on the M&A due-diligence team. Don't leave home without that talent.

Human Resources Must Be Reviewed

A human resource expert must review all significant personnel areas. These included compliance with statutes, labor union issues, pending unionization, strikes, slowdowns, and effects of industry changes and automation on competitors' costs.

THE MARKETING AND SALES EXPERT'S ROLE

All the good cost analyses in the world will not produce revenues. Without revenues you can forget the acquisition. So marketing analyses are very important to decide whether the target is in the correct market niche(s) for the buyer. These markets may or may not be the same ones with which the buyer has sufficient experience.

Explore the Target's Current Markets—Should It Leave Some? Should It Enter Others? Is There Synergy with Yours?

These questions must be addressed during the purchase investigation. Many buyers have in-house marketing talent, but others only have in-house sales expertise. Sales and marketing are not the same. If the buyer needs help, it is readily available from major consulting firms, smaller specialized firms, and individuals as is true for other functions being studied.

Explore the Target's Distribution System

Should the target use a direct sales staff? Should part or all of the sales effort be assigned to independent sales representatives? The seller should be prepared to defend its approach and the buyer should be sufficiently competent to question which method would be best after the deal is done.

The sales distribution system may benefit from integrating both companies' personnel or may be best left independent of one another. Separate identities in the marketplace may be more effective over time, even though that approach appears at the outset to cost more per dollar of sales.

Don't Presume You Know the Target's Market

Buyers must never assume they have complete knowledge about specific markets just because they are in the general industry niche.

For example, experience in the automotive aftermarket with chemical specialties may not assist the buyer in comprehending competitive strategies and customer demands for a target's market niche in front-end parts, tire accessories, or under-the-hood products. Distribution hierarchies may vary, specific major customers may be vulnerable, profit margins may be under attack by competitors, customers may be realigning with different suppliers—the list goes on.

Don't Presume You Can Profitably Obtain More Market Share

Many M&A deals will not realize the projected sales and profit potentials because sales volumes did not increase profitably. Why not? Unless you have more firepower in cash, sales effort, or technology, you will not reach the forecasted sales levels. Competition will not sit and watch you eat into their market share. They have been planning to take market share from the target. Just maybe they already are eating into it without any outsider's awareness.

THE FINANCIAL AND ACCOUNTING EXPERT'S ROLE

The chief financial officers (CFOs) of the buyer and the seller must be involved early on. Pro forma financial statements may be needed to recast the target's results of operations and financial condition for one period (often more) to best compute the true value of the target business. Perhaps nonrecurring expenses or income are in one or more recent year's income statement. Perhaps the balance sheet debt structure should reflect a possible or pending refinancing (types of debt, amounts, length of debt periods, and interest rates). International financing or currency translation gains and losses may be involved with currency risk. Such information can materially influence the perceived value by the buyer and the minimum acceptable value by the seller.

The cost analysis phase is included within the responsibility of the operations team member. Yet, the actual person doing the costing work may be the CFO or controller if separate jobs exist.

Independent certified public accountants (CPAs) are very important for both the buyer and seller. CPAs have broad experience in auditing, taxation, and operating systems. Some CPAs have a nose to smell problems. Many have performed numerous purchase investigations and know where to find the *Fatal Flaws*. Their client working papers are loaded with data of interest to all parties to an acquisition. Each significant asset and liability is detailed within their records. Revenues and all expenses are listed for applicable periods and profitability is analyzed. Use this information to your advantage rather than try to reconstruct it on your own. This applies to the buyer and the seller.

THE FEDERAL AND STATE TAXATION EXPERT'S ROLE

Income taxes materially affect the cash flow of every for-profit business. Tax planning can only take place after a clear understanding of the tax history. The seller's tax expert may be on the payroll or may be a consultant. The same goes for the buyer's tax expert.

Should the business be relocated in part or in total to another state or country to reduce taxes payable in the future? Should it be merged into the buyer's subsidiary or parent company? Should the acquisition be structured to be tax-free or tax-deferred for the buyer? Should tax-deferred or tax-free arrangements be sought overseas? Is a statutory merger or reorganization in order? Are assets of the seller adequately protected from excessive estate taxes? These and many other issues are commonplace when qualified tax experts review a business to buy it or position it for sale.

Do not wait too long to involve the best people available. The cost is small but it increases as the closing date approaches. It may soon become too late to change the deal.

THE LEGAL EXPERT'S ROLE

Good lawyers exist. Good lawyers are necessary and an integral part of any buy, sell, or merge transaction for the buyer and the seller. However, involve the lawyers at the right time and the proper place. By all means, keep your reins on them. They have an innate tendency to become aggressive and take over . . . just at the time that may kill the deal.

Yet, the lawyers have a ton of information at their fingertips to make available to the buyer in particular.

Some of the Legal Documents Needed

Literally small mountains of information and documents are needed to complete most acquisitions. These include

- Articles of incorporation and bylaws.
- Minutes of the shareholders and board of directors meetings.
- Registration forms showing the right to do business in various states and countries and fictitious name filings.
- Complete data about each class of capital stock, option plans, and debt securities.

- Copies of major contracts of all types, leases, titles, deeds, licenses, patents, trademarks, and franchises.
- Shareholders' lists.
- Employee agreements, union contracts and severance policies, bonus plans, inventions, and secrecy agreements.
- Affirmative action plans.
- Environmental reports.
- Insurance policies (medical benefits, life, liability, and others).
- List of all administrative proceedings, consent decrees, judgments, and claims and litigation pending or recently resolved.
- Representation letters sent to the company's independent CPAs.
- Corporate guarantees.

As this list shows, lawyers are an integral part of the buyer's and seller's teams. They have a lot to contribute. Just plan the quantity and timing of their participation. Be prepared to see costs escalate if your company is not in control over legal documentation, which it should have accumulated neatly over the years . . . somewhere.

THE INSURANCE EXPERT'S ROLE

The insurance area is very important in every M&A transaction. As in other areas, insurance expertise is readily available from third parties if it is not presently on the payroll. The time needed to perform due diligence as to insurance issues is not large, but the steps to be accomplished are highly important. See Appendix D for the due-diligence steps to accomplish.

SUMMARY

Every step in the acquisition process has a best pace, communication level, and style to keep momentum high but not off the scale. Certainly, the team should take its time to make certain all the bases are covered. Extra time and money are well spent by the buyer's and seller's team before the closing. Only regret results from a bad or mundane merger or acquisition. Again, this is like buying an insurance policy. For just a little more effort, you will receive a lot more benefit. Just do not fall in love too soon.

There may well be a *Fatal Flaw*. Where is it? What is it? Who is it? Who can find it?

CHAPTER 10

Sensitive Negotiating Issues

THE HUMAN SIDE OF ACQUISITIONS

A seller usually sells the same business only once. That is traumatic by and of itself. Some sellers are indecisive. Some sellers are uncertain of whether they should sell. Some sellers believe the real value of the business is yet to be seen due to future growth, more opportunities on the horizon, and so on. All sellers are convinced the buyer will not operate the business in the same way they did, regardless of how convincing the buyer tries to be to the contrary. Concerns abound around the negotiating table.

Surely, a buyer may be able to buy assets, but no buyer can buy people over the long term. The buyer just rents them for a while. The length of the rental period depends on how completely the owners tend to the employees' needs as well as on how well the employees serve the owners' needs.

People Are the Cornerstone

People make products. People create and deliver services. People make the cash flow positive . . . or negative. Machinery and plant facilities do not do anything on their own. So as a buyer or seller, spend a lot of time analyzing the party across the negotiating table. At the appropriate times, discreetly ask friends, secretaries, and business associates for their input concerning the type of person negotiating on the other side of the table—assuming it can be done in a totally confidential manner.

Acquisitions are most sensitive. Good, vibrant feelings about the other party (good chemistry) are very important. During the purchase investigation phase, buyers should spend considerable time and expense obtaining detailed knowledge about every key employee.

People are the foundation of the business and the secret to a successful acquisition.

Employment Contracts
Are Not the Solution

Employment contracts will not solve the human side of an acquisition. Legal documents rarely can solve that situation. Such agreements will not prevent an employee from leaving well before the specified termination date. Courts will probably allow the person to make a living in the same industry. No company wants a dissatisfied employee hanging around, potentially causing dissension with other key employees or disruption in the operations of the business.

In general, employment agreements do protect the employee much more than the employer. Check them with your attorney.

Retention Bonuses May
Be Appropriate

Upon or after the acquisition, bonuses may be needed to retain good people employed in the business. That is especially true if the buyer is a large conglomerate known to dominate its managers in businesses acquired. In addition, the acquired business may be operated virtually as a plant or department/small division after the closing—not a great prospect for those people in the target company.

WHO MANAGES AFTER THE CLOSING?

The term *acquisition* generally connotes that a buyer has or will acquire either the capital stock of a corporate business, some or all of a partnership's interest in assets and liabilities of a business partnership, or some or all of the assets and often the accompanying liabilities of any other legal form of a target business.

Acquirers Tend to Retain Control

The acquiring entity will normally be the survivor and will be in charge after the deal is consummated. However, the buyer's and seller's specific managers who will be in charge after an acquisition must be identified in advance of the closing. That should prevent internal operating confusion, provide a smooth transition after the acquisition is consummated, and apprise the customers, lenders, and vendors of the new structure.

After closing on the transaction, who manages depends on whether (1) the seller's business will be taken over completely and operated almost as a plant or integral division of the buyer or (2) the selling company's business will be a stand-alone business practically as it was before the acquisition. If managers with high ego levels lose their motivation, they can do substantial harm to the reputation of both buyer and seller companies.

Transitions are frequently built into a deal so the perception in the marketplace by customers, vendors, and lenders is one of acceptance and optimism.

FRIENDLY AND UNFRIENDLY TAKEOVERS (TENDER OFFERS)

In a friendly acquisition, the buyer and seller always agree early in the chase on how the combined businesses will be operated. If they cannot agree, the deal will not be done.

Usually, votes in favor of the deal by the shareholders of the selling company are needed before an acquisition can be effected. The votes of the buying company's shareholders are not usually required to acquire another business. The yes votes of the shareholders of all companies merging are needed before a merger can be effected. The majority percentage affirmative vote required will depend on the company's bylaws and related statutes.

Tender Offers

Tender offers occur when one company decides to acquire the outstanding shares of another publicly held company and contacts the shareholders of the target company offering to buy some or all of their shares at a stipulated price. Such a proposed procedure can be friendly or unfriendly, depending on whether the target company's board of directors and/or management approve the transaction in advance of the contact or ever. If not, the transaction is viewed as "unfriendly" or as "hostile."

HOSTILE TAKEOVERS COST DEARLY

Hostile takeovers can get mean and can lead to litigation. Such hostile takeovers (raids) will definitely cost each company a lot of money before some agreement is reached on whether to continue forward with the not-so-tender takeover offer.

Hostile Takeovers Damage Both Companies

Management of a target company facing a hostile takeover invariably wants to put out the word that the raider is not dependable, is not honorable, will not grow the business, will strip the company of its cash, and will abandon its strategic plans. Some use the media, government contacts, and other resources to influence shareholders, key personnel, and others to reject the offers of the takeover person or corporation. The stage is set to pit one faction against the other. Rarely does that bode well for either party in the long run.

If the deal goes through, many shareholders and employees of the target will feel they were losers in the deal. The price of the shares may have exceeded the real value of the target business. In that case, the acquirer's shareholders may feel they lost on the transaction (since they may expect lower future return on investment and possibly lower future dividends). Management of both sides must now try to build a bridge of mutual understanding. They now must pretend that the awful things they said about each other do not matter.

The raider will invariably install one or more of its best, most loyal managers into a lead position in the target so the policies of the raider are followed to the letter. Surely a number of very talented managers will depart voluntarily or be forced out in a "rightsizing" of the combined entities.

Hostile Takeovers Are Expensive

If the takeover did not succeed, much money of both sides was diverted to lawyers and others to defend against or promote the takeover. Those funds are no longer available to grow the business. Other raiders may now surface to start the ugly process all over again so more time will be taken away from the business and more money will be spent without benefit to the company.

Are Tender Offers Good for Anyone?

Some are good, some are bad, and others are neither. A number of studies have analyzed whether tender offers are beneficial to shareholders. Invariably a publicly held target's quoted market value goes up by 35 to 45 percent over the quoted price per share preceding the announcement. That is the good news. However, the impact on employees is not as clear since mergers or takeovers often result in downsizing the combined businesses to take advantage of cost reductions possible in various direct (production) and indirect (overhead) departments. That news is not good.

DIRECTORS INFLUENCE THE INITIAL AND FINAL OFFERS

Yes, directors do materially influence the offers! One of the most interesting recent studies of tender offers is *Do Independent Directors Enhance Target Shareholder Wealth during Tender Offers?* Dated May 1996, it was compiled by James F. Cotter, Anil Shivdasani, and Marc Zenner. They studied 169 tender offers from 1989 through 1992. Their analysis focused on the role of independent outside directors, who were defined as those directors who were not current or past employees of the companies, did not have substantial business or family ties to management, and had no potential business ties with the companies. Abstracts of their report follow:

> Finally, the shareholder gain from the inception of the offer to its resolution is 62.3% for targets with an independent board compared to 40.9% for targets without an independent board. (page 7)
>
> Thus, targets with an independent board are more likely to resist, obtain higher premium revisions, and experience larger shareholder gains than other targets. (page 7)
>
> More interestingly, however, the shareholder gains in successful tender offers for targets with independent boards are an additional 22 percentage points higher. (page 10)
>
> 5. CONCLUSION
>
> Tender offers can result in important conflicts of interest between the managers and shareholders of target firms. We examine whether independent

outside directors perform an important role in controlling these conflicts and enhance shareholder wealth during tender offers. We document that the target shareholder gains over the entire contest period are higher when the target's board is independent. In evaluating the source of these gains, we find that targets with independent boards extract both higher initial tender offer premiums and higher bid premium revisions than targets without independent boards. Targets with independent boards are not, however, more likely to be successfully taken over. In addition, the target shareholder returns of unsuccessful tender offers do not differ between targets with and without independent boards. These results suggest that the higher shareholder gains for targets with independent boards are driven by higher initial premiums and bid premium revisions, and not by better post-tender offer bid performance for targets that have not been successfully taken over. We also find that resisted offers and offers to targets with poison pills lead to higher target shareholder gains when the board is independent than when it is not. (page 19)

We conclude that independent outside directors play an important role during tender offers and that they enhance shareholder wealth during tender offers. Our evidence also suggests that when targets with independent boards resist, both bid premium revisions and target shareholder gains are higher than in resisted offers where the target's board is not independent. This result suggests that targets with independent boards are likely to resist to extract a higher premium for target shareholders rather than to entrench incumbent managers. (page 20).[1]

NEGOTIATING TECHNIQUES FOR THE BUYER AND SELLER

Some advantage can be gained by each of the parties during the negotiating phase by following a few good rules.

Deal with One Principal Initially

It is best to at least start negotiating with someone who has the responsibility for the entire transaction. Then you and the other person will get to know each other much better and learn how to deal with each other's hot button or sensitive issues. Multiple personalities can cause multiple problems.

---

[1]James F. Cotter, Anil Shivdasani, and Marc Zenner, *Do Independent Directors Enhance Target Shareholder Wealth during Tender Offers?* May 1996, to be published in *Journal of Financial Economics*, Elsevier Science, SA.

Be Yourself

If a negotiator tries to transform into a totally different type of person, his facade will crumble. Mistrust will develop since the other party will quickly realize the person is just role-acting. On the other hand, if the dealmaker or chief negotiator for your side is a just a body, a boring or overly aggressive persona, a person without a nice personality and warmth, a person who remains faceless . . . get another person for the job, an individual who will be remembered, trusted, and respected.

Be Positive

Nothing creative was ever invented by a negative thinker! Acquisitions take a lot of persistently positive attitudes and actions if they are to be consummated.

Involve a Mutual Friend

Try to get to know someone in the other company who has some authority. Then try to become good friends. That individual may be tremendously helpful in keeping the deal on track.

Meet the Spouse

Try to become acquainted with the spouse of every significant owner of the buyer. Rarely do large companies looking to acquire a business bother with the spouse. That can be a big mistake. Spouses can make the difference if the other buyers in the race for the business are just personas or have a *Fatal Flaw*. Just a little extra effort and hospitality in this area will greatly help you accomplish the mission of buying or selling a business.

Represent the Company Professionally

Both as a buyer and as a seller you should always present the best impression of your company. Do not be too modest about strengths, and do not overly stress weaknesses. Sell with enthusiasm. Tell why you are with the company, why you and the other key people like the business, what your plans are for growth, what the employees' strengths are, and so forth. Yet, do not oversell and leave the impression of being too aggressive.

Meet with a Purpose

Have a purpose for every meeting and leave the other party with some pleasant thoughts about your visit each time.

THE TRANSACTION MUST BE A GOOD DEAL FOR BUYER AND SELLER

The dealmakers (negotiators) for buyer and seller are the two most important people impacting whether a closing will occur. Each can personally foul up the transaction without trying very hard. *The more people involved in the negotiations, the greater the likelihood of fouling up the transaction.*

Mutual Respect Is Mandatory

Mutual respect and trust are critical at all times in the negotiating process. There should not be one winner. Both sides must be winners (a win-win situation) for the deal to have permanency. If somehow the contract was unfair or became so after signing, perhaps adjustments should be made voluntarily, if this is legally possible. Having the attitude of making a win-win deal (where neigher party loses) is a great test of fairness at the outset. Lawyers may disagree, but years of experience in the field clearly demonstrate that real trust and fairness should prevail during the negotiations. Deal fairly and quickly with aberrations and unplanned issues as they arise, whenever they arise.

Money Is Not the Only Criteria

Keep in mind that the seller will often be the one appointed to accomplish the goals for the newly acquired business. Therefore, the negotiations must be carried out professionally, honestly, and understandingly.

Money is not the only criterion the seller is using to measure a buyer's offer. The seller's perception of how a buyer will treat employees, deal with customers and vendors, and relate to the seller are critical issues. A seller should never, never take anything for granted in the negotiating process, even if it seems trivial. It may be important to the seller and differentiate the buyer from other buyers. The buyer must be a real person, not a persona who lacks individual personality and character.

SET THE STAGE AND STYLE, THEN CONTROL THE SHOW

The negotiating process is delicate, most sensitive and, if not carried out properly, can result in irreparable harm to both sides. The buyer and the seller have conflicting goals. One wants to buy at the lowest price and the other wants to sell at the highest price . . . if at all! Any one or a series of fairly small issues may trigger the other party to exit stage left from the scene. To allow the best chance of success, try to control the process in the following ways.

Establish a Time Line Early

The prime person responsible for acquisitions or an appointed dealmaker should establish a timetable for the due-diligence investigation, negotiation, and closing of the transaction. Responsibilities need to be assigned to each member of the acquisition team and to those on the seller's team. Prevent duplication, but bring in all who should be involved at the proper time.

Select the Proper Meeting Place

Where is the proper place to meet? It varies. An owner of a small enterprise may not be comfortable meeting a buyer for the first time on the owner's premises. Do not rush the acquisition process. A meeting at the seller's site can be arranged at a later date if the buyer and seller pass the first screening. Over time, arrange to meet at both the buyer's and seller's places of business. Being on-site at each other's locations will have a positive impact on both parties.

Remember That Attitude Affects Outcome

When meeting face to face, be as positive, frank, and open as is practical about your people, your operations, and your business culture. Above all, be honest! That approach will lead to a similar style by the other party. The attitudes of the representatives and negotiators on both sides are even more important than the meeting locations. Attitudes telegraph instantly and create good or bad negotiation atmosphere. Do not use a hostile, arrogant, or demanding approach. That gives the appearance and impression of trying to put the other party in a corner and invariably results in overly defensive or offensive responses from that party.

Do not set a negotiating tone where the other party cannot tell where the deal terms may end due to your changing stance on issues. If a point is resolved, try to let it stay resolved. If possible, try to have the detail negotiating accomplished one level below the owner and buyer or presidents, as the case may be. This allows them to resolve remaining issues if the issues are really important, while preserving their roles in the relationship to come after the acquisition as operating executives in top management positions.

Limit Attendance at Initial Meetings

Keep initial meetings to a small number of top-level people who have a distinct stake in the acquisition. This almost always excludes legal counsel, the controller, and independent certified public accountants! Plenty of time will be available for them to become involved in the process later or outside of the negotiating room.

Involve the Best People

Ultimately, the buyer and seller should have the best brains in the business; help them consummate the deal. However, timing their participation is critical. The timing totally depends on who the best brains are and how their personalities relate to the other party to the transaction.

With all due respect to the legal profession, lawyers cannot be expected to be good at everything and at all times. So, unless the lawyers for the seller and the buyer are really unique, unless they have simply wonderful charm and warmth, allow them to enter the scene after the initial meetings where the two parties have struck a deal in principle on major issues. The major issues include ballpark price range, general payment terms, and buyer and seller involvement after the sale. Details should be left to the accounting and legal staff to work out in later stages.

Again, insulate the owners and buyers from many meetings where staff personnel are hammering out lots of details. They should not have to negotiate smaller issues. In that way, the buyer and seller will not ruin their sensitive relationship and can keep their contact professional, yet warmly personal.

Be Informative Early On

The buyer should have sufficient data available to present the business in its best light, but without overstating or misrepresenting any facts. The buyer does not need to see basic financial statements in any detail at the first meeting. Summary highlights are sufficient. The main purpose of the first meeting is to allow enough exchange of information so the parties will be able to intelligently evaluate the potential for a possible transaction based on limited data and whether the parties hit it off well together. So-called chemistry (how the parties feel about each other) will be a very important emotional and highly qualitative element in the negotiating process.

Early discussions should always be quite open and frank. All major issues should be presented so obvious deal breakers are known early on.

Be Serious

If the seller can be made comfortable enough to mention a sales price, the buyer may have an advantage. One thing is certain: Once the other party offers or agrees to anything, including pricing, that issue will not be changed later without giving up something.

No one should waste the time of the other party. Question each other fairly quickly as to the ability and intent to consummate the transaction. Neither buyer nor seller should go to the meeting before being convinced each wants to and can accomplish the transaction. The meeting place is not the arena the seller should use to decide if the business is really for sale at any price! That decision should be made beforehand.

Solve Some Issues
and Delay Others

The parties should not agree to any issues that they may wish to decide differently at a later date. Once a point is discussed and resolved, it is extremely difficult to change it later without a high cost incurred by the person who wants to change the deal as it relates to that issue.

One party may agree to issues on a tentative basis subject to amicable resolution of other issues that the other party knows need resolution as well. To that end, list the more important issues early and let it be known that these are cut points or deal breakers. Then any items that seem to be problems requiring more discussion can be set aside as a group. They can be resolved as soon as the other major issues are resolved or agreed to, subject to mutually satisfactory resolution of the stickier items.

Secrecy Is Always an Issue

Do your absolute very best to maintain total secrecy about the discussions. Even having agendas or special reports typed can lead to unplanned disclosure to outsiders who do not need to know about the negotiations. Competitors will try to use the rumor to their benefit. Employees may become agitated and unsettled. Customers may start calling. None of that is desirable at this point in the negotiations. Carefully choose typists and control copies of acquisition- or sale-related memoranda and letters. Perhaps the services of a CPA or law firm are best used at early stages to maintain secrecy. Their personnel are trained in and required to maintain confidentiality and are independent of your personnel.

Use of a facsimile machine is great to speed communications, but the material being transmitted can be read by anyone passing the facsimile machine as the transmission is in process. E-mail is dangerous for confidential matters. Forget it until the transaction becomes public.

Be Quick but Deliberate

Button up the discussions, investigations, and negotiations as soon as is practical. Yet, do not rush, panic, or accept being pushed into hurried decisions. Be decisive.

Know What Is Important

Do not allow small, inconsequential issues to hold up the closing.

As is often the case, the ABC system continues to be effective. That is, approximately 65 percent of the importance or value of a process or group of issues is represented by only 10 percent or so of those issues or items called A items. They are high-value items. On the other hand, only about 10 percent of the importance or value of items or issues is represented by approximately 65 percent of the low-value issues or items called C items. B items are those in between (25 percent of the number of issues equals approximately 25 percent of the value or importance of the issues or items).

Stop wasting valuable deal-making time on issues that are not important. Issues that cannot possibly adversely impact the economics of the transaction to any material extent (C items) should be resolved quickly and fairly. Often the small issues become very aggravating to the seller or to the buyer, who erroneously decides the other party will be too tough to live with after the deal. Just one more issue sometimes triggers the hot button of either the seller or the buyer. The transaction goes to another buyer, or the seller stops selling . . . at least to you.

Keep on Track

Set the next meeting date when you conclude any meeting with the principals. Assign people on both sides to keep in touch with each other to save time and to prevent long delays in personal contact. It is vital to establish open and frequent lines of communication to keep the deal on track and to keep others out. Such communications should include the owners and their representatives and key managers.

EXTRA NEGOTIATING SENSITIVITIES WITH FOREIGNERS

In addition to the usual concerns in negotiating with sellers and buyers who are native to our country, we must be most sensitive when dealing with a foreign buyer or seller.

How Does the Other Person Think?

Keep in mind that the other party grew up in the educational, business, and social cultures of a different country. Cultures and ways of thinking vary even from region to region within the United States. That is why some people are still fighting the Civil War. That is why some people are not racing to openly accept those with different racial and language backgrounds. "After all, those people think differently than we do!" "They do not understand how to conduct themselves in our neighborhood!" Well, such impediments are magnified in the world markets of acquisitions. Every buyer and every seller thinks, acts, and reacts differently—even if they speak the same language. The same approach will not be in order for every available business due to the idiosyncrasies of the owners and the buyers.

Sensitive Issues with Foreigners

What are the most important sensitivities to be aware of when dealing with a foreigner?

- A contract in one legal system may not be adequate in another jurisdiction.

- Some foreigners are known for ignoring a contract or getting around it one way or the other. This is perhaps one of the most important points to worry about. Discuss the situation with other business owners and the U.S. Department of Commerce, state government agencies, or other government departments to learn background cultural information, negotiating practices, and contract experiences. Governments change, as do their policies, and business conditions are unstable in some countries, even on a day-to-day basis.

- A buyer or seller may not be dealing with anyone with the power to complete the transaction. Find out early on who has the decision power.

- Decide at the outset whether a transaction with foreigners is desirable. Over the long term will they be good to work with from a day-to-day management standpoint? Will employees care? Will customers care?

- Try to find out how those on the other side think and reason.

- Try to understand as much as possible about the culture of their country. Learn about the history, the politics, the hierarchy, the business and market processes, the legal system, the accounting practices and principles, and the system of taxation.

- Try learning at least a few basic sentences in the language of the other party. Perhaps the usual greetings and limited talk about the weather will suffice for a start. Do not try to joke in the language unless you are good at it. Jokes do not translate well and may not be in good taste in the native country. Be careful about the timing and type of gifts sent to some foreigners. Some presents may cause problems due to their color or type.

- Do not try to accomplish a lot at the first meeting. Often, the other person will be mainly trying to decide if trust is developing. If either person decides trust is not there, forget about doing business together. Leave a lot of time for unforeseen problems, side trips, and intentional delays on their part to pressure you, especially if the meetings are in their country. Avoid trying to match them in their drinking habits. Being inebriated does not foster the best negotiations and is not fair to the investors or owners.

- Try to conceal time schedules. They may wait until the last moment to spring some surprises in hope that the time pressure will get the deal done, perhaps unfairly. Time should not be the controlling element in deal making unless one party has had it and is making a last stand.

- Try to resolve the overall deal in general terms before going on to each individual point. Many do not want to resolve one issue at a time. International transactions often require highly qualified local attorneys, accountants, and bankers early in the negotiating process since local laws, accounting practices and principles, and lending regulations vary by country.

- Do not tell the foreigners everything wanted or known before they do likewise. Otherwise, they will know what you know and want, but you will not know what they want and know. This is really difficult for Americans who like to lay it all on the table up front. Generally, you lose a real advantage with this approach. You must be yourself, but throttle down the enthusiasm to tell all too soon.

- Do not be mesmerized by the foreign accent of their English. Crediting too much to them simply because of the fact that they can speak your language is dangerous. This halo effect of an accent may cloud other imperfections of much more significance.

- Be a good listener! Allow them to do all the talking at the outset. Try to find out where they are coming from. Learn what drives them.

- Do not be arrogant or talk down to them.

THE AUCTION PROCESS—USE IT OR NOT?

If the buyer instituted the search or is lucky, or if an intermediary treats a buyer first-class, the auction process may be avoided. If not, here is how the auction works.

Circulate Descriptive Literature and Information

The seller will create and circulate a well-prepared outline of the business to those potential buyers who appear logical and who have signed a confidentiality letter and asked for information. Usually, the package contains a letter describing the rules and timing for submitting bids, an executive summary highlighting the business, and a description of the markets (including customers and competitors), products, and services of the business along with financial statements for the past three to five years and projections for the next three to five years. Sometimes the data are bound in hardcover. Sometimes the data are in a three-ring binder. But they will always be circulated to many people.

Establish the Bid Schedule

Then the potential buyers will be given approximately one month to decide if they will bid on the business. If so, they send their sealed bids to the seller or the seller's representative for review. Frequently, the bidders will be called and asked to raise their bids, since a number of buyers may have evidenced real interest. This can happen even though the seller said it would not. Then the auction begins and some sellers drop out for fear that the price will be astronomical.

Too often, little concern is given to the managers and employees who are expected to remain with the business being sold. Many key employees are not introduced to the bidders until the very end.

The auction process scene involving so many buyers, lots of pressure to stay in the running, and time constraints established by the seller's representatives is perfect for overly anxious buyers. They become prey to the auctioneers.

Involve Legal Counsel before and during Auctions

If a buyer enters into the auction process, a good attorney should be involved. This is not the typical scene where a buyer is negotiating directly with the seller. Instead, the buyer (bidder) is going into a lion's den with other hungry and vicious lions and tigers. Many issues about the terms of a bid, the conditions of the business, and the warranties and representations of the seller need to be resolved. Due-diligence periods may be limited and documentation may be too incomplete to make an appropriate bid from a legal view. Confidentiality is often mentioned as the reason the bidders are not given full access to the financial records, the key people, and the facilities.

Occasionally, the seller gives a take-it-or-leave-it impression. It may well be best to leave the scene and allow the other bidders to be the feast. If a buyer decides to stay in the auction, the buyer's attorney should prepare or review the bid and all pertinent seller data, terms, and conditions. Certain factors will be more critical in the bidding process than others.

Concentrate on the critical issues and try to hedge the offer appropriately. Perhaps submit two offers: one with restrictions or caveats at a higher price and the other at a lower bid with few exceptions built in.

An Auction Is Dangerous for Buyer and Seller

Another concern about auctions occurs if the buyer's offer is accepted. Then the light goes on. The buyer just bought a business after most or all of the target's business plans, its pricing practices, cost data, and trade secrets were also presented during the bidding process to competitors or others who may become competitors. A number of key people in the target business were interviewed and could be hired by the bidders who were not successful in the auction but could become very successful in acquiring the best part of the business . . . the people. That is not good!

Usually, there is no commitment by the seller to sell or to take the highest bid. The letters written during the auction process should be carefully reviewed by attorneys. Buyers should avoid getting into the situation where they may have caused other bidders to leave the scene, then turn the purchase down for whatever reason, and expose themselves to potential liability for causing damages to the seller's business and so on.

Also as a seller and as a buyer, avoid situations where the selling process takes so long that employees and managers become disillusioned or frustrated and depart for the nearest competitor. Even employment contracts and agreements not to compete will not always offer sufficient protection. Attorneys will counsel about the rights of an employee to make a living in the same industry.

Ask the attorney about the rights of the seller to compete in some markets in the world, despite the broad geography covered in the noncompete agreement.

Limited Auctions May Apply

Limited auctions are stripped-down versions of the foregoing. The seller may limit the bidding in stages to a small number of serious qualified bidders. This reduces the negative aspects of a full-scale auction since it restricts the quantity of third parties. There are times when limited or full-scale auctions for businesses are appropriate. Before going that route, a buyer should again give the matter a lot of thought and ask legal counsel and the intermediary specialist about the ramifications.

Auctions Push Prices Up

The highest bid is usually, but not always, the one accepted. Financial condition, culture, and market expertise of the bidders are taken into consideration as are the feelings of key managers, on occasion. Nevertheless, not much money will be left on the table. A full price usually develops, much to the chagrin of the ultimate buyer.

WHAT POTENTIAL LIABILITIES MAY OCCUR EVEN WITHOUT AN AUCTION

Always take negotiating with a third party seriously. Lawyers have ways of helping clients find ways to sue for little provocation. The buyer is exposed to litigation in a number of ways during the course of the acquisition process. All employees involved in that process should know their responsibilities and not exceed them. Discussion with attorneys in advance of beginning the acquisition search and during the negotiations is highly recommended.

- **The confidentiality agreement may be too tough.** A buyer may sign a confidentiality agreement that is too encompassing and restrictive, thereby risking exposure to possible future liabilities if an action can be related to the data received during the due-diligence (purchase investigation) effort.

- **The buyer may be sued.** The buyer may be sued if it later decides not to buy the company after submitting a bid. Take time to write the bid appropriately.

- **The seller may be sued.** The seller may withdraw and not sell the company, and bidders may sue. The seller also needs good legal advice before and during the acquisition process.

- **The bid price may Be reduced.** The bidder may later decide to lower the bid based on new information discovered during a more relaxed period of investigation. This may appear justified but is a potentially litigious issue if not properly documented.

- **The letter of intent may lead to litigation.** If a letter of intent is signed by both buyer and seller, one could get into litigation with the other if the letter did not really reflect the intention of each party and if it was interpreted by the courts as an agreement to sell or buy, rather than as a simple letter of intent subject to one or more escape clauses.

Sample Letters of Intent

Appendix A's sample letters of intent are not intended to be the proper letter for any particular situation, but they present issues that might arise in certain situations. A letter of intent may not even be necessary. Certainly, not all acquisitions have letters of intent signed by one or both parties. Consult an attorney for the form and content of a letter of intent.

HOW TO GET TO PRICE DISCUSSIONS

Usually, the seller has a price in mind. The buyer or intermediary should ask whether a price exists, whether it is firm, and what range it falls in. If the price is not firm, the seller may choose a fairly broad price range sufficient to allow the buyer some room to come close. It takes time to get the price out of some sellers. The same can be true for getting a price out of the buyers. In some cases, they do not have a firm number. If that is the case, or perhaps in any case, the buyer or seller could offer computations along the lines of some of the valuation methods included in Chapter 8. That will focus the parties on one or more methods to value the company and offer a discussion vehicle of the most logical ways to get at the question of value from the buyer's and seller's perspectives.

Another way to get to the price discussion is to involve an intermediary who can discuss the subject individually with each party and help bring the two parties together on price. This approach avoids the embarrassing situation where one party may have mentioned a price too low or too high and ruined the negotiating atmosphere or harmed the long-term relationship of the two parties.

PROBLEMS OF THE SELLER

A seller may face numerous problems:

- Different culture from that of the buyer.
- Materially overstated positive side of the business and materially understated negatives or downside.

- Not being mentally ready to sell.
- No successor to the entrepreneur.
- Family relatives negatively impacting the business or the deal.
- Financial statements in poorly presented form:
- Not showing current interim period and five prior years.
- Omitting balance sheets, income statements, and cash flow analyses.
- Lacking pro forma statements for historical and future years.
- Poor advisors, inside and outside of the business.
- Estate not in order.
- Seller not positioned to sell due to
- Income tax fraud, usually relating to understated inventories, unreported assets, or nondeductible expenses for income tax purposes.
- Inadequate or no internal records for the buyer to review.
- Shareholder disputes.
- Abnormally low profits for a current or recent year.
- Old technology and aging product lines.
- Falling market share.
- No crisis plan for downturn in the business.
- No internal unit cost and unit shipment data by product line for the past three to five years.
- Not being up on competitors' actions in the marketplace.
- Losing credibility due to not really being for sale or because of overly optimistic forecasts.

After the sale, many owners and managers may leave because they are frustrated or planned to leave anyway. If the good ones leave, the business will lose much of its attraction to buyers and its value will also decrease markedly. Then the buyer will have paid too much, regardless of the price! The majority of buyers put in one or more managers to run the business before the end of the first three years.

PROBLEMS OF THE BUYER

A buyer too may face various problems:

- The purchase investigation may be insufficient, especially for a business related to the one now owned or known to the buyer. Too often a buyer thinks he or she knows all there is to know about the business niche and does not take the time to really dig in and analyze the target business in the same niche. Yet, customer relationships differ, pricing may differ, and other issues probably are present.

- There may be too many projections but not enough analysis of product unit costs and selling price trends for the past 5 to 10 years by product line.
- A buyer may lack real comprehension of the base business when compared to other segments. Few businesses have only one product or service. Each different product or service may well be another distinct business as perceived by the customer.
- Inadequate investigation may be made of the business by people experienced in the operations, sales, and administration of a similar business. They may not finish the purchase investigation with written reports by the various people who did the investigation.
- The buyer may lack understanding of the market conditions specifically applicable to the sellers' products and services.
- Current strategic plans of major competitors may be unknown.
- Customers' demands may be changing.
- Market share trends may be unknown.
- Profitability trends by product may be unavailable.
- **The buyer may fall in love too soon;** that is, the buyer may stop analyzing and start buying too quickly. Sometimes this occurs because of the intensity of the drive to buy a business due to the availability of funds or the frequently misguided belief that growth is easier via the acquisition route.
- The six most important items missing are

  People . . . people . . . people.

  Market share . . . market share . . . market share.

  Buyers must meet the key people if they expect to retain them. Also, the buyer must understand the vagaries of the market niches of the target business.
- Why the seller is selling may not be known.
- Involvement in the buying process by management personnel of the buyer may be too limited.
- Sellers may "go to the beach" after the sale.

- A deal structure may lack
- Golden handcuffs. Those are ways (bonus plans, earnouts, stock options, etc.) to keep the key people for a fairly long period after the sale.
- Pay plus incentives equal to past earnings.
- Annual and longer-term incentives.
- No attempt may be made to allow the present managers to manage, if they are capable.
- Buyer may forget to feed the ego of seller and key people of the target business.
- Negotiating style may be poor.
- There may be no noncompetition contracts for key people or agreements preventing them from investing in competitors' businesses.
- The best businesses may not be for sale. Well, let us say sellers do not want to give the impression that they are for sale. If a company looks good, be flexible and fast, and try to tie down an option to buy it as the purchase investigation continues before the pack comes in.

SUMMARY

The human factor is the single biggest influence on the ability of a buyer and a seller to successfully conclude an acquisition after finding each other. People always make the difference. Usually the seller does not have to sell. The buyer's team members will weld a deal together or blow it apart, depending on their personal approaches to the seller and the key managers of the target business.

A second large factor affecting success is whether the buyer can convince the seller (and vice versa) that the transaction proposed will be a good deal for both buyer and seller. If one side tries to outdo the other or get the upper hand, the deal will not take place or will not be as successful in later years due to unhappiness on the part of one of the parties. Do not try to be the only winner. Both sides must win or the ultimate loser may be the party once thought to be the winner!

The staging of the negotiations is very important. At all times be in control of the events needed to complete the transaction, so surprises and unplanned issues are minimized. The people, dates, times, places, and agendas for the meetings must be well planned in advance and should be scheduled and controlled.

Dealings between buyers and sellers from foreign countries are challenging. Laws, accounting principles and practices, and ways people think will differ markedly. Language will often be a barrier to communicating distinctly and precisely. Make sure the other party really does understand what you have proposed and want to accomplish. Listen a lot before telling foreigners all about the transaction and the other issues you believe to be important. Find out what they believe and have in their plans. In that manner, you will still know what you knew before and now know what the other party knows, or at least what they are willing to share. Try to speak at least a little of their language. The days of the ugly American are or should be over. The English language is not the only one in town.

The auction process is a tough one for the buyer. Competitive bidding will almost certainly drive the price up. Analysis is more strained and legal exposure more intense due to the time lines imposed by the seller.

The seller's image to a buyer during negotiations is affected mainly by the personal and business cultures, market share and trends thereof, internal records, planning levels, technological levels of products, potential loss of credibility due to overly optimistic forecasts, and general condition of the company if not positioned for sale.

The buyer's image during negotiations is mainly impacted by insufficient investigation of the target business, causing less-than-adequate understanding of the total business and the financial numbers of consequence. This can result in not really understanding the market conditions particularly applicable to the target firm, including the customers and competitors. In general, **the buyer often falls in love too soon.**

Then, too, the seller or key managers may "go to the beach" after they cash in on the sale of the business. Ways must be found to retain the key people if they are valuable. **Do not buy a business without the leaders, unless that is your plan.**

CHAPTER 11

Ways to Structure the Deal and Why

MAKE YOUR OFFER DIFFERENT

There is more than one way to do a deal. Many ways can be used to structure an acquisition. However, a few methods and techniques are probably best for a specific seller. The key is to find a way to make the transaction a good deal for both the buyer and the seller. That requires a great deal maker, measurable effort, and team planning. Successful acquisitions do not just happen.

A Unique Deal Maker Is Vital to a Good Deal

Sometimes the deal should be simple and other times not so simple. Some owners of smaller businesses believe that the buyer should give them cash in exchange for their shares of stock with, at the most, a very brief legal document containing the basic terms of the sale. Those owners do not want to agree to any future contingencies or restrictions which may decrease the purchase price. Acquisition terms can be complex. What does the seller want? What does the seller need? Is the underlying value at hand to pay for it upfront or must the buyer have time pass to determine the value? Creativity and the income tax laws are the only limits to the structural boundaries of the purchase agreement.

If you do not have a good deal maker on your team, employ one, rent one, but get one. A deal maker can expertly help package the important wants and needs of both sides in the transaction.

Deal the Right Cards

Try a new deck of cards for the instant deal. Maybe deal out a "mulligan" or trial hand to test the seller's reactions to your deal structure and type.

A proposal to buy a business should often differ from the usual, cold, impersonal, and standard approach most frequently used by the large corporate buyers. After all, the seller never sold the business before to anyone, much less to you. Large corporate buyers tend to possess and certainly exhibit little creativity in deal transactions. They see everything in terms of formula pricing, accounting debits and credits, and tax deductions. They simply treat all sellers the same.

That cut and dried approach to deal making is not effective in today's very competitive market for small to medium-size buyers. It works for megadeals, but how many of these truly large transactions occur in your company? Such deals are not a recurring item for sure. The standard, cookie-cutter approach is particularly ineffective in the small to medium-size transactions where one or a comparatively limited number of stockholders own or control all or most of the outstanding shares of stock of the selling company. In such companies, the owners are generally entrepreneurs. Entrepreneurs do not think like traditional stockholders of larger corporations. Yes, they do want a fair price for their shares. Yes, they do have some knowledge of the ways values are determined for similar businesses. However, they have a much closer attachment to the business and the employees than typical stockholders of large corporations have. They often want special attention, special consideration, and more stroking (personal interaction and support).

Make Your Offer Incomparable

No other point in this book merits more time on your part as a buyer. Sellers already know that if all offers are the same, or almost the same, top money upfront will win.

However, if the buyer offers terms that are not totally comparable to those of other real or potential bidders, the seller will take notice. That offer will be studied to see whether the overall price, terms, and conditions seem fair and whether the differences are pluses or minuses. Differences in the offers will be prominent in the mind of the seller. Such differences can include: benefits, terms of employment, the manner key employees are to be treated or perceived to be treated, length of the noncompetition period, the legal style or appearance in content of letters of intent (including whether a cash payment is offered with the letter of intent), the volume of pages in the offer document, the amount of cash upfront, and so forth.

Offers Should Include What the Seller Needs, Not Just What the Seller Wants

Stockholders/owners of small- to midsize businesses tend to lack adequate income tax and estate tax planning. Similarly, they may not have good pension plans to cover them after retirement. They do not think about retiring until it almost happens.

Sensitive and caring buyers (are those adjectives ever used to describe you as a buyer?) can cover these areas in discussions with the seller and include appropriate issues as part of the acquisition transaction. That approach will differ from those submitted by the pack. That different offer, if fair, will be remembered and be successful!

WHAT ARE THE SELLER'S WANTS AND NEEDS?

Nothing is more important in deal making, once the right business is discovered, than determining what the seller wants and what the seller needs. These two issues are not the same.

As a child the author wanted candy yet needed socks. The same statement holds true even today. The discovery of the seller's basic wants and needs is not a simple, easy process. Successful buyers excel at discovering the key trigger points of the seller, long before they start structuring and pricing the transaction. Lacking this capability, many otherwise astute buyers will lose the deal to competitors or structure the transaction incorrectly and ineffectively.

A publicly held corporation will operate differently in the acquisition marketplace, as either the buyer or the seller. Pressures by stockholders, corporate bureaucratic standard operating procedures, and regulatory agencies of the local, state, and federal governments influence the style, timing, and procedures that publicly held buyers or sellers are allowed to or do use.

The Key to Success in M&A

The real key is to discover what makes the other side tick. How do they think? What is important to them? What are their personal idiosyncrasies? What are their wants? What are their needs? This book cannot cover every way conceived to structure an acquisition agreement. However, the book and this chapter in particular do illustrate some major types of structures a buyer and seller should consider for many transactions.

There is no end to innovation in deal structuring. Some of it is good and some of it bad for the company, its shareholders, and its employees. Issues to review for potential inclusion in M&A deal structuring include

- What are the individual seller's income tax and estate tax considerations? Does the seller care about the tax consequences based on the price?
- What are the compensation issues of the sellers and key employees?
  - Management employment contracts.
  - Noncompete agreements.
  - Earnouts or contingent ways for the seller and/or key personnel to participate in future growth.
  - Some equity participation.
  - Deferred payments of the purchase price and deferred incentive awards. Are they preferred? Are they appropriate?
  - Deferred tax-deductible purchase price amounts including those for consulting services, director fees, royalties, license fees, pensions, and health care benefits.
- Will restrictions on continuing operations before and after closing be needed?
- Will the seller take only cash, only capital stock, part in interest-bearing notes receivable, or some combination?
- Are royalties and license fees for technology or other factors desired by the seller and attractive to the buyer?
- Does it make sense to have the seller continue to own the real estate and fixed assets (buildings, machinery, or equipment) and lease them to the buyer? This reduces the upfront capital needed to buy the business and may be of value to the seller from a tax standpoint.

THE M&A LEGAL AND TAX FORMAT

The legal form in which an acquisition or merger is documented depends on the intent of the parties. In the main, the choices are

- The acquisition of all or just certain assets and all, some, or none of the liabilities and contingencies.
- The acquisition of capital stock.
- A statutory merger, whereby owners of two or more individual corporations agree to exchange shares of their corporate capital stock with each other, and one corporation is merged into the other and ceases to exist as a separate legal entity.

The Form of the Acquisition Varies

The proper form depends on the intent of the parties and can be influenced by tax laws, pending or potential litigation, whether the shares of one party are publicly traded, and other factors. Consult investment advisors, taxation and accounting experts, as well as legal counsel to select the best form for particular circumstances.

Public securities laws apply to some transactions involving state and federal agencies. In addition, certain acquisitions and mergers require filings with regulatory bodies. Federal labor laws, union labor contracts, pension plans, and state laws relating to plant closures and so on may also impact the timing and the form of the transaction.

Further, some acquisitions may not be permitted under the laws of the country for security or other reasons. Acquisitions are not easy from any standpoint. Government rules, regulations, and reporting are just part of the maze. In certain cases, the seller and/or buyer may be required to obtain the approval of shareholders and/or financial institutions holding debt instruments prior to completing the sale.

Is the Deal to Be Tax-Free?

Then the need to structure the transaction to be taxable, partly taxable, or tax-free has to be resolved. A taxable transaction can result when either capital stock or assets are acquired. No taxable gain or loss is recognized if stock or securities in a corporation that is party to a reorganization is exchanged for stock or securities of a corporation that is a party to a reorganization (IRS Code Sections 354 and 361). To qualify as a tax-free acquisition it must fall into in one of seven qualified corporate reorganizations. These are referred to by letters in Code Section 368 as letters "A" through "G". The income tax laws are so complex and subject to such constant change that both buyer and seller should consult tax experts, before structuring the acquisition, for best net-of-tax results.

ACCOUNTING COMPLIANCE

Accounting for Acquisitions

The accounting for an acquisition varies by the underlying securities used. If the buyer corporation issues only voting common stock of the type outstanding and held by a majority of the stockholders in exchange for substantially all the voting common stock of a target corporation, a pooling of interests or purchase can usually be used. Normally, all other types of purchases will be treated as purchases for accounting purposes. The income tax ramifications may and often do differ from the accounting treatment.

Acquisition accounting for book and tax purposes can be difficult to keep track of but must be done correctly. Since income tax regulations and accounting standards change periodically, always have experts in taxation and accounting principles consult with you as buyer or seller.

Accounting Principles in M&A

Generally speaking, accounting principles for acquisitions are contained in Accounting Principles Board Opinions (APBs) of the American Institute of CPAs and, more specifically, APB Opinion No. 16, Business Combinations, and APB Opinion No. 17, Intangibles, and a number of interpretations by the various authoritative bodies. Income tax regulations applicable to acquisitions are mainly contained in various Code sections of the federal income tax laws.

In simple terms, APB No. 16 allows two main methods of accounting for business combinations: the purchase method and the pooling-of-interest method.

The purchase method of accounting requires the acquisition to be recorded at the buyer's purchase cost. Assets purchased for cash are recorded at the amount disbursed. If the asset is obtained as an exchange, without cash, cost is the fair value of the assets given up or received, whichever is clearer. If stock is issued in exchange for assets, the cost of the stock is determined by the fair value of the assets acquired. Liabilities are assumed to be priced at the present value of the amount that will eventually be paid. Any contingent issuable debt or equity security is recorded when the contingency is resolved. If the purchase price exceeds the fair value of the seller's assets, net of any liabilities applicable, the excess is recorded as goodwill. If the purchase price is less than the fair value of assets less liabilities, the difference usually is deducted from noncurrent assets.

Pooling of Interests

The pooling-of-interests method of accounting is intended to reflect a merger or adding together of the two businesses. Balance sheets are simply added together and results of operations are also added together to show the joint totals. All amounts are carried forward without restatement of amounts. The net result is as if the entities being pooled were always together even in prior years.

WHAT A WAY TO BUY

One novel approach used occasionally by venture capitalists and others is to buy a minority interest in quality companies at a very high price. Later the remaining shares outstanding are purchased on more favorable terms.

For example, let's assume a business has a current fair market value of $25 million. First, the buyer might offer, say, $19 million for 49.9 percent of the stock, which is only $6 million less than the value for 100 percent of the stock. The seller still has ownership control of 50.1 percent and operates the business as always. This appears to be very acceptable to many sellers. To make the economics work for the buyer, the buyer insists the purchase price of $19 million be entirely or almost entirely raised by pledging the seller's net assets and borrowing the rest at banks, insurance companies, or elsewhere. Perhaps the buyer need only come up with less than $5 million.

The business goes on, heavily saddled with debt, but the buyer expects the debt will be paid off out of cash flow, and the buyer's return on a relatively small investment will be high with little downside risk. Later, probably as provided by the original purchase agreement, the company may have its shares publicly traded, or the buyer or the selling corporation itself may have an option on the seller's remaining shares at a fixed or variable price, thereby permitting the original buyer to exit profitably via a public offering or acquire control. This is another innovative way to make the deal happen.

LBOs AND MBOs

In this period of high financing, unfriendly and friendly takeovers, and urges to buy with small down payments, a number of financing vehicles has arisen. Each has different implications and is tailored to the buyer with some attention to the seller.

Leveraged Buyouts

Leveraged buyouts (usually referred to as LBOs) can be either friendly or unfriendly as to their approach to management and the target company's board of directors. An LBO is most easily accomplished when the target company is asset-rich, is not heavily in debt compared to the underlying stockholders' equity (assets less liabilities), and has good cash flow prospects.

Banks, insurance companies, and other firms lend funds collateralized by the target company's net assets. The lenders receive a debt security (convertible for common and/or preferred shares or straight debt), capital stock (common or preferred shares), or a combination of those securities. Frequently, the investors will receive financing of 5 to 15 times the amount of the equity of the investors who are in charge of the acquisition. The cash flow of the operations pays off the lenders, and the investor group has a vastly enhanced ownership with minimum capital of its own at risk . . . hopefully.

Many LBO investors expect to realize a multiple of their investment in a three- to seven-year time frame. Taking the business public (that is, selling shares of capital stock on stock exchanges) or selling out to other third-party investors is the name of the game for them.

Management Buyouts

Management buyouts (MBOs) are similar to LBOs, except management, rather than third-party outside investors, intends to make the acquisition.

Then too, outsiders may ask management to participate in the buyout with the outside investors to insure their staying with the business and making the profits and cash flow happen. Such transactions are still

referred to as MBOs. The percentage ownership offered to managers
varies according to the specifics of the MBO offer. Whether the managers
have to pay for their shares at all, in the same proportion and way that the
LBO group does, or in other ways are variable issues. Once the debt levels
are more rational, and given a consistent track record of profits and cash
flow, the investor group may take the company public, sell it, or refinance
for additional acquisitions.

Management Buyouts May
Be Conflicts of Interests

MBOs can often be perceived as direct conflicts of interests when comparing the position of management with that of the present stockholders, unless those stockholders favor selling.

Do the managers see more value in the business than they have com-
municated to the stockholders? If so, why have they not informed the
stockholders? Nonetheless, if the business will be sold, the managers and
other key people represent a logical buying group. They should be able to
find the same amount of financing leverage available to an LBO group or
employ financial experts to structure the transaction and obtain the financing for them.

MBOs Are Often Successful

A comparatively high success rate follows MBOs since management does
in fact know the ins and outs of the business.

Perhaps the owners did not reinvest in its growth to retain market
share, did not fund adequate technology levels, lost key personnel, and
missed other opportunities. They may have drained its cash (milked the
cash cow) for other personal investments or a higher life style. Perhaps the
owners just did not want all their eggs in one basket. Maybe they desired
to get more liquid and get off the hook from corporate debt secured by
their personal guarantees.

For whatever reason, MBOs are a serious way for sellers to cash in at
once or over time via installment sales of stock. MBOs are also a great vehicle for outside buyers to come into ownership (minority or majority) of
the business—all the while insuring that management will continue on
due to the "golden handcuffs" of stock ownership. Management might negotiate for an increasing ownership percentage of the business upon meeting or exceeding certain goals mutually agreed on with the other outside
owners.

EMPLOYEE STOCK OWNERSHIP PLANS

These plans—referred to as ESOPs—are one of the few gifts from the U.S. Congress and the Internal Revenue Service. ESOPs are qualified retirement plans established as an avenue for employees to invest in an employer's capital stock.

They can be used as the company's retirement plan or in conjunction with a corporate retirement plan. In fact, the Tax Reform Act of 1986 permits ESOP participants to begin to diversify their investment after age 55 and before retiring from the company by selling shares of the employer back to it in accordance with certain conditions. See an income tax expert to check on the latest applicable tax regulations to keep current on this and other issues. An excellent general review of ESOPs is contained in chapter 30 of *Valuing a Business* (3d ed., 1996) by Shannon P. Pratt, Robert F. Reilly, and Robert P. Schweihs, published by Richard D. Irwin.

An ESOP can be used to finance the corporation's growth and the purchase of the business from the stockholders with good tax benefits to those selling stockholders. Banks lending the money to buy the stock and the employees, who can pay for the stock out of corporate cash flow, all receive substantial tax benefits. The specific tax incentives should be reviewed with expert tax advisors since the tax laws change.

Theoretically, employee productivity will increase since employees will remain with the business and own part of the profits and stockholders' equity. The selling stockholders and the employee stockholders will build capital appreciation over the long term in a tax-sheltered environment. The U.S. Congress has passed tax legislation many times affecting ESOPs, but each time the tax benefits have been retained or enhanced. That position could change so applicable regulations should be reviewed on a current basis.

ESOPs Defined

In simple terms, an ESOP is a benefit plan for all employees allowing them to own their employer corporation over time by paying for it out of the profits of the employer rather than out of their wages. It is really like a deferred-compensation profit-sharing plan that has, as its target, appreciation in value over time of the very company giving rise to the job of each person.

Whereas profit-sharing plans usually pay benefits in cash, an ESOP purchases and then distributes the capital stock of the corporation to the employees. ESOP plans do not permit discrimination in favor of highly compensated employees and must benefit a stipulated percentage of all employees of a certain type.

A definite formula for allocating stock to the member employees must be used. The formula is often based on the percentage an employee's compensation is to the total compensation of the members of the plan. There are restrictions on the amounts that can be distributed annually.

Some experts argue that substantial amounts of the assets of an ESOP can be invested outside of the employing company's own securities. That is not typical. Normally, the employer's securities are common stock or preferred stock that is convertible into common stock.

ESOPs May Offer Substantial Tax Benefits

The ESOP offers a number of tax benefits to employers, to selling shareholders, and to certain lenders to ESOPs or to employers funding them to acquire the employer's stock.

■ The corporation can borrow the money to buy the stock from the owner and pay the indebtedness in pretax dollars since contributions to the ESOP are tax-deductible for federal income tax purposes. A leveraged ESOP can result in both interest payments and principal repayments that are deductible for income tax purposes by the corporation, which is not true for more traditional forms of borrowing.

■ Employer contributions are tax-deductible whether in the form of cash or its own stock. Using its stock conserves cash for the employer while adding a tax deduction, which increases cash net of taxes. Corporate contributions to an ESOP are usually limited to 15 percent of the total employee payroll, except under some conditions.

■ Another benefit comes from lower interest rates charged by the lender on borrowings. This should follow because only 50 percent of the earned interest for funds loaned by banks and other specified lenders is taxable to them. So lending money for ESOP purchases of an employer's stock is attractive to the qualified lenders who do receive a deduction for interest on funds they may have borrowed to fund the ESOP loan amount in the first place.

■ Another potentially super benefit to the seller is the provision in the federal income tax code allowing proceeds from the sale of the stock to the ESOP to be invested by sellers as tax-deferred if the proceeds are reinvested in securities of many U.S.-based corporations within a short period of time. It requires a filing of a tax reporting form during the year of the sale.

The seller thereby converts a possibly illiquid position with a cost basis (normally resulting in a high capital gain tax upon sale) in a single corporation to a very liquid investment in one or more publicly traded securities. This requires certain compliance such as sale of at least 30 percent of the corporation to the ESOP. Additional sales of stock will also receive the tax-deferred treatment as long as the ESOP continues to hold at least 30 percent of the outstanding shares of the company. Taxation will only result when and if the seller sells the securities purchased with the ESOP funds.

- Dividends paid to participants or to the ESOP and in turn redistributed within 90 days after the plan year are tax-deductible expenses, for federal income tax purposes, by the employer corporation. These dividends would not be deductible if paid to outsiders as is common in publicly held corporations. Dividends paid to make debt service payments on loans used by the ESOP to acquire the company's shares are also tax-deductible.

- Certain estate tax benefits may also be available. Consult a good tax attorney or tax accountant to review these areas in detail under the then-applicable tax laws.

An ESOP's Shares Can Be Acquired

One requirement of an ESOP is that the shares owned by an ESOP have to be valued annually by an independent, qualified valuation expert. That annual appraisal must be filed each year with the Internal Revenue Service (IRS). The IRS income tax code regulations specify the qualifications of an independent appraiser.

Nevertheless, any third party can offer to buy the shares owned by the ESOP. Just keep in mind that differences between a buyer's valuation and offer to buy will come under close review by every employee and the federal government. That additional scrutiny usually is absent when ESOPs are not involved, except for scrutiny by the Securities and Exchange Commission when publicly held companies are involved.

Valuing ESOP shares can include factors for minority position (lack of control) and for lack of marketability (no public price established). Yet, the ESOP may have an option to "put" the shares back to the employer at a stipulated price or prices. This put is required under certain circumstances, which again require the buyer to involve tax experts and consider the selling company's value in light of any significant puts outstanding, which may affect the company's liquidity and thus its value to a third party.

How ESOPs Can Decrease
Seller's Value

A company may have a leveraged ESOP with related debt on its balance sheet. If the total debt level of the seller is excessive as perceived by buyers due to normal business debt plus the ESOP-related debt, then the value of the business may suffer and drop due to the level of debt service requirements. This is certainly applicable if the company finds itself in an economic downturn causing operating cash flow to decrease.

Past and future cash expenditures for personnel, property, plant and equipment, marketing, or product development may have been or are hampered by the cash needed to service ESOP-related debt within the company. That can reduce the seller's value. Therefore, a seller should not adopt an ESOP without considering its long-term consequences. If sale of the business is on the horizon, stop. Why bring broader ownership of the business into the scene? ESOPs are not deal breakers or barriers, but they are impediments. One more owner is one too many.

Should Earnings of the Seller
Be Adjusted Because of ESOPs?

Not necessarily. However, let's talk about it.

If earnings from prior years or the current year are the basis of valuation multipliers, the buyer may adjust the earnings upward or downward, assuming the ESOP will not exist after the sale. Perhaps employee benefits will decrease to bring them more in line with the buyer's policies. On the other hand, employee benefits may increase since the seller may not have been adequately compensating the employees overall. Still, the debt level of the target seller may be so high considering it leveraged itself to fund the ESOP, that the seller's value should be decreased.

What will the future net-of-tax and net-of-debt service cash flow be after the seller takes over? That is a good criterion for deciding if adjustments to the purchase price are in order.

CAPITAL STOCK ACQUISITION VERSUS ASSET PURCHASE

Many buyers of small- to midsize businesses want to buy assets instead of capital stock to avoid contingent or real unrecorded liabilities that would go with the business if they bought capital stock.

On the other hand, if the target business has operating losses that can be carried forward and used to offset future profits, such losses are potentially valuable to the buyer and can be carried forward into the acquisition only if the acquisition is properly structured. An income tax expert is needed to assist in determining under what circumstances tax loss carryforwards can be used by buyers. Asset purchases do not qualify to allow use of a seller's loss carryforwards on the acquirer's income tax returns.

Also, a buyer may want to preserve a special business license or the corporate charter for banking, insurance, or other reasons so buying capital stock would be in order.

BUYING ASSETS—FLEXIBILITY

Some buyers structure the acquisition as a purchase of certain assets rather than buying capital stock of the target company. Then they structure the deal to fit their particular preferences if the seller is flexible.

Less Risk in Buying Assets Instead of Capital Stock

It is usually desirable to purchase assets. Part of the purchase price can probably be allocated to depreciable assets if the transaction is so structured. Further, buying assets generally insulates the buyer from corporate liabilities, whether or not recorded on the books of the buyer, and from other real or potential contingencies. Check to see if any liens or other claims are attached to the assets by searching for such at local court houses.

Contracts not desired by the buyer are also so excluded. Such business contracts could include those applicable to labor unions, social benefits, leases, purchase orders, and others.

The purchase agreement is simpler in wording if only assets are purchased. However, the asset purchase requires that many details be resolved concerning the registration of the assets into the new owner's name, clearance from security collateral arrangements if any, and other matters.

If only assets or assets and specific liabilities are designated as being purchased instead of capital stock, be sure to include trade names, trademarks, patents, corporate names, and know-how if desired and if appropriate.

Buy What You Want

For example, a buyer's offer might exclude purchasing the accounts receivable. This eliminates concern by the buyer as to the collectibility of the accounts and also reduces the cash required up front to finance the deal. Such an offer could and probably should allow the buyer to collect those accounts receivable from the customers and remit the proceeds intact to the seller as collected. This procedure keeps direct contact with the customers under the control of the buyer, who will want their future business.

In the case of inventories, the buyer could offer to pay only for the inventories as they are used in the business (entered into the production cycle or sold to customers). Thus, the buyer is protected from purchasing potentially obsolete items or those units that are slow-moving inventories. The initial purchase price is also less since payment by the buyer for the items will be made only when the items in inventory are used.

Accounts payable could also be excluded from the purchase so all purchases from vendors begin anew with the buyer of the business and old lingering disputes with vendors are excluded from the acquisition transaction.

Bank loans and other unsecured debt might be excluded from the acquisition. Again, this approach will modify the acquisition price at settlement, and it will allow the buyer to refinance the entire acquisition without the limitations of the seller's current borrowing agreements, if not included in the transaction and if allowed by the buyer's lender.

Union labor contracts and other contractual obligations as well as real or contingent liabilities are avoided if assets are purchased instead of the capital stock of the corporation. The ramifications of this could be rather important to the buyer. However, it is not easy to avoid union labor commitments without a lot of effort and a ton of luck.

ASSIGNMENT OF VALUES BY CONTRACT TO SPECIFIC ASSETS

Assigning specific values within the acquisition agreement may influence the taxation of the sale of the business at federal, state, and local levels of taxation.

If apportionment of all or some of the purchase price is stipulated within the purchase agreement, the tax basis of those items may carry over to the corporate and personal income tax returns of buyer and seller. Consult a qualified income tax expert on how to determine the best ways to treat such issues for tax purposes. But do not allow taxes to foul up a good deal for your business and for you.

Sometimes, the seller wants and may need to continue to own the real estate or some of the property, plant, and equipment after the sale. Related debt, possibly a mortgage, normally follows the applicable asset and is also then excluded from the items covered by the acquisition agreement. Naturally, the purchase price will be reduced, assuming related debt does not exceed the fair market value of the related assets.

If some of the products or processes are patented, the seller may prefer to retain ownership to such patents and grant licenses or rights to the buyer to use such assets and pay for the use over time via royalties or other means. So-called black-box technology or know-how can be treated in the same manner. These arrangements for intangible assets will reduce the amount of cash, notes payable, or securities required at closing. Also, the buyer can then pay for the use of those assets as the business generates the funds, unless such intangible assets prove to have little or no value.

ALLOCATION OF PURCHASE PRICE
FOR TAX PURPOSES

Since the Tax Reform Act of 1986, many allocations once deductible for income tax purposes are no longer available to reduce taxable income. See an income tax advisor for the best allocations to include in the agreement of sale.

CAPITAL STOCK FOR CAPITAL STOCK

In this scenario, the seller and buyer exchange shares of capital stock with each other as a pooling of interests or as a purchase.

Usually, the pooling transaction can avoid taxation until the respective shares are resold. Further, the transaction is quite simple, easily understood, and not too difficult to handle from a bookkeeping standpoint. Part of the proceeds can even be paid in cash in the case of a statutory merger and a transfer to a controlled corporation. Expert tax advice is required to avoid unplanned taxation, and accountants are needed to advise on the bookkeeping.

CASH (OR PART CASH AND PART STOCK) AT CLOSING

This is a fairly simple way to effect the purchase, but the amount of stock used will impact tax and accounting treatment. Many sellers prefer cash. Stock prices vary over time and are not controllable by the recipient due to the influence of the economy, market conditions, technology, and other outside factors. In addition, some stock certificates are subject to restrictions on resale of the shares received. The amount of stock versus cash received will affect the taxation of the transaction. Due to the unpredictable dynamics of taxation, always involve tax advisors early on before structuring a transaction to acquire a business.

CASH AND NOTES PAYABLE

The use of cash and cash-equivalent interest-bearing notes that equate to cash is simple, yet it allows the buyer an amount of comfort because the seller is still looking to the buyer for cash when the notes come due and collectible.

This method often eliminates the need for an escrow of part of the proceeds at settlement, since the buyer still owes part of the consideration and might offset the notes payable if misrepresentations were made by the seller or in the event of other disputes. Owing money to the seller after the date of sale is one good way to keep the seller honest and interested in the future success of the business. Keep it in mind. Having the seller provide some of the leverage is usually cheaper, is less restrictive, and affords some advantages later on if the deal goes sour due to misrepresentations by the seller.

FORGIVENESS AMOUNT FOR ERRORS OR ADJUSTMENTS

Financial statements are not always accurate to the decimal point or even to the nearest $10,000. They do contain estimates of realizable amounts such as uncollectible accounts receivable, obsolete inventories, overstated assets, and/or understated liabilities. Frequently, the actual value of such items cannot be known until weeks or months after the date of financial statements containing the book amounts.

Allow a Margin of Error to Simplify the Deal and Save Money Later

Reduce the amount of extra work by auditors and attorneys by using a "basket" clause in the agreement.

A buyer and seller should usually agree to having a pool of forgiveness (a basket) provided for in the M&A agreement. That basket could be in the range of $5,000 to over $1,000,000 depending on the size of the transaction. A percentage of the purchase price (say, 3 to 8 percent), could be used for that purpose. This clause in the agreement allows for generally minor adjustments to the books and records of the target company without adjusting the purchase or exchange price of the total deal. If the errors are tolerable in amount, the financial statements, on which the price of the transaction was determined fully or in part, can be allowed to contain fairly small individual or cumulative errors without disrupting the transaction's timing or price.

Such a proviso is highly recommended for most acquisition agreements in order to keep the deal on stream and not allow it to derail due to fairly insignificant errors or omissions.

CONTINGENT PAYMENTS AND EARNOUTS— "GOLDEN HANDCUFFS"

The term *golden handcuffs* is one the author may have created and is not to be confused with golden parachutes, which refer to substantial payments to those individuals covered by them in the event the business is purchased by others and the individuals are terminated by the new buyer. The holders of such parachutes can leave (bail out) with handsome rewards paid out of the corporate treasury.

The concept of golden handcuffs is to have the buyer pay a reasonable price up-front for the business, yet have substantial funds due to the seller and/or other key people at a later date or dates, say, three to five years.

Such incentive funds may be payments based on attainment of future goals for operating revenues, profits, and/or cash flow of the business purchased. These contingent payments are also referred to as earnouts. They are due to be paid only if the targets are attained or exceeded. The payments could also be represented as deferred consulting fees or pension-type payments, or they might be based on other contingencies. Such contingencies might require a stipulated period of employment, a non-competing period, the resolution of litigation, the achievement of certain business goals, or the resolution of other items before the deferred payment becomes due.

The Reason to Use Golden Handcuffs

The main reason for the buyer to provide golden handcuffs is to keep the seller and/or other key people active and motivated in the business.

Retaining consulting services of the seller and other key personnel over a number of years after the acquisition may be vital. Their technical assistance may be needed. Access to new technology or innovations may be facilitated by the seller or the key people after the sale date. After all, these people grew the business to the point that the business became of interest.

Deferring Payments Has Advantages

From the seller's standpoint, such deferred payments and contingent payments may be acceptable or desirable. For example, income tax rates may be expected to decrease or be eliminated on some formerly taxed classifications of income. Capital gains is one type of income that may or may not be taxed in future years. Also, the seller might expect net income to increase materially in the coming years and favor participation in that upside potential gain in value.

Many earnout clauses in acquisition agreements potentially add from 15 to 50 percent or more to the initial base purchase price, if the targets are achievable.

Deferring Payments May
Have Disadvantages

The seller, in accepting deferred potential payments, risks having received a lower initial base price for the business and may not be entitled to further payments due to poor economic conditions, increased competition, technological changes, or poor performance by the new owner.

Another very possible complication for earnouts is the difficulty in tracking revenues and related costs if the buyer sells or merges the business with another, changes manufacturing and distribution methods or locations, does not invest in efficient production equipment, charges different management fees or interest charges than before, or changes accounting principles and practices. Perhaps the most serious problem could be the failure of the buyer to pay the seller future earned amounts due to (1) disputes between the parties relating to the original sale (seller's warranties and so forth) or (2) the buyer becoming insolvent or bankrupt.

So cash on the barrel may be the right answer if any real doubts exist about whether certain earnout amounts may ever be collected.

Earnouts need to be very carefully defined in the acquisition agreement. Examples of how the computations are to be made should also be included in that agreement to avoid misunderstandings later.

Golden Handcuffs Can Offer Leverage

The golden handcuffs can offer some buyers between 15 and 50 percent or more of the financing of the total purchase price established by the seller. The exact amount is a matter of negotiation.

Part of the golden handcuffs could be notes payable for a portion of the price, and part could be in the form of an earnout. This substantially reduces the amount needed from other sources at probably higher interest rates or tougher lending terms. Collateral for the notes payable, which are usually issued by the target company being sold, is usually the company itself. Its capital stock can be pledged. Personal guarantees are sometimes included in smaller transactions. The shares of stock may be pledged subject to other agreed-on debt restrictions from banks or other sources.

This is a significant area to explore with the seller and should be given much attention. It is important as a financing vehicle and has great impact on the seller's involvement and attention after the sale.

Use Ingenuity to Make the Deal Happen

Creativity is the only limit in how to structure each acquisition. The seller's wants and needs must be determined and dealt with appropriately.

All contingent payments will have income tax consequences that may differ. Some will be treated by the tax authorities as additional purchase price and may or may not be deductible for income tax purposes or may be deductible over a series of years. Other payments will represent deductible items of expense when payment is made or due.

EXAMPLES OF DEFERRED PAYMENT DEAL STRUCTURES–EARNOUTS/GOLDEN HANDCUFFS

Assume a business was acquired for $10 million in cash or cash equivalents (secured interest-bearing notes). Also, assume that results of operations for that business for the five years following the acquisition are as shown in Table 11–1.

The following section offers a series of examples to stimulate the buyer's imagination as to how to structure incentives to retain the seller and/or key people at the seller's company. These are only a few of the ways to consider. Use the buyer's company goals or those of the target business to create the best incentives for a particular transaction. The incentive contingent payments could be applied as additional purchase or as actual bonus incentives (normally tax-deductible) representing the only incentive plans of Company Sold, or they could be added to the already existing incentive systems in that company. The use of three- and five-year periods is not necessary or even appropriate for every business purchase. These are merely examples. Use the right number for your particular transaction.

TABLE 11–1

Incentive Earnout
Company Sold (Dollars in Thousands)
Assume a Buyer's Base Purchase Price of $10,000

Years	Revenue	Gross Profit $	Gross Profit %	Income after Tax	Generated Cash Flow	Cash Dividends
First	$12,000	$ 4,800	40.0%	$1,000	$1,100	$ 900
Second	11,000	4,070	37.0	900	1,010	910
Third	13,000	5,200	40.0	1,300	1,420	1,200
Total	36,000	14,070	39.1	3,200	3,530	3,010
Fourth	15,000	6,150	41.0	1,400	1,530	1,230
Fifth	17,000	7,140	42.0	1,600	1,740	1,340
Total	$68,000	$27,360	40.2%	$6,200	$6,800	$5,580

Example 1. Contingent Payment Based on Growth in Revenues

A contingent payment could be due if cumulative revenues for the three years ended after the acquisition date exceed $36,410,000 (a 10 percent compounded annual growth rate from $10,000,000 for the year before the sale date).

Actual revenues per Table 11–1 totaled $36,000,000, so no payment became due for the first three years. However, if the agreement required the same 10 percent growth for the five-year period, the minimum target is $67,156,100 in cumulative sales for the five years. Therefore, a payment would be due based on a percentage of the excess of $843,900. Perhaps 20 percent of the excess would be fair. In that case, 20 percent of $843,900 is $168,780 due to the seller after year 5.

Example 2. Contingent Payment Based on Gross Profits

Assume a contingent payment is due if cumulative gross profits for the first three- and five-year periods exceed $5 million per year ($15 million for first three years and $25 million for the five years).

Actual gross profits were only $14,070,000 (Table 11–1) for the three years, so no payment is due. However, the gross profits for the five years were $27,360,000 ($2,360,000 higher than $25 million), thereby earning a payment from the buyer of that excess times a percentage. If that percentage was 10 percent, the seller would receive $236,000 at the end of the fifth year—which is well worth staying around for.

Another way to use gross profits in contingent earnouts is to base the payment on a percentage of revenues. If in the earlier case, the percentage would have been 39 percent per year on average (assume it is the historical average), then the actual percentages for the three- and five-year periods exceed the target of 39 percent by .1 and 1.2 percentage points, respectively. (See Table 11–1.) Suppose the buyer agreed to pay the seller $100,000 for each percentage point or fraction thereof per year in which the actual gross profit exceeded 30 percentage points. Then 0.1 percent times the $100,000 base (or $10,000) is due for each of the three years payable at the end of the third year (or $10,000 times the three years, which totals $30,000). At the end of five years 1.2 percentage points (40.2 less the 39 percent base target) times the $100,000 base is due (or $120,000) for each of the five years for a total of $600,000.

Increasing gross profit margin percentage rates is not an easy task.

Example 3. Contingent Payment Based on Growth in Income after Tax

In this case, assume the contingent payments are based on income after taxes exceeding $1,000,000 average per year for the three- and five-year periods. For each dollar over that goal, the seller agreed to pay the same multiple (10 PE) paid at the outset based on historical profits.

In the earlier case (Table 11–1), the cumulative income after tax for Company Sold was $3,200,000 for the first three years. The target is $3,000,000 total for the three years and the seller is due 10 times the excess amount ($3,200,000 less $3,000,000 = $200,000) or $2,000,000. For the five years, the seller was more fortunate and Company Sold had income after tax of $6,200,000, $1,200,000 more than the target. As a result, the seller is due 10 times that amount, $12,000,000. That type of golden handcuffs would probably keep most sellers working diligently to grow the business profitably.

Example 4. Contingent Payment Based on Dividends to the Buyer (Cash Generated by Company Sold less All Its Business Needs for Reinvesting in Working Capital, Facilities, Equipment, Etc.)

Cash flow is a great scorecard measuring the real success of a business. Suppose the buyer establishes or adopts the cash flow targets of Company Sold. One contingent payment plan could be based on sharing 50 percent of the net cash available for dividends exceeding $900,000 per year on average for the three- and five-year periods. Therefore, the targets are $2,700,000 and $4,500,000 for the three- and five-year periods, respectively.

How was the $900,000 established? It is purely discretionary. It may represent the minimum acceptable amount of return on investment to the buyer.

The actual cash available for dividends at Company Sold for three years was $3,010,000 and was $5,580,000 for the five years per Table 11–1. The contingent payments would be $155,000 (or $3,010,000 less $2,700,000 times 50 percent) for the first three years and $540,000 (or $5,580,000 less $4,500,000 times 50 percent) for the full five-year period.

Example 5. Contingent Payment Based on Growth in Generated Cash Flow

This example is not shown but could be an appropriate one to employ in the right circumstances. Use of imagination is the only limiting factor. The actual cash flows generated would be compared to bonus targets and excesses shared to whatever extent agreed upon.

Example 6. Contingent Payment Based on Return on Investment (ROI) at Cost and at Fair Market Value

Shareholders of any company can measure and compare their ROI in two readily available ways. One way is the cost basis and the other is the fair market value basis. Shareholders of privately held corporations must determine the fair market value basis by assuming the fair market value to be a multiple of after-tax income or by some other method.

Let's look at these methods. One, the investment at original cost basis, simply compares the yearly returns (net income and/or net income plus dividends) to the original cost plus later investments at cost and less dividends/distributions received. The second method is a portfolio approach that compares the estimated value of the investment at a given date, which may be higher or lower than the cost basis, to the returns.

In this case, assume the contingent payments to the seller were payable if the actual ROIs exceeded the goals cumulatively for the three- and five-year periods. The payment could be $100,000 per year on average for each one percentage point over the goal and proportionate payments for fractions. As stated previously, these payments could also be part of an incentive plan for key people to retain and motivate them as they assist in achieving the overall corporate goals of the buyer.

Based on the formula relating to return on investment on the cost basis, the three- and five-year actual ROIs did exceed the goals. See Table 11–2. Payments due to the seller at the end of year 3 would be 2.9 (or 19.9 less 17) times three years times $100,000, or $870,000. At the end of year 5, 5.4 (or 22.8 less 17.4) times five years times $100,000 (totaling $2,700,000) becomes earned.

For the ROIs on the fair value method, payment due to the seller at the end of year 3 would be 1.8 (or 18.8 less 17) times three years times $100,000 (totaling $540,000), and for five years the payment would be 1.3 (or 18.7 less 17.4) times five years times $100,000 (totaling $650,000).

USE CREATIVITY IN TAILORING ACQUISITION AGREEMENTS TO FIT BUYER AND SELLER

This chapter was presented to stimulate your imagination to work diligently at structuring the acquisition agreement to be a good deal for buyer

TABLE 11–2

ROI Earnout

	At Cost		Return on Investment at Fair Value	
	Goal	Actual	Goal	Actual
First	17 %	9.0%	17 %	9.0%
Second	17	–0.9	17	–1.0
Third	17	51.5	17	40.0
Total	17	19.9	17	18.8
Fourth	18	21.9	18	15.9
Fifth	18	32.3	18	20.9
Total	17.4%	22.8%	17.4%	18.7%

and seller. Selecting the best type of acquisition format is vital. Deciding on whether to exchange stock or cash or both is just one important step with differing tax and accounting results. Structuring the transaction as a regular purchase, LBO, MBO, or ESOP definitely affects the future of the business, the owners' rewards, and the ultimate happiness of the people at the business acquired.

Built-in incentives to supplement the initial fair price by means of contingent purchase price and/or other incentive payments allow for upside potential to keep the seller and management very motivated to make the acquisition successful for all parties. The payments could be in cash, capital stock, or combinations. As in so many areas of life, creativity and carefully planned and timed effort will make the difference in success in acquisitions as a buyer, seller, or employee.

Go for it! Beat the competition. Close the deal at a fair price to both seller and buyer.

CHAPTER 12

Managing the Closing and Postclosing Issues

CONTROLLING THE TIME TO NEGOTIATE AND CLOSE THE DEAL

Schedule the Acquisition and Keep to Schedule

The best way for a buyer and a seller to be sure to close on an acquisition transaction is to settle on it with some urgency.

Too much haste may cause the deal to become a bad one through lack of adequate investigation. Yet, the deal must be kept on a track. Otherwise, it may wander into the hands of another buyer, lose a qualified and interested buyer, or allow the seller to constantly change from selling it to not selling it. Unscheduled and constant delays are not in the best interests of the buyer or the seller.

The timing and scheduling of responsibilities without surprises are all important. Assign dates and give people specific duties for both the buyer and seller. Keep in contact with key people throughout the process. High touch by the buyer with the seller's key people is important at all times, especially during the purchase-investigation stage and the early postclosing times.

A number of acquisitions are lost or almost lost between the date the buyer and seller first meet and the closing or settlement date. Such disasters after significant investment of time and expense by both parties

are mainly due to lack of managing and staging the events to cover and
the issues to resolve. One person from the buying company and one from
the selling company should be delegated to keep the negotiations and
purchase investigation proceeding with diligence and in a professional
and personal way.

USE TIME LINE CONTROL

Table 12–1 illustrates one simple way the necessary controls can be in effect, in evidence, and planned for success by the buyer. The buyer and the
seller can each use separate time lines or share one listing all significant
events. The table presumes the first introductory meeting has occurred and
the parties wish to proceed to the next level of the acquisition process. Although the time line control seems rudimentary, it is easy to prepare and
keep up to date—and it works.

WHEN TO STOP NEGOTIATING

Stop Bad Deals in Their Tracks Fast

If the party with whom you are negotiating lies, tries to cheat you, misrep-
resents material issues, and/or is always fighting over every inconsequential issue instead of sticking with the larger, more important items, you
may want to exit. No explanations are necessary. They will know they
overstepped their bounds. Some deals are not destined to be made. You do
not want to make a contract with anyone who is not forthright and honest
in all respects. If one side is always trying to get the best of the other side,
one will be a loser—and that is not good. One of the two parties may not
be realistic and will only hamper future negotiations. You might as well
leave them to their type of people. Your culture will not mesh . . . now or
later.

Keep Up the Pace

If, on the other hand, the major issues were identified and are resolved, try
to wrap up the deal at a resonable pace. Prolonging the negotiating time is
dangerous. The price may change, other buyers will come along, or the
seller may get tired of the process.

TABLE 12–1

Acquisition Time Line Control

Responsible Person	Matters	Final Date	Status and Action Needed
Buyer—W	Set date and agenda—2d mtg.	1/15	
Buyer—X	Arrange tour—manufacturing, including engineering; interview key people.	1/19	
Buyer—X	Review production costs, vendor arrangements, statistics; prepare report on manufacturing, including engineering.	2/15	
Buyer—Y	Meet with seller's CPA.	1/25	
Buyer—Z	Meet with seller's marketing and sales key people.	1/19	
Buyer—Z	Complete market study.	2/14	
Buyer—Z	Interview major customers.	2/14	
Buyer—Z	Report on marketing/sales position.	2/15	
Buyer—Y	Review finance, accounting, tax, and insurance dept. people and reports.	2/15	
Buyer—Y	Prepare report on finance, tax, accounting, and CPA issues.	2/15	
Buyer—T	Review management information systems dept. and prepare report.	2/15	
Buyer—X	Complete negotiations with seller.	2/16	
Buyer—X	Prepare final report proposing or rejecting acquisition.	2/17	
Buyer—V	Meet with seller's legal counsel, reach agreement as to who will prepare each closing document and the documents for notifying and clearing with stockholders, lenders, and regulatory agencies.	2/8	
Buyer—V	Review all necessary legal documents such as articles of incorporation, bylaws, and statutory filings.	2/12	
Buyer—V	Prepare first draft of acquisition agreement.	2/13	
Buyer—V	File any needed reports with regulatory agencies and stockholders.	2/18	
Buyer—X	Obtain approval to acquire.	2/18	
Buyer—V	Clear all changes in acquisition agreement with seller's counsel.	2/26	
Buyer—X	Clear closing date with all parties.	2/26	
Buyer Each person	Complete due-diligence review of interim operations.	2/27	
	Closing—determined by legal approvals.	?	Target is 3/15.

Note: The time line control should be issued no less than every two weeks, showing date issued and status of each step.

Prioritize the Unresolved Issues

Use the ABC system to identify and evaluate all pertinent M&A issues. This is being repeated here since it is such an important technique. Prioritize issues into two (A and B) or three classifications (A, B, and C) according to their importance. Keeping each issue in perspective will assist in getting a good deal to be consummated.

Issues classified as "A" could represent individual dealbreakers, "B" could stand for those that are important enough individually that if several or more are not resolved to your satisfaction, the deal could go down. Normally, "A" items will only represent about 15 percent of the issues, but each is important in its own right. "C" items are individually and collectively minor and may represent around 65 percent of the total number of unresolved negotiating issues, but perhaps only 10 percent of the value of the transaction. Those would not normally stop the transaction. Resolve the big ones, and let the small ones be resolved with dispatch!

Someone from each side, perhaps the deal makers, should be working on a resolution to each open item. The time to stop negotiating must be recognized by both seller and buyer. Prolonging this phase is deadly once the major issues are resolved. Is a delay in anyone's best interest? If not, get on with resolution.

OPERATING DECISIONS DURING A HIATUS

Seller Is in Charge before Closing

The closing or settlement date normally occurs 15 to 60 days after the buyer and seller each verbally agree to the terms of the acquisition. The interim period varies in length depending on the ownership of the companies (publicly held or privately held), the complexity of the agreement, and possible regulatory approvals required. Legal contracts and supporting exhibits, mailings to shareholders, as well as government disclosure filings for certain acquisitions of size are finalized then. During this period (referred to as the hiatus period), the seller's management continues in control, manages the target business, and must continue to manage it. However, certain operating decisions should be cleared with the buyer during this same period.

Buyer Can Be Informed and Active Too

Occasionally, the buyer will be permitted to place one or more persons with operating experience on site at the seller's main place of business. This is not the rule. It is indeed an exception, which, as an accommodation, must be approved in advance by the seller.

The seller risks giving the buyer hands-on knowledge of possible sensitive processes and data when there is still the possibility that the buyer may call off the transaction but still possess valuable new information.

The purpose of apprising the buyer of major operating issues and decisions is for the seller to inform the buyer of significant matters that will affect the period of ownership by the buyer or impact future operating results. Such issues should normally include

- Payment of any dividends or other distributions to stockholders. This provision is meant to prevent the seller from stripping the corporation of its assets, unless it is agreed to by the buyer.
- Wage and salary changes and negotiations on all wage and salary employment contracts.
- Changes in labor benefit programs.
- Financing agreements and sales of any type of capital stock shares.
- Guarantees and other contingent liability agreements by the corporation.
- Substantial agreements and related commitments and orders with vendors, in excess of stipulated amounts agreed to in advance.
- Acceptance of large customer orders. This is important since the buyer can then review sales backlog orders that may materially (adversely or beneficially) impact the future profits of the business after the acquisition. An occasional seller will accept a low gross profit margin order to increase the sales order backlog and thereby impress the buyer. Often, the backlog does not show the estimated profitability, just the sales value. After the acquisition date, those orders will be produced and shipped at abnormally low profits or even losses. Who needs that surprise?
- Changes up or down in selling prices of the target's products.
- Litigation.

- Acquisitions and divestitures of business segments and product and service lines of business. Every buyer is entitled to be informed of what product or service lines of business are being disposed of or acquired before the buyer assumes control.

FINANCING

Do Not Waste Time with Shoppers

Sellers need to screen out buyers who are just shopping for information and those who do not really have the funds to buy at the right price.

Such shoppers will disrupt the operation and waste management's time in the selling company. They will attempt to garner all competitive information available to them. Meanwhile the seller may incur substantial professional fees before it is obvious that the buyer lacks the interest or money to do the deal.

Sellers must ask tough questions and perhaps even obtain a letter from the buyer's financial backer as to the availability of equity funds and credit arrangements for borrowed funds to be used in the transaction. Do not hesitate to ask for the financial statements of the buyer at the outset. Once the closing takes place, the seller is out and the buyer is in. The seller's days of control are over. If the buyer used notes payable or other securities to pay for the business, the seller is exposed. Will the notes or securities be converted timely and in full for cash?

Go to Traditional Financing Sources

A myriad of ways exist, and more are being invented each week, to finance a purchase of assets or capital stock of a target business.

The best sources of financing are the sellers, your banks, insurance companies, investment bankers, and venture capitalists. Yes, friends and relatives can be included in a list of potential financiers on small deals, but do not count on them staying your friends or admitting to being your relative for long after the financing. Your telephone bill will skyrocket, as will your blood pressure, when the business fails to meet the planned growth and profitability, or if more capital is needed to ensure survival in the morass of your marketplace.

Consider Various Financing Methods

How to finance—whether that includes leveraged buyouts (LBOs), cash, cash and notes payable, all debt (convertible features could be used), and/or various types of capital stock—is an issue so dependent on the underlying business that it cannot be covered in this book. Again, talk with several or all of the sources of financing listed previously before deciding on the most appropriate way to go.

Some thoughts about using leverage and its impact on returns on investments in acquisitions are presented in Chapter 8's section "How Using Leverage Affects the Rate of Return on an Investment." In addition, banks, insurance companies, venture capital companies, commercial loan companies, finance and leasing firms, and the federal government's Small Business Administration are other usual sources that the buyer's accountant or attorney may recommend.

SELLER FINANCING

Insofar as the seller is concerned, the financing issues will include whether the seller insists on all cash, all stock of the buyer's corporation, or a combination of those methods of payments. Further, some of the proceeds might be payable over time as predetermined amounts (notes payable), according to a formula earnout, or as some form of compensation.

Notes payable by the buyer will undoubtedly be interest-bearing at rates falling between those established by tax authorities and the short- and long-term rates for similar securities in the marketplace. Those interest rates could be based upon specific securities with fluctuating interest rates over time.

Other seller financing issues are

- The amounts being financed.
- The conditions of the financing:
- Periods covered.
- Scheduled serial or variable amounts of each payment.
- Guarantees and security covering the notes payable to the seller.
- Conditions of breach and default, ways to cure them, and penalties or consequences resulting from them.

Those main issues can normally be easily handled with the aid of expert attorneys and cooperative buyers and sellers. The terms are important since other financing within the target company will be directly influenced by the acquisition terms with the seller. Subordination of the notes to the seller will be demanded by third-party financiers to the target business, unless stock warrants or options or shares are included.

CLOSING DOCUMENTS MUST BE ASSEMBLED AND READ

Legal Issues and Documentation Make Closings Difficult

Legal documentation of the merger or acquisition will vary from state to state, from country to country, and from one merger/acquisition agreement to another. The sheer volume of legal documentation will put fear into the hearts of anyone. Asset and liability assignments and transfers can be complex. Then there is the matter of the buyer and seller warranties. Sellers just want the money and/or shares. Buyers want free title. Lawyers want to document the transaction.

What Are the Basic Documents Called for by Most M&A Agreements?

The mountain of papers attached to or incorporated by reference in the merger or acquisition agreement will be awesome. It is tempting not to read them thoroughly. Each party to the deal must have one or more responsible officers or employees read every document. The more important ones are

- Patents, licenses, royalty agreements, trade names, and trademarks.
- Labor and employment agreements.
- Leases.
- Mortgages, loan agreements, and lines of credit.
- Stock and bond commitments and details.
- Supplier and customer contracts.
- Distributor and sales representative agreements.
- Stock option and employee incentive plans.
- Health and social benefit plans.

- Complete description of all foreign patents, facilities, and investments.
- Intermediary fee arrangements.
- Warranty and guarantee agreements.
- Insurance policies, coverage, and claims pending.
- Litigation pending for and against each party.
- Environmental compliance issues resolved or on track to be resolved.
- Seller's corporate minutes of the board of directors and any other significant committee.
- Articles of incorporation, bylaws, stock certificate books, and seals.

Now, who is going to read each of these on the buyer's and seller's teams? One and hopefully more than one person from each side should read every document before they are submitted to the other party to the transaction. This tough, tedious job must be done carefully and thoroughly for everyone's protection.

POSTCLOSING ISSUES

How to Run the Business after Closing

Buyer and seller must clearly know how to operate the business after the sale. They should agree in advance as to new procedures, paperwork, and timing requested by the buyer for spending for people, facilities, equipment, and materials. All should be aware of the quantitative and qualitative goals and targets of the new owners. A corporate calendar should be prepared identifying deadline dates and times for all routine operating and financial reports. Discussions must be held and plans implemented to deal effectively with the new organization, internally with the employees and facilities and externally with the customers, vendors, regulatory and taxation agencies, and news media.

A Checklist of Important Issues to Control

All real risk issues or potentially high-risk items should be identified and addressed. A consistent position should be agreed to regarding communications with employees, customers, vendors, and the news media.

Outplacement programs may be needed for employees who might be displaced by the merger of the businesses.

The best way to make certain that all significant issues are or will be promptly addressed is to appoint a team to be responsible for all aspects of integrating the acquired business or ensuring it is not integrated and will remain independent as planned. This team can be two or more people as needed to address the following questions:

- What will be the operating style of the new owner? Will it be strong centralized or decentralized control of operations? Of finances? Of sales pricing policies and practices? Of credit policies? Of sales contracts? Of vendor contracts? Of taxes? Of legal issues? Of insurance? Of employment (hiring, terminations, and promotions) and of salary and wage levels? Of labor union contract plans? Of incentive plans? Of retirement plans? Of health care plans? Of stock option plans? Of ESOP plans? Of data processing?

- Will the representatives of the new owner supervise the business? How? From what location?

- What operating and financial reports will be required? How often? What format? What accounting principles and practices are to be followed?

- What fees and expenses will be billed or charged by the buyer to the seller's operations after the sale that impact cash, financial stability, incentive plans, and similar items?

- Will the cash funds be merged into those of the buyer? How? Will the seller be permitted to disperse funds and pay bills and payrolls? Sometimes the buyer will place the seller on a zero balance bank account wherein the seller can still write checks against a bank account with a zero balance, and each check as it clears is paid for by automatic transfers from the parent company's (buyer's) bank account to that of the target company's to exactly reimburse that account.

- How will customers and suppliers view the change in ownership?

- Will the seller's research, design, and development abilities and expenditures be augmented or restricted by the acquisition?

- How will minority shareholders view the change in ownership? Will any shareholders of the seller's company have appraisal rights to different values for their shares?

- Will the seller's company have its own board of directors? If so, who can appoint the members? Can outsiders be or remain on the board?

PITFALLS FOR THE UNWARY

The acquisition process is typically on a short and fast schedule. It is hectic. It can be crisis-oriented. Often, an auction atmosphere (either real or imagined) engulfs the process. Seller-supplied data are the only show in town. Buyers are at the mercy of that data. They are in unfamiliar territory. The industry or market niche may be new or fairly unknown. Nevertheless, the decision has been made to enter the scene and spend thousands, millions, or billions of dollars on a target company.

Do You Have Sufficient Data to Buy?

The owner of the target company wants to sell. Why? The owners apparently are more pessimistic about the business than the buyers and know more about the business. That should be enough for buyers to worry about.

The temptation to grow by acquisitions and to fall in love too soon is real. The buyer may expect too much added value. Market share growth can be bought, but to grow that share to another higher level without buying yet another business is the real trick! Implementation problems can arise. Competitors are probably meeting in their offices, strategically planning to take market share away from the target business.

Management may "go to the beach"—it may just walk out and possibly become a competitor disguised as a son-in-law, friend, affiliated investor, or a newly formed business having too much data about the target business. Now then, why would any buyer want to face those unknowns? Tough question. It needs a good answer.

The real proof of a good acquisition is whether it will ultimately meet or exceed the buyer's target returns on the investment, create the synergy planned, gain the market share, or result in better technology. Unfortunately, those events will only occur in the future, long after the closing date.

THE USUAL MERGER AND ACQUISITION PITFALLS

- Thinking that growth is easy by buying businesses.
- Competition from other buyers.

- Acquiring the business after many prospective buyers visited the operations and were given perhaps too many details. After digesting all that data, these current or potential competitors learned too much about its people, customers, pricing policies, costs, and future plans. That is why it does not pay to simply price your business via the marketplace before you are serious about selling it.
- Lack of understanding of the business in detail. . . market niche by market niche and product costs by line item.
- Not knowing the right questions to ask.
- Not asking the right questions.
- Not knowing if the answers to the right questions are correct.
- Not meeting several levels of management before buying. People, not facilities, make sales, profits, and cash flow.
- Not knowing why the seller is selling. Why is this particular company for sale? No single other question is more important for the average small to midsize acquisition.
- Falling in love too soon.
- Not being able to retain the good people after the acquisition.
- Poor communications with owners and managers during and after the period of the purchase investigation and closing.
- Not acting decisively and quickly when a good acquisition candidate is available.
- Buyers and sellers need to be opportunistic. When the right buyer or great business comes along, jump on it if it fits. Maybe the acquisition will lead to a totally different arena in the marketplace where higher cash flow and better returns on investment are probable.
- Not understanding the level and age of technology.
- The hype of the high technology or higher technology businesses sounds very attractive. These businesses might be the way to go for your competitors or business associates and friends. That does not mean that such investment is for you or your business. Too often, high technology businesses have low to negative cash flow . . . for a long time . . . maybe forever. When you enter the wrong business, each day seems to be weeks long. Aggravation and negative cash flow have a way of draining the lifeblood out of you 24 hours a day.

- Cost to move and relocate a business and the problem of having machinery and equipment perform up to prior standards.
- Falsely assuming that present tax regulations—including income and other taxes at the local, state, and federal levels—will stay the same.
- Union contract issues.
- Overstated assets.
- Understated liabilities and commitments:
- Unfunded or underfunded pensions.
- Severe income tax issues, mainly in the case of buying capital stock rather than assets.
- Stockholder lawsuits.
- Leases.
- Purchase contracts.
- Guarantees.
- Violations of various laws protecting the environment.
- The major laws include Occupational Safety and Health Act (OSHA), the Clean Water Act (CWA), the Clean Air Act (CAA), the Resource Conservation Recovery Act (RCRA), the Comprehensive Environmental Response, Compensation, and Liability Act (CERCLA), the Hazardous Materials Transportation Act (HMTA), and the Federal Insecticide, Fungicide, and Rodenticide Act (FIFRA). Many other laws are administered by regulatory agencies such as the Environmental Protection Agency (EPA) and the Occupational Safety and Health Administration (OSHA). Does anyone understand all of these laws' implications for an acquisition? No, but the law is clear that the buyer must beware. Good legal counsel is needed when acquiring any business affected by these laws. Most are so affected.
- Missing the *Fatal Flaw*.

POSTCLOSING REVIEW

Do a Postaudit

After the acquisition has settled down and things appear to be on a normal course, an evaluation should be made of the negotiations, the closing, and the economics of the transaction.

What can be learned from those events and issues to make the next acquisition even better and go even more smoothly?

Every acquisition should be revisited in some detail at least once for each of the first three years of ownership. The purpose is to see whether the acquisition was a success, a failure, or just an event.

Here are the important areas to look at from an acquisition decision standpoint:

■ First, the financial projections upon which the acquisition was based should be compared to the actual financial results of operations.

How did the business do compared to what was expected financially? Are the returns on the investment adequate? If not, why not? What can be done to at least attain the financial goals?

■ Second, are the base business operation and overall business still desirable?

Has the buyer learned more about the industry, the market, or the business that requires a second guess about staying with the business and the market niche?

■ Third, are the experienced people on board to run the business profitably, given the buyer's system of reporting and controls? Can they do the job? Will they remain?

■ Last, should the next potential merger/acquisition be managed better and the candidate analyzed differently? Should it be measured against tougher standards? Should it be less acceptable if submitted by X because that person seems to bring in losers but is so convincing and good at selling the buyer on values that are not real?

Get Over a Bad Deal Fast

There is little to be gained in outlining various measuring yardsticks or forms some buyers use to reevaluate the acquisitions. Cash flow is good, bad, or blah. The buyer knows that instinctively.

Can the business with a cash flow that is poor or even blah be turned around now that the deal is done? If not, the buyer should probably turn the cow over to some other pasture, liquidate it, or give it away. Even cows have to be fed.

Do not let the bleeding or out-of-control cash consumption go on. Cut the losses, if appropriate. Better to admit to a bad acquisition than live with it forever. By unduly diverting and wasting your time and attention on a poor acquisition, you lose the time advantage to acquire and grow a better acquisition. That is a double loss, which neither you nor your company can afford.

SUMMARY

Nothing about an acquisition should be left to chance. That begins with screening out the sellers and the buyers. Do not deal with the pack. Find the right one for the business, one that fits the strategic plan and fulfills the needs of seller and buyer.

Plan every detail. Detailed planning of how to accomplish the transaction in the best way for both seller and buyer is mandatory.

If proper, adequate thought is given to the parties and the business before the closing, the transition will be smooth and the acquisition will have a much better chance of success. If one business is to be integrated or merged into another, the issues are even more sensitive and require excellent planning.

Many different influences will converge on the buyer and seller as the acquisition closing date comes and passes. Each significant influence should be planned for. People should be assigned to accomplish detailed action steps and tactics according to quite specific time lines.

Make the acquisition a good deal for both sides. Plan and administer the details of smoothly integrating the acquired business. Care about and for the people, make some money on the deal, and have fun doing it!

Find the *Fatal Flaw.* If a buyer continues to look for the *Fatal Flaw* at all times during the due-diligence investigation, and if the buyer has qualified investigators who take sufficient time to discover the problems, the acquisition will most likely produce what is expected of it.

No perfect investigative programs or flawless M&A procedures combined with excellent binding acquisition contracts can cover every exposure a buyer and a seller face in the acquisition arena. *Fatal Flaws* abound in the world of deals on both the buyer's and seller's sides. Containment is one object. Try to make sure that the worst errors in judging the target company or buyer will not result in adding more than an acceptable range of risk in terms of dollars to the transaction.

Remember that people problems will be the cause of failure. People will more than likely be the root cause of the misjudgment of the buyer or seller.

Management deficiencies, cultural differences, rapidly changing markets, competitors, and technological changes are all closely aligned with less actual return on investment than planned. Most, if not all, of these impending conditions could have been and should be seen prior to closing the deal, if the buyer and seller are careful, diligent, and prudent.

Time makes up for considerable deficiencies in the acquisition program. Many issues—almost all, in fact—surface simply by the passing of time. The manufacturing efficiency drops, the inventory is not sold for a profit, the accounts receivable do not get collected, the customer demand sours, the income tax authorities audit the records, the . . . that is enough.

The picture is drawn. *People make haste! Haste makes waste and bad acquisitions. Fatal Flaws* are patient. They existed before the transaction and may live on after it.

Manage the transaction and avoid the *Fatal Flaw*.

LETTERS OF INTENT

The letters of intent included in Appendix A are samples only. They are not intended to be used or to be appropriate for use in any particular transaction or acquisition. These examples are presented to give the reader some ideas of the types of items sometimes included in such letters of intent. Consult an attorney for the appropriate approach and proper documentation. Not all acquisitions provide for letters of intent.

LETTER OF INTENT 1—NO PAYMENT AT SIGNING

Name and address of seller

Dear _____:

As you are well aware, you and I have been negotiating seriously for some time for the possible acquisition of your business by (*insert buying entity's legal name*) or by an affiliate.

One purpose of this letter is to confirm that we continue to be very seriously interested in having you, your people, and the business join us.

The other purpose is to state the agreement between us that, in order to give us time to proceed with our negotiations in an orderly fashion, you will neither negotiate nor discuss with any other person or entity the sale of all or part of your business listed below for a period of 90 days (*the number of days is negotiable*) from the date hereof. We will target a closing date earlier than 90 days. Unless required by law, you and I and our associates will also keep our discussions concerning the proposed transaction strictly confidential.

Prior to our signing a definitive agreement, a series of steps will need to be accomplished including, among other things, finalization of terms of the transaction, obtaining financing, audit of financial statements, and a detailed review of the business.

Briefly, we contemplate a transaction whereby the purchase price for 100 percent of the capital stock of (*insert legal name of seller's business and any subsidiaries includable in the acquisition*) will be (*insert dollar amount*) cash-equivalent (*or cash and notes or the number and description of capital shares of the buyer to be issued*). In addition, we expect to have a profit sharing/bonus plan for you and key people wherein (*insert a brief description of the plan*). Please acknowledge your agreement with the contents of this letter by dating and signing the enclosed copy and returning it to me.

Very truly yours,

(Name and title)

Agreed to on _____

_____
(Name)

_____
(Company)

LETTER OF INTENT 2–OPTIONAL PAYMENT AT SIGNING

Name and address of seller

Dear _____:

As you are well aware, you and I have been negotiating seriously for some time for the possible acquisition of your business by (*insert buying entity's legal name*) or by an affiliate. One purpose of this letter is to confirm that we continue to be very seriously interested in having you, your people, and the business join us.

The other purpose is to state the agreement between us that, in order to give us time to proceed with our negotiations in an orderly fashion, and in consideration of our payment herewith to you of (*insert amount*), you will neither negotiate with nor discuss with any other person or entity the sale of all or part of your business listed below for a period of 90 days (*the number of days is negotiable so insert the number you want*) from the date hereof. We will target a closing earlier than 90 days. You and we will also keep our discussions concerning the proposed transaction strictly confidential.

Prior to our signing a definitive agreement, a series of steps will need to be accomplished including, among other things, finalization of terms, obtaining financing, audit of financial statements, and a detailed review of the business.

Briefly, we contemplate a transaction whereby the purchase price for 100 percent of the capital stock of (*insert name of seller's business and any subsidiaries includable in the acquisition*) will be (*insert dollar amount*) cash-equivalent (*or cash and notes or the number and description of capital shares of the buyer to be issued*). In addition, we expect to have a profit sharing/bonus plan for you and key people wherein (*insert a brief description*).

The (*insert amount*) paid herewith will be applied against the purchase price at closing. If closing does not take place due to our actions, you may retain this sum. If the closing does not take place due to your actions or because of misrepresentations by you, you must return such funds to us within 15 days of our request in writing.

Please acknowledge your agreement with the contents of this letter by dating and signing the enclosed copy and returning it to me.

Very truly yours,
(Name and title)

Agreed to on _____

_____
(Name)

_____
(Company)

LETTER OF INTENT NUMBER 3–ALTERNATE FORM

Name and address of seller

Dear _____ :

We hereby confirm that XYZ Corporation (XYZ) is willing to purchase (*insert name of seller's corporation*) and its wholly owned subsidiaries (collectively known as seller) on the terms and subject to the conditions set forth in this letter, subject to our further investigation of seller and to negotiation and execution of a definitive acquisition agreement containing representations and warranties acceptable to us.

We believe the terms of the acquisition should be as follows:

1. In exchange for 100 percent of the capital stock of seller, we will pay an aggregate purchase price of (*insert dollar amount*) cash and interest-bearing notes at closing and a contingent payment to be made in the fourth year thereafter.

2. The contingent element of the purchase price would be calculated by reference to the profits earned, during the three calendar years following closing, from the seller's product lines based on the present key manager profit-sharing plan you described as now being in effect at seller.

3. The owners of the capital shares will enter into four-year (*the number of years is negotiable; advantages and disadvantages exist for long and short periods depending on the individuals*) employment agreements with XYZ. The employment agreements will provide for compensation at no less than that presently being paid by seller to the owners.

4. The owners will enter into a five-year (*the number of years is negotiable, but longer is better than shorter in general*) noncompetition agreement with seller or XYZ.

In order to enter into a binding agreement with seller, XYZ will need to make the following further investigations:

A. Talk to all key employees of seller.

B. Review seller's key patents, licenses, and know-how and have the opportunity to discuss them with all relevant parties.

C. Review in detail the seller's financial statements and income tax returns for the five years ended December 31, (year), and those for all interim periods from the last calendar year to the date of closing. XYZ needs to make such investigations of those financial statements as deemed by XYZ to be necessary to ascertain that such financial statements accurately portray the financial position, results of operations, and cash flow for the seller, in accordance with generally accepted accounting principles consistently applied during those periods.

Because XYZ needs to make further investigations and to negotiate the details of the proposed transaction, this letter should not be regarded as an offer that your acceptance would make the above terms legally binding on XYZ and on seller. However, we sincerely hope our further discussions with you will lead to the execution of a binding acquisition agreement for XYZ of seller.

Very truly yours,

(Name and title)

Agreed to on _____

_____
(Name)

_____
(Company)

Note to the reader: An optional payment at signing to show the serious nature of the proceedings and to give the seller an incentive to not negotiate with others could be made and incorporated within the text of this letter if deemed desirable. See the preceding letter of intent.

Confidentiality Agreements

The confidentiality agreements included in Appendix B are samples only and are not intended to be used or to be appropriate for use in any connection with any particular transaction or acquisition. These examples are presented to give the reader some ideas of the types of items sometimes included in such confidentiality agreements. Consult an attorney for the appropriate approach.

CONFIDENTIALITY AGREEMENT 1

Name and address of buyer

Dear _____:

In connection with your consideration of a possible transaction with (*insert the legal entity's name*) ("seller") pursuant to a purchase of the stock of the seller (*or insert the description of the transaction planned*), you have requested and have been furnished or will be receiving financial and other information concerning the business and affairs of the seller. As a condition to the seller furnishing you and your representatives such information that has not heretofore been made available to the public, you do agree to treat such information and data as "evaluation material" and

1. You agree that the evaluation material will be used solely by you for the purpose of evaluating a possible transaction between the seller and you. You further agree that you, your directors, officers, employees, agents, and representatives of your advisors, herein collectively referred to as "your representatives," will not disclose any of the evaluation material now or later, except as required by applicable laws or legal processes, without the prior written consent of the seller. However, any such information may be disclosed to your representatives who may need to know such information for the purpose of evaluating a possible transaction with the seller and who agree to keep such information confidential and to be bound by this agreement to the same extent as if they were parties thereto.

2. You recognize and acknowledge the confidential nature and competitive value of the evaluation material and the damage that could result to the seller if information therein is disclosed to any third party.

3. In addition, without the prior written consent of the seller, you and your representatives will not discuss or disclose to any person either the fact that discussions or negotiations are taking place concerning a possible transaction with the seller, or any terms or conditions thereof with respect to any such possible transaction, including the status of it.

4. In the event that the transaction contemplated by this agreement is not consummated, neither you nor your representatives will for a period of (*insert years knowing seller will want a long period and buyers will want a short period, which may prevent their taking over the seller via unfriendly takeover or other means*) from the date of this agreement, without prior written consent of the seller, (a) proceed with or seek to cause any transaction looking to the acquisition of the seller or any interest in the seller or (b) acquire or offer or propose to acquire, directly or indirectly, by purchase or otherwise, the seller or any interest in the seller.

5. In the event that the transaction contemplated by this agreement is not consummated, neither you nor your representatives will, without the prior written consent of the seller, use any of the evaluation material now received or to be later obtained from the seller or its representatives for any purpose.

6. In the event the transaction contemplated by this agreement is not consummated, all evaluation materials (and all copies, summaries, and notes of the contents or parts thereof) will be returned promptly and not retained by you or your representatives in any form or for any reason.

7. You and your representatives will have no obligation hereunder with respect to any information in the evaluation materials to the extent that such information has been made public, other than by acts by you or your representatives in violation of this agreement. Kindly acknowledge your agreement to the foregoing by countersigning this agreement in the place provided.

Sincerely,
Seller's corporate name

By _____

Title _____

Received and consented to on *(insert date)*:

Company name _____

By _____

Title _____

CONFIDENTIALITY AGREEMENT 2

Name and address of buyer

Dear _____:

(*Name of the intermediary and/or the seller*) will furnish confidential information to you or the corporation you represent upon the following conditions and applicable terms:

1. The undersigned understands and agrees that any information with respect to (*insert legal name of the selling corporation and refer to its subsidiaries being sold in some way*) (seller) furnished to the undersigned is highly sensitive and strictly confidential, and the undersigned will maintain such information in the utmost confidence. The undersigned understands that all such information is being furnished solely at its request in connection with its consideration of an acquisition of or related transaction with seller. The undersigned agrees to take such action to ensure that such information about seller obtained by it or any of its directors, officers, employees, agents, representatives, and attorneys shall remain confidential and shall not be disclosed or revealed to outside third parties or used in any manner inconsistent with this confidentiality agreement without the prior written approval of seller. The undersigned understands that any unauthorized disclosure will constitute a material breach of duty owed to seller.

2. Seller makes no representation or warranties as to the information furnished with respect to the data. Any and all representations and warranties by seller shall be made solely by seller and a buyer in a signed acquisition agreement and be subject to the provisions thereof.

3. The undersigned further agrees and acknowledges its sole responsibility to perform a due-diligence review prior to any acquisition of seller.

4. In the event that the transaction contemplated by this agreement is not consummated, all evaluation materials (and all copies, summaries, and notes of the contents or parts thereof) shall be returned promptly and not be retained by the undersigned or its representatives in any form or for any reason.

5. The undersigned and its representatives shall have no obligation hereunder with respect to any information in the evaluation materials to the extent that such information has been made public, other than by acts by the undersigned or its representatives in violation of this confidentiality agreement.

If the foregoing correctly states your understanding, please sign this agreement and return one copy to me.

Sincerely,

Name _____

Title _____

Seller's company _____

Accepted and agreed on (*insert date*):

Name _____

Title _____

Buyer company _____

Address _____

_____

Typical Acquisition Contract Issues

The agreements to purchase a business must be tailored precisely to the particulars of the specific transaction.

Typical issues normally covered within a purchase agreement are included in this appendix. These are samples only and are not intended to be used or to be appropriate for use in any particular transaction or acquisition. For example, some agreements contain employment or consulting contract clauses while others may have such issues covered by one or more contracts. These examples are presented to give the reader some ideas of the types of items frequently included in purchase agreements. Consult an attorney for the appropriate approach.

The following outline is designed to list the most important issues covered by many purchase agreements. Not every item will be necessarily covered in each acquisition agreement, but these offer much to think about and negotiate on as the day of the closing for an acquisition draws near.

GENERAL STATEMENT

Describe the nature of the agreement and the legal names of the parties to it as buyer and seller. Within this opening paragraph of the agreement, the collective names of the owners are often specified to be referred to in the rest of the documents as "seller". Additionally, the names of the buyers are generally referred to from that paragraph on as "buyer." The target company being sold is often referred to as the "company." The date of the agreement is also listed.

DESCRIPTION OF THE TRANSACTION

The next section of the document often describes

- The contemplated transaction, such as a sale and purchase of capital stock, a sale and purchase of assets, a merger, and so forth.
- The consideration (purchase price).
- Deposits, if any.
- Escrow agreement referred to, if applicable.
- Closing date, time, and place.
- Items seller will deliver at closing:
- Free and clear title to the assets being sold.
- The capital stock certificates being sold.
- Opinion of seller's legal counsel including
  1. Stipulation of the seller's ability to sell.
  2. A statement as to the type and number of capital stock shares of the company issued, in treasury and outstanding, including a reference to stock options, warrants, and other related commitments.
  3. A statement as to the company's state of incorporation and the legality of the capital stock shares being sold.
  4. A list of states and other jurisdictions where the company is qualified and authorized to do business.
  5. A statement that the purchase agreement being signed contemporaneously by buyer and seller is enforceable and so forth.
  6. A statement that the articles of incorporation and the bylaws of the company allow the transaction.
  7. A statement that the transaction is not prohibited or affected by indentures, mortgages, loans, credit agreements, or other agreements.
  8. A statement that the company has good title to the assets.
  9. A list of any litigation pending, outstanding, or adverse actions known.
  10. A statement that the company holds all permits, licenses, approvals, and so on required by law.
  11. A statement of significant issues and events not covered by the letter.

- Items buyer will deliver at closing:
- The proceeds to pay for the company according to the terms of the agreement.
- Employment agreements or consulting agreements, if provided for in the transaction. (Many buyers prefer to separate these types of agreements from the purchase agreement for several reasons, including the fact that the separation keeps the acquisition terms more distinct from the employment terms for default or breach purposes.)
- Other documents required.

TERMS OF DEFAULT BY BUYER OR SELLER

- There is a statement that failure of any party to the agreement insisting upon strict performance of the provisions of the agreement shall not be construed as waiving their rights under it.
- There is a statement that default by either party in their performance of any provisions in the agreement constitutes legal basis for the recission or termination by the other party.
- Usually a period of time is stipulated (30 days, for example) for the party defaulting to cure or remedy the default.

REPRESENTATIONS AND WARRANTIES OF THE SELLER

This section of the purchase agreement containing the representations and warranties of seller can be brief or very extensive, depending on the negotiating skills of the parties and the expertise of the attorneys. Some agreements contain all the provisions on one page, whereas others contain 20 or more pages.

Representations and warranties typically cover

- Ownership of the assets and/or capital shares being sold, company's authorized capital stock issued, outstanding, or in the treasury, and whether any stock options, rights, warrants, or commitments are outstanding.
- Right to sell those assets or shares.
- Company's organization and incorporation in a specified state and its powers and authority to operate.

- List of subsidiaries and affiliates.
- Statement as to whether fees are due to intermediaries in connection with the transaction.
- Declaration that financial statements for the years and for any interim periods that seller delivered to buyer are complete, correct, and prepared in accordance with generally accepted accounting principles consistently applied for the periods covered, and that the statements fairly present the financial condition of the company and the results of operations for the periods covered.
- List of any previously undisclosed liabilities and litigation except those recorded on the books of the company, reflected in the financial statements submitted, or disclosed in the purchase agreement.
- Disclosure of events that have occurred subsequent to the date of the last balance sheet requiring adjustment to or disclosure in the financial statements.
- List of changes of any material adverse nature to the financial condition of the company, its assets, its titles to assets, and so forth.
- Statement as to any decree, order, claim, action, suit, government investigation, proceeding, or any matter regarding the legal validity of the purchase agreement or any possible impediment to the transaction.
- Disclosure of any tax matters relating to taxes of all types imposed by the United States, a state, or other taxing authority that have not been paid in full and settled, and a statement that all tax returns have been correctly completed, filed on time, and paid on time with no outstanding issues being claimed or contested.
- Real property description and title issues to all assets.
- List of leases.
- Disclosure that no representation, warranty, exhibit, or schedule to the purchase agreement contains any untrue statement of a material fact, omits one, or is misleading and prevents the buyer from obtaining adequate and complete information about the company and its affairs.
- Contracts and agreements of significance.
- Statement as to compliance with government regulations and laws such as those relating to the environment, labor agreements, and pensions.

- List of patents, licenses, trademarks, trade names, and intellectual property.
- Statement as to compliance with all applicable laws, and statement as to any government consents needed and who is to file for them.
- Comments as to insurance and other items as appropriate.

REPRESENTATIONS AND WARRANTIES OF THE BUYER

- Statement that the execution, delivery, and performance of the purchase agreement has been authorized properly and is a valid and legally binding obligation of the buyer.
- Statement that all government authorizations or consents have been obtained.
- Statement concerning whether any intermediaries are due fees in connection with the purchase/sale transaction.
- Disclosure of any action, suit, or proceeding instituted or threatened by a court or government agency or body that casts doubt on (1) buyer's ability to conclude the transaction or (2) its legality or validity.

OBLIGATIONS OF THE SELLER AND THE COMPANY

- Statement that all laws have been and are being complied with.
- Statement that all asset transfers will be done.
- Conduct of the business prior to closing to be in ordinary course of events, consistent with prior practice. Business will be kept intact with employees, suppliers, landlords, and customers. Seller will assist buyer in obtaining employment agreements or other agreements, if needed, with certain or all officers and employees.
- Limits on declaration and payment of dividends or distributions of any assets or funds prior to concluding the transaction.
- Best efforts to provide buyer with full access to books, records, and latest financial statements.

OBLIGATIONS OF THE BUYER

- Compliance with applicable laws.
- Completion of the transaction as contemplated.

CONDITIONS AS TO CLOSING

- A list of whatever buyer and seller have to execute or do prior to closing, including the transfer of assets.

INDEMNIFICATION

- Seller to indemnify buyer against losses or costs arising out of (1) liabilities that were not contemplated or disclosed but that should have been, (2) misrepresentations, or (3) breaches of warranties.
- Provision for an allowance based on a percentage of the purchase price or a flat amount under which no adjustments to the purchase price are to be made and paid by seller. This provision, frequently referred to as a "basket," can save much time and expense. Otherwise, the attorneys and accountants may have to spend inordinate amounts of professional time looking for any size of adjustments to the financial statements that might qualify as items requiring adjustments to the purchase price.

COSTS AND EXPENSES

- Cost and expense sharing or allocations in connection with performance and compliance with purchase agreement.

MISCELLANEOUS

- Nature and survival of representations and warranties.
- Noncompetition clause (omitted if covered by a separate agreement).
- How to communicate notices, requests, and demands in writing and to whom to address them.
- The agreement to bind the legal successors and assignees.

- The agreement and attached exhibits and schedules to be complete, to represent everything, and to supersede other prior agreements and understandings.
- State and country of the governing law.

EXHIBITS

- Articles of incorporation with amendments and bylaws as amended.
- The corporate capital stock ledgers and certificates.
- Minute books of all meetings of the stockholders, directors, and committees of directors of the company.
- All employment contracts and engagement contracts with employees and consultants.
- Pension, retirement, deferred compensation, profit sharing, bonus, stock option, or other employee benefit plans.
- All material contracts of the company including those with vendors, licensors, lessors, distributors, customers, venture partners, investors, labor unions, insurance, loans and financings, and so forth.
- Intercompany contracts.
- Confidentiality agreements.
- List of trademarks, trade names, copyrights, and other intellectual property.
- Financial statements of the company for the years and periods requested and agreed to.
- Litigation issues.
- Regulatory items including important licenses, permits, orders, approvals, zoning matters, and documents or filings with government regulatory and compliance agencies.
- Annual reports to stockholders as requested.
- Titles and title reports and maps for real property.
- Insurance policies for years relating to claims and the current year.
- Other items appropriate for the particular acquisition.

Due-Diligence Program

INTRODUCTION

Every merger and acquisition should be subjected to the scrutiny of a detailed business review. That may include an audit by an independent certified public accounting firm, but is *never* limited to that type of an audit due to the nature of an audit when compared to other reviews necessary to obtain satisfaction that the target company is suitable for acquisition or merger. The extent of such a review will and should vary according to the circumstances of the target business including the internal controls operating within it and external influences from customers, competitors, vendors, regulatory bodies, and the economy. Look for the *FATAL FLAW.*

The due-diligence scope could range from a sophisticated purchase investigation with a written report, to reliance on previously certified financial information, a brief visit to the target company, and representations in the acquisition contract. The program depends on the size and quality of the target company, the availability of reliable financial and market data, the type of transaction, and other factors. Before the investigative team spends a lot of time getting involved in a myriad of financial numbers, they should ask the seller and as many key people as possible to talk at length about the business, the key wants and needs of the seller, sensitive issues, competition, and other issues. From such a discussion a number of matters will eventually evolve and surface that should be added to the investigative program.

EXECUTIVE SUMMARY

Regardless of the extent of the investigation, a summary of basic data should be written including

- Company (companies) name(s) and address(es) and state(s) of incorporation, and telephone, facsimile (fax), and electronic (E-mail) numbers.
- Persons and their titles to contact at company's or owner's location.
- Acquisition intermediary's name, address, and telephone, fax, and E-mail numbers.
- Investment banker's and any outside experts' names and telephone, fax, and E-mail numbers.
- Attorney's name, address, and telephone, fax, and E-mail numbers.
- Accounting firm's person to contact with address, and telephone, fax, and E-mail numbers.
- Ownership and brief synopsis of history of company and why the business is for sale.
- A brief description of operations outlining the industry, principal markets, and products, including product line characteristics.
- An overall company or divisional chart showing the various operating groups and plants targeted for acquisition.
- An overall personnel organization chart showing departments and numbers of people.
- Major customers' profiles.
- Major competitors' profiles.
- Assessment of the attractiveness of the market for the target business and current market shares held.
- Human resource evaluation of top management, all key managers, and issues of consequence.
  - Include a statement on who runs the business in fact. Is it dominated by one or several individuals? Is the person (those persons) vital to the business?
  - Assess whether the company and its business units are managed on a decentralized or highly central control structure.

- Determine whether management acts or reacts to change. Is it effectively decisive in short time periods?

- Discover whether any top-level persons were involved in criminal matters, regulatory investigations, or civil litigation.

- Obtain a biography of each key executive and key manager. Were any of them promised stock ownership by the owners or other arrangements that might create dissatisfaction if the company is sold or merged?

■ Assessment of property, plant, and equipment as to capacity and condition.

■ Assessment of significant legal and regulatory issues.

■ Synopsis of results of operations, cash flow, financial condition for the past five years, and forecasts for at least three to five years.

■ The range of per share capital stock traded prices for the past three years if a public company.

■ Summary highlights of the long-range plan, business plan, and budget, and comments on the major issues within them.

■ Management's list at the target company of what the most important uses of funds would be if made available in excess of those currently available and planned to be invested. Use rational increments starting at $1 million (less or more depending on size of the target).

■ Reasons to reject or propose the acquisition or merger including major risks and rewards and any minority opinions to the contrary.

■ Overall evaluation checklist as proposed in Table D–1.

OWNERSHIP AND HISTORY

■ The ownership of the company should be described briefly with names of those holding significant numbers of shares. The buyer may know some of the stockholders that could be helpful at some point in the investigation and negotiation processes.

■ Summarize the history, since inception, of the company, its subsidiaries, and its affiliates.

TABLE D-1

Acquisition Evaluation Summary Checklist

	Product Lines				
	X	**Y**	**Z**	**Other**	**Overall Business**
Markets					
Share	___	___	___	___	___
Growth	___	___	___	___	___
Price integrity	___	___	___	___	___
Customer mix	___	___	___	___	___
Customer desirability	___	___	___	___	___
Distribution strength	___	___	___	___	___
Subjection to much regulation	___	___	___	___	___
Cash Flow Characteristics					
Ability to generate cash	___	___	___	___	___
Discretionary cash available?	___	___	___	___	___
Cash for dividends	___	___	___	___	___
Product Lines					
Proprietary	___	___	___	___	___
New product development history	___	___	___	___	___
Patent position	___	___	___	___	___
Know-how	___	___	___	___	___
Technological obsolescence exposure	___	___	___	___	___
Labor intensity	___	___	___	___	___
Commodity pricing	___	___	___	___	___
Management					
Entrepreneurial	___	___	___	___	___
Quality	___	___	___	___	___
Will stay	___	___	___	___	___
Work Force					
Unionized	___	___	___	___	___
Quality level	___	___	___	___	___
Will stay	___	___	___	___	___
Capital Intensity of Investment					
Possibility for Above-Average					
Profitability	___	___	___	___	___
Return on buyer's investment	___	___	___	___	___

Notes:

1. Rating choices are Strong, Average, Weak, Yes, No, or N/A (not applicable).

2. Add comments on attached pages.

3. Discretionary cash flow is net income after income taxes plus depreciation and amortization, less working capital needs within the business, but excluding property, plant and equipment expenditures.

MARKETING AND SALES

Industry

- Major influences (population demographics, technologies, style sensitivities, competition, and similar issues).
- Past and projected trends, growth, and cycles.
- Market sizes.
- Profitability.
- Capital intensity.
- Commodity versus value-added pricing market influences.
- Distribution channels.
- Dominant customers.
- Dominant competitors.
- Dominant vendors.
- Regulatory influences.
- Major trends within the industry and its segments worldwide.
- Merger and acquisition trends.
- Business successes and failures.
- Is the industry market/sales-driven or technology-driven?

Specific Market Niche Analysis

- Summarize target company's marketing and sales plans for the next three to five years.
- Is the target company market/sales-driven or technology-driven?
- Historical product line sales should be summarized for at least three (preferably five) preceding years along with best estimates of the market share changes during the period. See Table D–2.
- List the projected product line sales for three to five years by major product line. Also include current and projected market shares for each product listed. See Table D–3.
- Historical product line sales should be summarized for at least three and preferably five preceding years along with best estimates of the market share changes during the period. See Table D–4.
- List the projected gross profit for three to five years by major product line. See Table D–5.
- List sales dollars by major customer with appropriate comments. See Table D–6.

TABLE D-2

Historical Product Line Sales

	Product Line Sales Dollars					Market Share %	
Product Lines	5 Yrs. Ago	4 Yrs. Ago	3 Yrs. Ago	2 Yrs. Ago	Last Yr.	5 Yrs. Ago	Current
Product X							
Domestic							
Region A	_____	_____	_____	_____	_____	_____	_____
Region B	_____	_____	_____	_____	_____	_____	_____
Region C	_____	_____	_____	_____	_____	_____	_____
Region D	_____	_____	_____	_____	_____	_____	_____
International							
List places							
	_____	_____	_____	_____	_____	_____	_____
	_____	_____	_____	_____	_____	_____	_____
	_____	_____	_____	_____	_____	_____	_____
Product Y							
Domestic							
Region A	_____	_____	_____	_____	_____	_____	_____
Region B	_____	_____	_____	_____	_____	_____	_____
Region C	_____	_____	_____	_____	_____	_____	_____
Region D	_____	_____	_____	_____	_____	_____	_____
International							
List places							
	_____	_____	_____	_____	_____	_____	_____
	_____	_____	_____	_____	_____	_____	_____
	_____	_____	_____	_____	_____	_____	_____
Product Z							
Domestic							
Region A	_____	_____	_____	_____	_____	_____	_____
Region B	_____	_____	_____	_____	_____	_____	_____
Region C	_____	_____	_____	_____	_____	_____	_____
Region D	_____	_____	_____	_____	_____	_____	_____
International							
List places							
	_____	_____	_____	_____	_____	_____	_____
	_____	_____	_____	_____	_____	_____	_____
	_____	_____	_____	_____	_____	_____	_____
Other Lines							
Domestic							
Region A	_____	_____	_____	_____	_____	_____	_____
Region B	_____	_____	_____	_____	_____	_____	_____
Region C	_____	_____	_____	_____	_____	_____	_____
Region D	_____	_____	_____	_____	_____	_____	_____
International							
List places							
	_____	_____	_____	_____	_____	_____	_____
	_____	_____	_____	_____	_____	_____	_____
	_____	_____	_____	_____	_____	_____	_____
Total	_____	_____	_____	_____	_____	_____	_____

TABLE D-3

Projected Product Line Sales

Product Lines	Product Sales Dollars					Market Share %	
	Year 1	Year 2	Year 3	Year 4	Year 5	Current	Year 5
Product X							
Domestic							
Region A	_____	_____	_____	_____	_____	_____	_____
Region B	_____	_____	_____	_____	_____	_____	_____
Region C	_____	_____	_____	_____	_____	_____	_____
Region D	_____	_____	_____	_____	_____	_____	_____
International							
List places							
	_____	_____	_____	_____	_____	_____	_____
	_____	_____	_____	_____	_____	_____	_____
	_____	_____	_____	_____	_____	_____	_____
Product Y							
Domestic							
Region A	_____	_____	_____	_____	_____	_____	_____
Region B	_____	_____	_____	_____	_____	_____	_____
Region C	_____	_____	_____	_____	_____	_____	_____
Region D	_____	_____	_____	_____	_____	_____	_____
International							
List places							
	_____	_____	_____	_____	_____	_____	_____
	_____	_____	_____	_____	_____	_____	_____
	_____	_____	_____	_____	_____	_____	_____
Product Z							
Domestic							
Region A	_____	_____	_____	_____	_____	_____	_____
Region B	_____	_____	_____	_____	_____	_____	_____
Region C	_____	_____	_____	_____	_____	_____	_____
Region D	_____	_____	_____	_____	_____	_____	_____
International							
List places							
	_____	_____	_____	_____	_____	_____	_____
	_____	_____	_____	_____	_____	_____	_____
	_____	_____	_____	_____	_____	_____	_____
Other Lines							
Domestic							
Region A	_____	_____	_____	_____	_____	_____	_____
Region B	_____	_____	_____	_____	_____	_____	_____
Region C	_____	_____	_____	_____	_____	_____	_____
Region D	_____	_____	_____	_____	_____	_____	_____
International							
List places							
	_____	_____	_____	_____	_____	_____	_____
	_____	_____	_____	_____	_____	_____	_____
Total	_____	_____	_____	_____	_____	_____	_____

TABLE D-4

Gross Profit by Product Line—Historical

Product Lines	5 Yrs. Ago	4 Yrs. Ago	3 Yrs. Ago	2 Yrs. Ago	Last Yr.
Product X					
Domestic					
Region A	_____	_____	_____	_____	_____
Region B	_____	_____	_____	_____	_____
Region C	_____	_____	_____	_____	_____
Region D	_____	_____	_____	_____	_____
International					
List places					
_____	_____	_____	_____	_____	_____
_____	_____	_____	_____	_____	_____
_____	_____	_____	_____	_____	_____
Product Y					
Domestic					
Region A	_____	_____	_____	_____	_____
Region B	_____	_____	_____	_____	_____
Region C	_____	_____	_____	_____	_____
Region D	_____	_____	_____	_____	_____
International					
List places					
_____	_____	_____	_____	_____	_____
_____	_____	_____	_____	_____	_____
_____	_____	_____	_____	_____	_____
Product Z					
Domestic					
Region A	_____	_____	_____	_____	_____
Region B	_____	_____	_____	_____	_____
Region C	_____	_____	_____	_____	_____
Region D	_____	_____	_____	_____	_____
International					
List places					
_____	_____	_____	_____	_____	_____
_____	_____	_____	_____	_____	_____
_____	_____	_____	_____	_____	_____
Other Lines					
Domestic					
Region A	_____	_____	_____	_____	_____
Region B	_____	_____	_____	_____	_____

Region C	___	___	___	___	___
Region D	___	___	___	___	___
International					
List places					
___	___	___	___	___	___
___	___	___	___	___	___
___	___	___	___	___	___
Total	===	===	===	===	===

TABLE D–5

Projected Gross Profit by Product Line

Product Lines	Year 1	Year 2	Year 3	Year 4	Year 5
Product X					
Domestic					
Region A	___	___	___	___	___
Region B	___	___	___	___	___
Region C	___	___	___	___	___
Region D	___	___	___	___	___
International					
List places					
___	___	___	___	___	___
___	___	___	___	___	___
___	___	___	___	___	___
Product Y					
Domestic					
Region A	___	___	___	___	___
Region B	___	___	___	___	___
Region C	___	___	___	___	___
Region D	___	___	___	___	___
International					
List places					
___	___	___	___	___	___
___	___	___	___	___	___
___	___	___	___	___	___
Product Z					
Domestic					
Region A	___	___	___	___	___
Region B	___	___	___	___	___

Region C	____	____	____	____	____
Region D	____	____	____	____	____
International					
List places					
____	____	____	____	____	____
____	____	____	____	____	____
____	____	____	____	____	____
Other Lines					
Domestic					
Region A	____	____	____	____	____
Region B	____	____	____	____	____
Region C	____	____	____	____	____
Region D	____	____	____	____	____
International					
List places					
____	____	____	____	____	____
____	____	____	____	____	____
____	____	____	____	____	____
Total	════	════	════	════	════

TABLE D–6

Major Customer Sales

Customer Name	4 Years Ago	3 Years Ago	2 Years Ago	1 Year Ago	Last Year
____	____	____	____	____	____
____	____	____	____	____	____
____	____	____	____	____	____
____	____	____	____	____	____
____	____	____	____	____	____
____	____	____	____	____	____
Others in Top 65% by:					
Number	____	____	____	____	____
Dollars	____	____	____	____	____
All Others by:					
Number	____	____	____	____	____
Dollars	____	____	____	____	____
Total sales	════	════	════	════	════

- Risks associated with present and projected customer base (mix).
- Order backlog status (sales and estimated gross profits) by product line as of current date and at the date just prior to settlement and comments. See Table D–7.
- Competition's sales and profitability by product line. Comment on competitors, pricing, sensitivities, cost trends, and related matters. See Table D–8.
- Sales price changes, including collection terms and discounts by product line. Comment on competitors, pricing, sensitivities, cost trends, and other issues. See Table D–9.
- Competitor comparisons and comments. See Table D–10.

TABLE D–7

Sales Order Backlog

Product Line	Sales	Gross Profits
Product X	$ _____	$ _____
Product Y	_____	_____
Product Z	_____	_____
Other	_____	_____
Totals	$ _____	$ _____

TABLE D–8

Competitive Data

Product Line	Competitor Name	Competitor Owned by	Sales in Thousands	Market Share	Trends
Product X	_____	_____	_____	_____	_____
Product Y	_____	_____	_____	_____	_____
Product Z	_____	_____	_____	_____	_____
All others	_____	_____	_____	_____	_____
Total	_____	_____	$ _____	100%	_____

TABLE D—9

Percent Changes in Unit Sales Price

Product Line	3 Yrs. Ago	2 Yrs. Ago	Last Year	Year 1	Year 2	Year 3	Year 4	Year 5
Product X	____	____	____	____	____	____	____	____
Product Y	____	____	____	____	____	____	____	____
Product Z	____	____	____	____	____	____	____	____
Other	____	____	____	____	____	____	____	____
Total	====	====	====	====	====	====	====	====

TABLE D—10

Competitor Comparisons

		Competitors			
Issue	Target	X Co.	Y Inc.	Z Ltd.	Others
Gross profit %	____	____	____	____	____
Selling % sales	____	____	____	____	____
Admin. % sales	____	____	____	____	____
Pretax % sales	____	____	____	____	____
Sales growth, 3 yrs. compounded	____	____	____	____	____
Sales growth, last year	____	____	____	____	____
Pretax growth, 3 years compounded	____	____	____	____	____
Pretax growth, last year	____	____	____	____	____
Market share by product line	____	____	____	____	____
Product X	____	____	____	____	____
Product Y	____	____	____	____	____
Product Z	____	____	____	____	____
Others	____	____	____	____	____
Quality position	____	____	____	____	____
Price position	____	____	____	____	____
Low-cost producers—rank	____	____	____	____	____
Dollars of sales per employee	____	____	____	____	____
Working capital ratio	____	____	____	____	____
Receivable days outstanding	____	____	____	____	____
Inventory turns	____	____	____	____	____
Accounts payable days outstanding	____	____	____	____	____
Debt equity ratio	____	____	____	____	____

- Describe each major competitor in detail. One example of a brief but useful profile is shown in Chapter 5.
- Historical gross profits by product lines in percentages. See Table D–11.
- Gross profit by product line, projected in percentages. See Table D–12.
- Percentages of sales for products introduced in the past five years.
- Warranties, returns, and allowance history and status. Show history and comment thereon.
- Seasonality and cyclicality of the business.
- New products planned for the next three years.
- Relationship to leading, coincident, and lagging economic indicators, if any.
- Technology and evaluation of remaining life of major products, by product line.
- Status of patents and know-how.
- Brand and trade names and their importance.
- Barriers to entry for competition now or in future.
- Risks surrounding this investment.

Personnel and Policies

- List key marketing and sales department personnel. Comment on prospects for retaining them. Record your evaluations of the individuals based on personal interviews by someone on the due-diligence team. See Table D–13.
- Chart the marketing and sales department organization showing position, number of people, and salary levels for all personnel. This may be included as an exhibit. Comment on the procedures and controls as well as the quality.
- List the significant points covered and conclusions as a result of our discussions (or those of the marketing research firm) with major customers. This step is only authorized after obtaining the approval of the seller in advance.
- Discuss results of market research regarding sensitivity of customers to price, quality, brand name, delivery, and service.

TABLE D-11

Historic Gross Profit Percentages

Product Line	5 Years Ago	4 Years Ago	3 Years Ago	2 Years Ago	Last Year
Product X	_____	_____	_____	_____	_____
Product Y	_____	_____	_____	_____	_____
Product Z	_____	_____	_____	_____	_____
Others	_____	_____	_____	_____	_____
Total	======	======	======	======	======

TABLE D-12

Gross Profit By Product Line
Projected in Percentages

Product Line	Last Year	Year 1	Year 2	Year 3	Year 4	Year 5
Product X	_____	_____	_____	_____	_____	_____
Product Y	_____	_____	_____	_____	_____	_____
Product Z	_____	_____	_____	_____	_____	_____
Others	_____	_____	_____	_____	_____	_____
Total	======	======	======	======	======	======

TABLE D-13

Key Marketing and Sales Personnel

Name	Function	Age	Salary	Experience	Evaluation
_____	_____	_____	_____	_____	_____
_____	_____	_____	_____	_____	_____
_____	_____	_____	_____	_____	_____
_____	_____	_____	_____	_____	_____
_____	_____	_____	_____	_____	_____
Overall:					
Marketing	N/A	_____	_____	_____	_____
Sales	N/A	_____	_____	_____	_____

TABLE D–14

Advertising Program

Type	Amount	Details
Trade shows, publications	_____	_____
Media	_____	_____
Promotion programs	_____	_____
Other	_____	_____
Total	_____	_____

- Comment on review of the sales representatives' and distributors' agreements for selling the products (commission rate structure, exclusive territories or customers, termination clauses, products and territories covered, and so forth).
- List credit policies, practices, and bad debt experiences.
- List sales office locations.
- Give location and adequacy of distribution facilities, warehouses, and other facilities and any significant leases for those facilities.
- List marketing and sales department incentive programs.
- List advertising programs by type. See Table D–14.

- Assess status and aging of company's catalogs, sales tools, service manuals, pricing sheets, parts lists, and application engineering manuals for customers.

- Identify strengths and weaknesses of the marketing and sales departments and major improvements needed.

- Ask the department managers for their individual "wish lists" for the business. Ask what action plan they would develop if they had an additional $1,000,000 (more or less depending on the size of the department budget) in their budget for next year.

- Assess synergies with buyer's current or planned businesses.

ENGINEERING, DESIGN, AND RESEARCH AND DEVELOPMENT

The target business may or may not have separate engineering departments for basic research, design, manufacturing, application engineering, and developmental projects. Rarely do many businesses have basic and fundamental research projects even if the name "research" is included in the title of a department or person.

As part of due diligence, determine just what amount of funds have been expended over the past several years for each of those functions. Some sellers make the bottom-line income numbers look attractive and healthy by cutting back on one or more of these functions as a sale or merger date looms. Others may have reduced such expenditures in recent years to push up net income as they positioned the business for sale. Still others may have reclassified engineering to put the best light on a certain category. For example, did the company reclassify customer service engineering and product service engineering into a research and development classification? Old technology really ages if that is the case in the target company.

- List engineering, design, and research and development department personnel (key people) and salary levels. Comment on the prospects for retaining these personnel. See Table D–15.

TABLE D–15

Engineering, Design, and R&D Personnel

Name	Function	Age	Salary	Experience	Evaluation
_____	_____	_____	_____	_____	_____
_____	_____	_____	_____	_____	_____
_____	_____	_____	_____	_____	_____
_____	_____	_____	_____	_____	_____
_____	_____	_____	_____	_____	_____
Overall:					
Engineering	N/A	_____	_____	_____	_____
Design and R&D	N/A	_____	_____	_____	_____

- Provide engineering, design, and research and development organization chart(s) showing function, number of all people, and salary levels. This may be included as an exhibit. Comment on the procedures and controls as well as the quality of the people and projects.

- Obtain a summary of the current projects and those planned for the next three years as to

  – Manufacturing engineering work orders.
  – Redesign or design projects.
  – Development projects.
  – Basic research projects.

- List the products introduced within the past five years by dollar amount of sales for the past year.

- Give engineering, design, and research and development spending levels for the past five years. See Table D–16.

- Determine from the numbers and by discussion with company personnel whether the company has deferred projects to increase income prior to planned sale or merger of the business. Frequently, the managers of the above departments will volunteer information on deferred projects they wish to reinstate pending funding.

- Compare the facilities for these functions to those of competitors and to those of the buyer.

TABLE D–16

Engineering Design and R&D Spending

	5 Years Ago	4 Years Ago	3 Years Ago	2 Years Ago	Last Year
Mfg. engineering					
Redesign or design					
Development					
Basic research					
Total $ as % of sales					

- Describe the facilities as to age, condition, adequacy, and perceived usage for the purposes intended.
- Comment on the control procedures and on the capability to meet the needs of
- Manufacturing.
- Market demands for present and emerging markets and future growth in sales.
- Application engineering and technical service to customers.
- The customers and the company to comply with the laws, regulations, and rules of all applicable regulatory agencies.
- The company by providing commercial products sufficient to meet the sales targets of the company in the future.
- Are the manufacturing engineering drawings current and usable on the factory floor?
- Does the company try to standardize component parts for the manufacturing process?
- How do these functions compare to those of the competition and to customers' needs? Are they adequate? If changes are needed, list them and the estimated costs to install those changes.■ Patents pending and received should be reviewed—particularly as to the ability of the company to maximize them and other proprietary know-how in the United States and international markets.
- Describe black-box technology and know-how special to this company.
- List known litigation relative to alleged, real, or potential patent and trademark rights infringements.
- Describe controls on design, research and development, and projects approved. Review the postaudits of them after completed.
- Ask the department managers for their individual "wish lists" for the business. Ask what action plan they would develop if they had an additional $1,000,000 (more or less depending on the size of the department) in their budget for next year.
- Conclude as to the track record of successes and failures, strengths and weaknesses, and adequacy of the departments for the business at hand and planned for the next three years. Is the company a leader or a follower in this area?

MANUFACTURING AND SERVICE OPERATIONS

- Describe the manufacturing processes in general, list the plant facilities by location, and comment on capacity utilization. Accompany the write-up with appropriate photos.
- Show the major cost components of the major product lines. See Table D–17.
- List the personnel (key people) in the various manufacturing and service departments. Give salary levels and comment on the prospects for retaining them. These departments normally include purchasing, receiving, inventory control, information systems, scheduling, manufacturing engineering (if not covered separately), quality control, expediting, and shipping. Interview key people and record an evaluation of each. See Table D–18.
- List the major fringe benefit programs including incentives, health, and welfare.
- Ask the department managers for their individual "wish lists" for the business. Ask what action plan they would develop if they had an additional $1,000,000 (more or less depending on the size of the department) in their budget for next year.
- Attach manufacturing and service organization chart(s) showing function, number of all people, and salary levels. This may be included as an exhibit. Comment on the procedures and controls as well as the quality of the people and perceived operating controls

TABLE D–17

Cost Components by Product Line

Cost Component	Product Line X	Product Line Y	Product Line Z	Others
Direct material	_____%	_____%	_____%	_____%
Direct labor	_____	_____	_____	_____
Direct overhead	_____	_____	_____	_____
Indirect overhead	_____	_____	_____	_____
Total mfg. cost	100%	100%	100%	100%

TABLE D—18

Key Manufacturing and Service People

Name	Function	Age	Salary	Experience	Evaluation
Overall:					
Manufacturing	N/A				

for scheduling, shop loading, on-time delivery, and rework. Is scrap reporting adequate? Is scrap too high? Why?

- Comment on labor relations for the past five years including strike periods or other labor stoppages. What are the employee turnover rates for the past three years by department?
- List pending union or other labor negotiations coming up in the next three years. Is the work force readily available to handle the production needs at the present locations?
- List and comment on direct and indirect factory departmental wage rates and incentive systems. List all unions and contract expiration dates. See Table D–19.

TABLE D—19

Plant Wages and Incentives

Department	Number Direct	Number Indirect	Total Union	Average Pay Rate	Incentive System	Turn- over

- Purchasing function, including the procedures and controls, should be reviewed. Discuss personnel if not included elsewhere, covering age, experience, salary level, and adequacy. Other issues to cover are
- Centralized versus decentralized purchasing.
- Competitive bidding practices.
- Incentive systems for department personnel.
- Nature of important contracts with vendors, including discounts.
- Use of more than one source of supply.
- Procedures to insure lowest cost for quality materials and supplies.
- Issuances of purchase contracts as to: types, specific ones of size, length of time covered, and internal controls.
- List the 10 largest, or most important, vendors and the major raw materials, supplies and components purchased last year. Cover others if purchases are cyclical. Note those that are critical to the operation, the history of shortages in availability, large cyclical price swings, and the risks involved due to the nature of the materials. Describe the vendor evaluation program. See Table D–20.

TABLE D–20

Significant Vendors

Name	Ship from	Materials	Yearly Purchases	Contract Terms
		$		

- Describe significant intercompany and intracompany purchases and their pricing.
- Describe use of and list the main subcontractors.
- Cost efficiency, productivity, and value-added engineering programs should be reviewed for the past two years and commented on. Are any programs in process? Are make-or-buy decisions adequate?
- Describe the inventory cost accounting method(s) used. Are the costing methods appropriate for the processes and products? Have they been consistently applied in recent years?
- Review inventory turns by product line and by stage of inventory (raw materials, work in process, and finished goods). See Table D–21.
- Review company's record with regulatory agencies as far as production processes and products are concerned. Cover at least Environmental Protective Agency (EPA), Occupational Safety and Health Administration (OSHA), and Equal Employment

TABLE D–21

Inventory Turns

	Current Year		Last Year	
	Dollars	Inventory Turns	Dollars	Inventory Turns
Inventory Stage				
Raw materials	_____	_____	_____	_____
Work in process	_____	_____	_____	_____
Finished goods	_____	_____	_____	_____
Total	_____	_____	_____	_____
Inventory Lines				
Product line X	_____	_____	_____	_____
Product line Y	_____	_____	_____	_____
Product line Z	_____	_____	_____	_____
Others	_____	_____	_____	_____
Total	_____	_____	_____	_____

Opportunity Commission (EEOC). Are employees tested for potential contamination during production? Is drug testing conducted? If so, describe.

- Review the current sales order backlogs. Comment on present position and forecasted situation for the rest of this year and next year.

- Describe the technology level and risks associated with the principal products.

- Describe the strong and weak points of each important department and functioning of the manufacturing process and its group of departments.

- Analyze the record of quality production by reviewing the quality control function as it exists and the amount of rework, warranty claims, and customer allowances resulting from faulty products.

- Review all physical inventory shortages and overages for the past two years compared to the book inventory figures. Does the company cycle count inventories? Does it use the ABC or a similar system of controlling and reporting inventories by relative importance as to usage dollars or dollars in the inventory?

- By observation, discussion with appropriate individuals, and review of spending, determine the adequacy of repairs and maintenance of the machinery, equipment, and facilities.

- Describe the capitalization versus expense policies for the business. Do any "hidden" assets exist due to conservative policies?

- Describe the depreciation and amortization policies for book and tax reporting. Are they conservative?

- Obtain copies of all significant leases of facilities and equipment.

- List the major capital expenditures for each of the past five years and comment thereon. See Table D–22.

- Abstract all licences and cross-license agreements for the manufacture or sale of the products of the target company or those that company has rights to.

- Conclude as to the adequacy of the existing manufacturing plant, machinery, equipment, and land for the operation now and as projected for the next three to five years. Comment on the operating condition, age, and location of major facilities. Also list possible

TABLE D–22

Major Capital Expenditures

Year	Item	Location	$ Amount
Total for 5 years			

sales value of excess real property. Add a schedule of major facilities and equipment as to whether owned or leased. Such a list may become an exhibit to the purchase agreement.

- Conclude as to the track record of successes and failures, strengths and weaknesses and, adequacy of the manufacturing operations and facilities for the business at hand and planned for the next three years.

MANAGEMENT INFORMATION SYSTEMS

Management reports are prepared by various departments in a target company. Also, the information a buyer needs to evaluate a business or the seller needs to manage that business is not generated by only one particular department. Nevertheless, this separate section of the due-diligence investigation is included to highlight the issues relating to management information a seller should review before a full investigation can be deemed to be complete. The data will be obtained by different people at different times, yet it needs to be consolidated to focus on whether management is preparing and using, on a timely basis, those important reports key to effective control of that business.

- List the personnel (key people) in the department and salary levels and comment on the prospects for retaining them. Interview key people and record an evaluation of each. Record turnover statistics for the personnel. See Table D–23.

- Review a copy of every important management report. These reports can be summarized as shown below. Comment on the adequacy of the data including whether they include adequate departmental expense reports comparing actual costs to budget and to prior periods. See Table D–24.

- Obtain a list or summarize the major hardware and software used in any centralized system as well as a distributed system. See Table D–25.

- Summarize the MIS expenditure levels for the past two years. See Table D–26.

- Ask the department managers for their individual "wish list" for the business. Ask what action plan they would develop if they had an additional $1,000,000 (more or less depending on the size of the department) in their budget for next year.

- Conclude as to the track record of successes and failures, strengths and weaknesses, and adequacy of the department for the information needs of the business at hand and planned for the next three

TABLE D–23

Key Management Information Systems People

Name	Function	Age	Salary	Experience	Evaluation
Overall:					
MIS	N/A				
People					
Evaluation					

TABLE D-24

Key Management Reports

Title of Report	Contents	Frequency	Distribution

years. Also conclude as to whether the facilities and expenditures could be merged with, reduced, or eliminated as a result of the merger or acquisition.

- If all MIS is distributed on a decentralized basis, comment on the efficiency and effectiveness of the system.

TABLE D-25

Major Components of Management Information System

Type and Vendor	Location	Application	Own or Lease
Hardware			
Software			

TABLE D-26

MIS Expenditures

Expenses	Last Year	This Year
Salaries and wages		
Fringe benefits		
Hardware		
Software		
Supplies		
Outside services		
Other		
Total		

INSURANCE

The insurance area is one requiring expert assistance in the investigation due to the special knowledge of applicable laws and insurance policy coverages, which may differ from state to state, country to country, and business to business. In general, the following data are appropriate initial information. Sometimes the insurance claims and resulting losses will arise long after the sale of the products to the customers. It is vital to determine whether the seller or the buyer may be liable for claims involving products sold and delivered to the user prior to the acquisition date. Determine which insurance company is responsible for coverage under different claim incidences if carriers have been changed in recent years.

- List the personnel (key people) in the department and their salary levels. Comment on the prospects for retaining them. Interview key people and record an evaluation of each. Record turnover statistics for the personnel. See Table D–27.
- List the more important policy coverages in effect for the prior three years. See Table D–28.
- List the loss and claims experience for the past five years. See Table D–29.
- Conclude as to whether the company is and has been adequately insured, based on the type of transaction the seller contemplates (capital stock purchase or pooling versus an asset purchase). Is

TABLE D–27

Key Insurance Department People

Name	Function	Age	Salary	Experience	Evaluation
Overall:					
Overall	N/A				

TABLE D–28

Insurance Coverage

Coverage	Values	Premiums	Insurance Co.	Insurance Broker	Expiration Date

TABLE D–29

Insurance Claims

Describe Claims or Losses	4 Years Ago	3 Years Ago	2 Years Ago	I Year Ago	Current Year

there evidence of potential claims or lawsuits relating to any aspect of the company's operations, especially those involving product warranties, investor lawsuits, labor conditions, workers, compensation insurance, professional liability, general liability, fire and theft insurance, fidelity bonding, self-insured claim areas, and other possible exposure areas? Are reported and unsettled and unreported claims likely to be material in amount? Are insurance premiums expected to rise or fall in the next several years?

LEGAL AND REGULATORY CONCERNS

The litigious nature of the U.S. business world presents the buyer with a whole arena of concerns. Some concerns involve customers and users of their products and services. Other areas of legal exposure involve investors in the corporation or investors in corporations that have dealings with the target company. Still other sensitive areas involve local, state, and federal regulatory agencies controlling securities and environmental matters. In addition to notifying shareholders of acquisitions or sales of assets of size or the business itself, stockholders' approval may be needed in advance depending on the bylaws and other legal constraints. The buyer and seller must consult with legal and accounting experts before initiating a transaction in order to make certain that all necessary filings with regulatory agencies and notices to stockholders are made in proper form and content and are timely filed.

Do not sign any acquisition agreement without expert legal and accounting advice and assistance. That assistance will be inexpensive "insurance" considering the total transaction value.

■ Obtain an organization chart of the personnel in the legal and regulatory department(s). List the specialty, age, years of service, and salary for each person in related professional work.

■ Securities issued, exchanged, or purchased in an acquisition, statutory and other mergers, consolidation of securities, pooling of interest, and sale, transfer, or exchange of assets are usually subject to securities regulation under the Securities Act of 1933 and the Securities Exchange Act of 1934 of the Securities and Exchange Commission (SEC) as well as "blue sky" laws of the state governments, which broadly overlap the SEC laws. These laws in part require filings of information prescribed in the regulations, notices to stockholders of certain impending acquisitions, and many other actions of consequence to the acquiring and selling corporations. Many states have taken action to make U.S.- and some foreign-based companies planning takeovers publish pre-offer notices, lots of disclosure filings, and in general to allow the target board of directors more flexibility in warding off takeovers. This regulatory involvement is changing rapidly and needs checking with experts in detail at the appropriate time.

Also, the rules and regulations of each of the stock exchanges provide for certain filings, stockholder rights, and restrictions on trading the securities of subject corporations. The Hart-Scott-Rodino Act and the regulations applicable to it require companies and transactions of a certain size to supply information to the Federal Trade Commission (FTC) to see if the transaction will be allowed by the FTC or the U.S. Department of Justice. Such acquisitions cannot be consummated until a stipulated number of days after the filing of the report. The Food and Drug Administration of the federal government may also be involved prior to an acquisition, merger, or transfer of securities under certain circumstances. As usual, nothing is ever simple in the acquisition or merger business. That is another reason to make an acquisition or merger worth it by choosing the right partner, buyer, or seller in the first place. As in the case of marriage, the right partner is great, but the wrong one leads to divorce or years of frustration and unhappiness.

- List the nature and status as well as the expected results of all known litigation or potential litigation. This information can be obtained by talking with the target company's legal counsel and auditors as well as the management, by reading the certified annual reports of the company, or by reviewing its filings with the SEC. Note whether the business of the target company or the actions of the management appear to abnormally expose the owners to litigation.

- Obtain a copy of the articles of incorporation and/or charter and bylaws of the selling parent corporation and each of the subsidiaries. Review them for unusual restrictions and provisions.

- Read the minutes of the parent company being sold and of each subsidiary for at least five years. Look for major long-term contracts, significant licenses, legal issues, commitments, and contingencies.

- List states in which the company is registered and authorized to do business.

- List classes of stock and rights of each class. Briefly describe stock option and stock incentive plans.

- Obtain and review copies of all major contracts, leases, licenses and franchises, patents issued and pending, and trademarks.

- Conclude as to the legal and regulatory posture and potential exposure of the company and its operations.

TAXATION ISSUES

The impacts of income and estate taxes of each acquisition or merger in their various forms should be reviewed by both seller and buyer with the assistance of competent tax advisors. Sometimes the parties can defer or prevent imposition of taxes by the structure adopted for the transaction.

In addition, the tax picture of the target business should be reviewed by a tax expert in a number of areas. The purpose of such a review is to determine (1) the possible tax exposure of the target company for current and prior years and (2) whether tax deferrals and savings might be possible in future years by different tax-planning methods. Federal income tax returns are vital. Also, a number of states have become quite aggressive in seeking tax revenues from any firm doing business within their boundary.

- Obtain a tax department organization chart and, if appropriate, determine the adequacy of the personnel in that department. List the names, ages, salary levels, and years of experience in the taxation area.
- Obtain and review copies of all federal, state, and local income tax, franchise, capital stock, and sales/use tax returns filed for the past three years, unless waivers were signed by representatives of the company to extend the review periods. Also review and list the more important issues in all income tax deficiency reports and proposed tax adjustments and settlements for the past six years. Were the returns filed timely, completely, and accurately?
- What are the major differences between the books of record, including the financial statements, and the tax returns for the past three years? Are there any permanent differences between the books and the tax returns?
- What is the position of the company concerning federal and state income tax loss carrybacks and carryforwards?
- Analyze the reserves for all income taxes as of a current date. Determine the adequacy of those reserves for the purposes intended.
- Review the auditors' working papers and determine and conclude from the review and from discussions with the independent auditors and management whether any tax exposure exists that is not accrued for. Also determine whether the company has potential

deductions not claimed in prior periods or overreported taxable income.

FINANCIAL REVIEW

The target company may have financial statements audited by independent certified public accountants (CPAs) or at least reviewed by them. The working papers of the CPA firm will contain very informative analyses covering a number of years which will help the buyer evaluate the risks associated with the current financial position and the results of operations of the company for as many periods as appropriate.

A meeting with the CPA is in order. The CPA will clear the discussions with the client in advance since the data are otherwise confidential.

Buyers often demand certified financial statements as of a fairly recent date or at least a limited review by independent CPAs of the interim financial statements of a recent period. These financial statements will probably be attached to the purchase or merger agreement along with the other certified statements, if available. If the seller is contemplating a sale of the business, a certified audit is often in order prior to the sale to lend credence to the historic results of operations.

Regardless of whether a meeting with the buyer's representatives and the CPA firm's representatives is possible, the buyer and/or a CPA acceptable to the buyer will generally want to check on the following issues prior to the closing date for the acquisition. Include appropriate schedules and analyses.

Personnel and Policies

- Obtain an organization chart of the personnel in the controller, accounting, and finance department(s). List the ages, years of experience, and salary levels of the key people. Interview key people and assess the capabilities of the applicable staffs for the various financial functions of the company.
- Accounting policies:
- List the major accounting policies and procedures of the company, especially those peculiar to the industry, those recently changed by the company, and those that differ from the normal ones used in the industry. These include accounting principles relating to when

a sale is a sale, capitalizing versus expensing items and projects, depreciation and amortization of assets, and cost accounting methods and procedures.

– Ascertain that interim financial statements are prepared in accordance with the same accounting principles used for the annual statements.

■ Obtain the representation letters given by management to the auditors and legal letters received by them from company's legal counsel (internal and external).

■ Obtain copies of the past year's letters from the auditors to management containing suggested changes in procedures and accounting policies. Determine whether items of significance exist affecting the merger or acquisition. If an audit committee exists, ask for copies of their minutes.

■ Were the independent auditors changed in the past five years? If so, why?

Financial Statements

■ Balance sheet. Obtain the balance sheets for all interim periods of the current year and those for the past five full years.

■ Cash.

– Balances can be traced to the bank statements and confirmations received from the banks. Name the major bank accounts. Are there compensating balance requirements?

– Determine if any blocked currencies exist in foreign countries.

– Review the average cash and cash equivalent accounts for the past two years to see if borrowings are indicated at certain times of the year or due to levels of business.

– Is excess cash available for dividends or distributions to the owners?

– What are the terms of any lines of credit or debt instruments?

– Does the target company or any of its shareholders guarantee debt of the company?

■ Marketable securities and notes receivable.

– Confirm that they exist.

- – Determine if they are at cost or fair market value and draw conclusions.
- ■ Accounts receivable may be overstated if fictitious, may not be collectible in full, may be subject to discounts or rebates, or may have warranty claims and returns of the applicable products potentially reducing their value.
- – Obtain a copy and review a current listing of accounts receivable by period due. Do they appear collectible? Are any customers in default of the collection terms? Are there any special categories of receivables?
- – Consider confirming some or all of the account balances with customers.
- – Review the accounts at a later date to check on their being collectible prior to closing the deal.
- – List the bad debt write-offs and customer allowances for the past five years. Were the allowances due to production problems or billing issues?
- – What are the terms given for payment, sales return and allowances, and discounts on sales price? What is the impact on profits of granting dating for payment? Does the company lose sales opportunities because of too stringent pricing, credit, and collection policies?
- – List the largest customers of the target company representing, say, 65 percent of the sales volume for each of the past three years. The purpose is to look for significant variations and trends in sales to the major customers and the causes. A downtrend in sales or cessation of sales to a particular customer might signify dissatisfaction, merger with a competitor, or other serious issues.
- – Conclude as to the realizability of the receivables and the adequacy of reserves for bad debts.
- ■ Inventories may be understated by some private corporations to understate income and understate the related income taxes. This is accomplished by not recording some inventories as assets when purchased, not recording them at the physical inventory dates, writing down or off too many slow-moving items, reducing the inventories for excessive obsolescence, and undercosting the items.

- The inventories may be overstated if the items are obsolete, nonexisting, overcosted, or not salable due to condition, technology, or other reasons.
- Obtain summaries for the past three years of the inventories by major product line, by classification (raw material, work in process, and finished goods), and other categories as appropriate. One such set of categories could be materials, labor, and overhead. Review the summaries for information as to mix, turnover rates, levels commensurate with the business for the periods, and indications of problems.
- Review the reconciliations of the book to physical inventories for the past two or three years to see how accurate the inventory control records and procedures have been.
- Arrange to have a physical inventory count taken, observed independently, costed out, and tied to the books of record. Determine the method of costing for the inventories (last in and first out [LIFO], first in and first out [FIFO], or average costs).
- Review how direct and indirect costs and expenses are allocated to the inventory costs. Are these fair and proper methods?
- Compare the recent costed physical inventory to net selling prices to determine if a reasonable gross profit margin is expected when the inventories are sold.
- Review the inventories for slow-moving or obsolete merchandise or products. What are the company's procedures for writing off inventories that are not full realizable as to the costs on the books?
- Does the company have consigned goods or inventory stored off the premises?
- Has quality control been a problem based on review of scrap reporting, returns and allowances, and discussions with personnel in responsible positions?
- Are purchase commitments outstanding in abnormal amounts?
- Draw conclusions as to the inventory purchasing and control procedures, the costed amount of inventory on hand, and the potential to sell it at a reasonable profit.
- Prepayments and other current assets.

  Assess the realizability of such assets and whether they should be classified as current assets.

- Property, plant, and equipment.
- Obtain a summary of the major classes of property by type, location, and use as of a current date, showing original cost and accumulated depreciation, and the methods of depreciation used for income tax and book purposes.
- Where possible, obtain square footage measurements of floor spaces and the age and condition of all significant assets. Are the facilities constructed to be multipurpose or special-purpose?
- Note if any of these assets are leased, mortgaged, or pledged to secure personal or business borrowings.
- Determine if recent reliable appraisals are available.
- Were the assets recently physically accounted for?
- Are major renewal, replacements, or additions needed to handle expected levels of operations?
- What levels of capacity are now being used?
- List the capital expenditures for each of the past five years and note what the main items were. Do contractual commitments exist for the purchase or lease of additional assets of these kinds of fixed capital assets? Are major items needed for the next three to five years?
- Are the assets adequately insured?
- Assess the existence and costing of assets, the consistency of asset depreciation methods used, and the realization potential of the investment in these assets.
- Other assets and investments.
- Obtain a schedule of these assets and verify their realizability and classification. Some may be deferred research and development expenses or deferred consulting costs that are not realizable. Others may reflect investments in third-party companies or assets that are not fully realizable.
- Review all patents, copyrights, trademarks, and know-how areas for value. Judge whether lawsuits might arise as a result of them.
- Determine whether the company has been consistent in accounting for such assets.
- Draw conclusions.
- Unrecorded assets.

Obtain a list of significant unrecorded assets.

Draw conclusions.

- Current liabilities.
  - Obtain a summary of all accounts payable and accruals as of a current date. Verify the amounts by checking supporting documents and/or confirmation with vendors.
  - Obtain a list of the top 10 vendors and the amount of purchases from each for the past two years. Determine if the company is too reliant on one vendor, too susceptible to a single source of supply being cut off, or too exposed because of buying unusual raw materials, which inherently have a risk associated with the the ability to purchase them at consistent, predictable costs. Lead, copper, and other materials are just a few materials having wide pricing changes in short time periods.
  - Abstract terms of any major contracts with vendors.
  - Verify the outstanding balance of notes payable to third parties.
  - Examine borrowing documents for terms, pledges, conditions, liens, and guarantees.
  - Conclude as to (1) the amounts of such liabilities and their classification as current liabilities and (2) impact on the financial condition of the company.
- Income, sales/use, and property taxes.
  - Determine if the target corporation has filed sales/use and property tax reports and paid them on a timely basis.
  - Are there any tax matters in dispute? Obtain copies of the latest tax settlements and determine what years are still open for the tax authorities to question and adjust. What was the nature of the changes and adjustments made or proposed by the tax authorities?
  - Review the tax reserves on a recent balance sheet and determine whether they are adequate for the purposes intended. Are any tax reserves needed for items that were incurred in the past, but were deferred as to tax, due to differences between tax and book treatment on a timing basis?
  - Draw conclusions.
- Long term liabilities.

- Obtain summaries of these liabilities showing the type of items. For debt instruments, list
  a. The interest rate.
  b. Maturities.
  c. Principal and interest payments for each of the next three to five years.
  d. Restrictive covenants and collateralized or pledged assets.
  e. Default provisions.
  f. Prepayment provisions.
  g. Conversion privileges.
  List lines of credit and terms.
- List all guarantees made by the company. These will restrict its borrowing capacity.
- List all commitments for capital additions, inventory purchases, sales and advertising programs, customer arrangements, hedging contracts, and other significant matters.
- Review all leases, franchises, and royalty agreements.
- List all off–balance sheet financing along with terms.
- Summarize the pension plans and short- and long-term incentive compensation plans.
- Draw conclusions.
- Possible or potential unrecorded liabilities.
- Review history and judge the exposure of the company to the following matters:
  a. Environmental matters such as disposal of sensitive materials as a result of production processes or products that are sold containing sensitive materials.
  b. Consumer-sensitive issues (including truth in lending and in advertising) and product safety exposure.
  c. Product liability lawsuits, claims, and potential claims for product and service warranties, defective workmanship, and re-work.
  d. OSHA, EEOC, occupation-related injuries and illness, and other employee-related claims or potential claims.
  e. Underfunded or unfunded pension and employee benefits.

f. Pending union negotiations that may result, when concluded, in unexpected increases in near- and long-term costs.

- List unrecorded litigation costs and exposure facing the company due to prior events or due to the nature of the industry in which this business operates.
- List contracts with vendors, consultants, directors, customers or others that represent commitments of the company.
- Review the adequacy and cost of insurance coverage on products, operations, and assets.
- Draw conclusions.
- Stockholders' equity.
- Describe the classes of securities, their owners (largest block of share owners, at least), and pertinent provisions, including stock options and convertibility or "put/call" features of the securities.
- If pertinent, analyze the stockholders' equity accounts since inception to determine how the balances arose.
- Detail dividends and distribution to stockholders for the past five years.
- Summarize the average and high/low trading values of publicly traded shares for the past two years.
- Draw conclusions.
- Income statement—accounting for income and expenses.
  Determine through analysis plus discussion with the auditors and management that the accounting policies and practices employed in accounting for the operations were in accordance with generally accepted principles and were consistently applied.
- Income statement—revenues and cost of goods sold.
- Determine (1) by analysis of the sales and gross profits for the past five years by product line, testing to the extent needed or (2) by reliance upon the independent CPAs that sales are recorded properly and that applicable costs and expenses are also recorded properly to match costs with related revenues in correct time periods. Obtain management's explanations of major variations in profitability included in reports to the stockholders or reports filed with the SEC.
- Look for major variations in sales volume and profitability that need explanation.

- Obtain a schedule of intercompany sales to competitors of the buyer and subsidiaries and affiliates of the seller for the past year or two. Will the acquisition affect any of these?
- By analysis and discussions, determine how much sales dollars in the past five years were impacted by unit price changes compared to real volume fluctuations. When were selling prices last increased?
- Review operating expenses for the past five years by department for unusual variations and obtain explanations. Chart them or prepare them in a table for the periods covered.
- Determine which expenses may not continue at the same level (going neither higher or lower) after the acquisition. List them along with explanations of each one's amount of change over the next five years. Such expenses could include the payroll and fringe benefits of the owners or their relatives, yachts, cars, abnormal travel, entertainment, charitable contributions, and nonrecurring legal and accounting costs among others. Determine the impact of these potential changes in the level of expenditures. See Chapter 8 for common examples of pro forma adjustments to the recorded book amounts.
- Other pro forma adjustments could include changes in revenues, expenditures for fixed assets, and working capital due to changes contemplated by the merger or acquisition. These could include eliminating or merging marketing, sales, production, administrative, and data processing departments and facilities.
- During the past five years, were there changes in the nature of the operations such as discontinuance of businesses, plants, or offices? Similarly, were any started or significantly enlarged or reduced in that time frame? Determine the impact of the changes.
- Draw conclusions.
- Cash flow statements.
- Cash flow is the acid test as to whether the business can be successful over time. Nothing is more important than understanding the generators and users of cash over the years and for future years. Accruals may be high or low, but cash in the bank is for real.
- Obtain analyses of the cash generated and used for each of the past five years. Does the business appear to be capital-

intensive? Does it have good positive cash generation characteristics? How likely is it to have similar cash flow traits in the
next five years?
- What were the most important sources and uses of funds in the
  past five years?
- Financial highlights.
- Significant financial ratios and charts should be included in this
  section of the acquisition investigation if not previously included.
  The other major statistics not shown in the prior sections of this
  chapter that are normally useful follow:
- Working capital ratio (current assets divided by current liabilities)
  for the past five years and projected for three to five years.
- Accounts receivable days outstanding for the past five years and
  projected for three to five years.
- Bad debts as a percentage of sales for the past five years and projected for three to five years.
- Inventory turnover (cost of goods sold divided by weighted average inventory, except raw materials should be divided into
  purchases of same) by major product line and by class (raw materials, work in process, and finished goods) for the past five years
  and projected for three to five years.
- Depreciation compared to property, plant, and equipment expenditures for the past five years and projected for three to five years.
- Debt coverage (income before interest and income taxes divided
  by the amount to service the debt, including interest and principal
  payments as they fall due).
- Debt to equity ratio (all debt divided by stockholders' equity).
- Compound annual sales growth for the past five years and
  projected for three to five years.
- Gross profit margins as a percentage of sales for the past five years
  and projected for three to five years.
- Operating income (excludes interest and income taxes and
  unusual nonoperating charges and credits) as a percentage of sales
  for the past five years and projected for three to five years.
- Pretax income as a percentage of sales for the past five years and
  projected for three to five years.
- Draw conclusions.

Use of Charts Aids Comprehension

Charts of some items covered in the previous sections are presented for illustrative purposes. Many more could and should be prepared. Properly constructed, charts present more data in less space than any other format. Comments on such tables and charts should be in writing in a report to management of the buying or merging company. The following charts illustrate simple, effective ways to depict some very informative data.

For example, in Figure D–1 sales have been fairly flat—a negative trend if inflation in selling prices would be deleted from the chart. Meanwhile, historical gross profits have declined as a percentage of sales from 53 percent in the fifth year to 48 percent for the current year. Yet, the forecast projects a rise in gross profit margins during the next five years to the former levels of 53 percent. Why? How will unit prices be raised in what appears to be a declining price market? Similarly, pretax margins were more than halved in percentage terms from 20 percent

FIGURE D–1

Sales Dollars, Gross Profit Percentages, Pretax Percentages

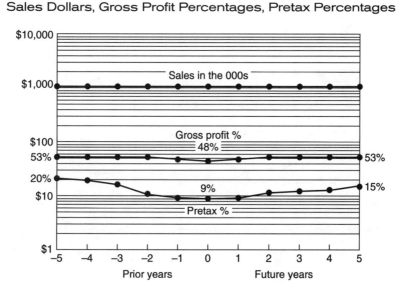

FIGURE D-2

Depreciation-Capital Expenditures

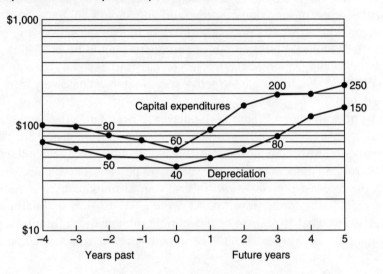

FIGURE D-3

Cash Flow

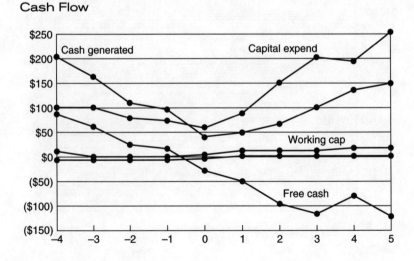

to 9 percent. Why are these margins to increase to 15 percent of sales by the end of the fifth year in the future? Is this optimism or does management have programs ready to turn the margins around? How have unit sales been trending?

When looking at Figure D–2, the buyer's analyst could question the consistent drop in capital expenditures over the past five years and try to determine if that tied in to pumping up cash flow to make the company look better. Such decreases over the years in plant and machinery investments may have caused a drop in manufacturing efficiency and increased unit costs, resulting in lower gross profit margins.

In the projections for the next five years, the forecast shows the need for renovations and more capital expenditures. Seems logical. What are the specific needs and projected benefits of investing in those capital assets? Are they mandatory?

The cash flow chart in Figure D–3 is prepared on a linear scale where every block is equal in size. The chart in Figure D–2 showing depreciation and capital expenditures is plotted on a semilogarithmic scale which shows the individual plot marks proportionate to each other since the rate of change or percentage change from one line to another vertically is the same. Use of the semilogarithmic approach is preferable for many applications. It is easy to grow $1 to $2, yet the percentage growth is high. It is much more difficult to grow sales at $1 million by that same percentage growth since it requires doubling sales to $2 million! The semilogarithmic chart keeps all dollars proportionate to all other dollar amounts so the rate of growth is highlighted if it is fairly large, and it is downplayed if it is small as a percentage growth when compared to the other plot points.

The cash flow chart in Figure D–3 does tie in to the previous charts showing lower profit trends, less cash generated, less cash used for capital expenditures, but a consistent level of working capital tied to sales. Again, cash available for other expenditures or for dividends is on the road down. Will the transaction price reflect it?

Not a pretty picture, but the buyer must beware. Some real investment capital must be injected into this company to revive it—the price should reflect the condition it is in. Do not pay for the business twice: once to buy it at a high price, and the second time to invest more funds into it to make it competitive and grow it once again.

SUMMARY

This sample due-diligence program is just that—a sample. It is not designed to be sufficiently comprehensive to fit all business investigations. As the buyer, prepare a *written program* to suit the situation and to discover the major problems and concerns about the business.

Spend the money on the investigation before the closing. It may well pay off in big dividends either by convincing a buyer not to buy or to buy at a different price. Above all, take the time and find the *FATAL FLAW*.

Standard Industrial Classification Codes

In order to organize your efforts in diversifying and in acquiring a business within business niches you are now in or plan to be in, the following standard industrial classifications (SIC) are generally accepted and used in the United States for all businesses. Those below are abstracted from the *Standard Industrial Classification Manual* by the Executive Office of the President, Office of Management and Budget. Not all account codes are listed.

Sic Codes	Business Niche
	A. Agriculture, Forestry and Fishing
0100	Agricultural production—crops
0200	Agricultural production—livestock
0700	Agricultural services
0800	Forestry
0900	Fishing, hunting, and trapping
	B. Mining
1000	Metal mining
1200	Coal mining
1300	Oil and gas
1310	Crude, petroleum, and natural gas
1320	Natural gas liquids
1380	Oil and gas field services
1400	Nonmetallic minerals, except fuels
1440	Sand and gravel
1450	Clay, ceramic, and refractory minerals
1470	Chemical and fertilizer minerals
1480	Nonmetallic mineral services
1490	Misc. nonmetallic minerals
	C. Construction
1500	General building contractors
1600	Heavy construction, excluding building
1700	Special trade contractors

D. Manufacturing

2000	Food and kindred products
2010	Meat products
2020	Dairy products
2024	Ice cream and frozen desserts
2030	Preserved fruits and vegetables
2040	Grain mill products
2050	Bakery products
2060	Sugar and confectionery products
2070	Fats and oils
2080	Beverages
2082	Malt beverages
2084	Wines, brandy, and brandy spirits
2086	Bottled and canned soft drinks
2090	Misc. food and kindred products
2099	Food preparations, other
2100	Tobacco
2200	Textile mill products
2250	Knotting mills
2260	Textile finishing, except wool
2270	Carpets and rugs
2300	Apparel and other textile products
2400	Lumber and wood products
2430	Millwork, plywood, and structural members
2500	Furniture and fixtures
2510	Household furniture
2520	Office furniture
2530	Public building and related furniture
2540	Partitions and fixtures
2591	Drapery hardware, blinds, and shades
2599	Furniture and fixtures, other
2600	Paper and allied products
2610	Pulp mills
2620	Paper mills
2630	Paperboard mills
2650	Paperboard containers and boxes
2700	Printing and publishing
2710	Newspapers
2720	Periodicals
2730	Books
2740	Miscellaneous publishing
2750	Commercial printing
2760	Manifold business forms
2770	Greeting cards
2800	Chemicals and allied products
2810	Industrial inorganic chemicals
2820	Plastics materials and synthetics
2830	Drugs
2840	Soaps, cleaners, and toilet goods
2850	Paint and allied products
2860	Industrial organic chemicals
2870	Agricultural chemicals
2890	Miscellaneous chemical products
2891	Adhesives and sealants
2893	Printing ink
2900	Petroleum and coal products
2950	Asphalt paving and roofing materials
3000	Rubber and plastics products
3010	Tires and inner tubes
3020	Seals
3050	Hose and belting and gaskets and packing
3060	Fabricated rubber products, other
3100	Leather and leather products
3200	Stone, clay, and glass products
3250	Structural clay products
3290	Miscellaneous nonmetallic mineral products
3300	Primary metal industries
3310	Blast furnace and basic steel products

3320	Iron and steel foundries	3650	Household audio and video equipment
3330	Primary nonferrous metals		
3350	Nonferrous rolling and drawing	3660	Communications equipment
		3670	Electronic components and accessories
3360	Nonferrous foundries (castings)		
		3690	Miscellaneous electrical equipment and supplies
3390	Miscellaneous primary metal products		
		3700	Transportation equipment
3400	Fabricated metal products	3710	Motor vehicles and equipment
3410	Metal cans and shipping containers	3720	Aircraft and parts
		3730	Ship and boat building and repairing
3420	Cutlery, hand tools, and hardware		
		3740	Railroad equipment
3430	Plumbing and heating, except electric	3750	Motorcycles, bicycles, and parts
3440	Fabricated structural metal products	3800	Instruments and related products
3450	Screw machine products, bolts, etc.	3810	Search and navigation equipment
3460	Metal forgings and stampings	3820	Measuring and controlling devices
3470	Metal services, other		
3480	Ordinance accessories	3827	Optical instruments and lenses
3490	Miscellaneous fabricated metal products		
		3840	Medical instruments and supplies
3500	Industrial machinery and equipment		
		3850	Ophthalmic goods
3510	Engines and turbines	3860	Photographic equipment
3520	Farm and garden machinery	3870	Watches, clocks, watchcases, and parts
3530	Construction and related machinery		
		3900	Miscellaneous manufacturing industries
3540	Metalworking machinery		
3550	Special industry machinery	3910	Jewelry, silverware, and plated ware
3560	General industrial machinery		
3570	Computer and office equipment	3930	Musical instruments
		3940	Toys and sporting goods
3580	Refrigeration and service machinery	3950	Pens, pencils, and office and art supplies
3590	Industrial machinery, other		
		3960	Costume jewelry and notions
3600	Electric, electronic, and other equipment		
			E. Transportation and Public Utilities
3610	Electric distribution equipment	4000	Railroad transportation
3620	Electrical industrial apparatus	4010	Railroads
3630	Household appliances	4100	Local and interurban passenger transit
3640	Electric lighting and wiring equipment		

4120	Taxicabs	5180	Beer, wine, and distilled beverages

4130	Intercity and rural bus transportation

G. Retail Trade

4140	Bus charter service	5200	Building materials and garden supplies
4150	School buses		
4200	Trucking and warehousing	5300	General merchandising stores
4300	U.S. Postal Service	5400	Food stores
4400	Water transportation	5500	Automotive dealers and service stations
4500	Transportation by air		
4600	Pipelines, except natural gas	5600	Apparel and accessory stores
4700	Transportation services	5700	Furniture and home furnishings stores
4800	Communication		
4900	Electric, gas, and sanitary services	5800	Eating and drinking places
		5900	Miscellaneous retail
		5910	Drug stores and proprietary stores

F. Wholesale Trade

5000	Wholesale trade—durable goods	5920	Liquor stores
		5930	Used merchandise stores
5010	Motor vehicles and supplies	5960	Nonstore retailers
5020	Furniture and home furnishings	5980	Fuel dealers
5030	Lumber and construction materials		

H. Finance, Insurance, and Real Estate

5040	Professional and commercial equipment	6000	Depository institutions
		6020	Commercial banks
5050	Metals and minerals, except petroleum	6030	Savings institutions
5060	Electrical goods	6080	Foreign banks and branches and agencies
5070	Hardware, plumbing, and heating equipment	6100	Nondepository institutions
		6140	Personal credit institutions
5080	Machinery, equipment, and supplies	6150	Business credit institutions
5090	Miscellaneous durable goods	6160	Mortgage bankers and brokers
5100	Wholesale trade—nondurable goods	6200	Security and commodity brokers
5110	Paper and paper products		
5120	Drugs, proprietaries, and supplies	6300	Insurance carriers
		6310	Life insurance
5130	Apparel, piece goods, and notions	6320	Medical service and health insurance
5140	Groceries and related products	6330	Fire, marine, and casualty insurance
5160	Chemical products	6350	Surety insurance
5170	Petroleum and allied petroleum products	6360	Title insurance
		6500	Real estate

I. Services

7000	Hotels and other lodging places
7010	Hotels and motel
7200	Personal services
7210	Laundry, cleaning, and garment services
7300	Business services
7310	Advertising
7320	Credit reporting and collection
7330	Mailing, reproduction, and stenographic services
7340	Services to buildings
7360	Personnel supply services
7370	Computer and data processing services
7372	Prepackaged software
7375	Information retrieval services
7380	Miscellaneous business services
7500	Auto repair, service, and parking
7600	Miscellaneous repair services
7800	Motion pictures
7900	Amusement and recreation services
8000	Health services
8050	Nursing and personal care services
8060	Hospitals
8070	Medical and dental laboratories
8080	Home health care services
8090	Health and allied services, other
8100	Legal services
8300	Social services
8600	Membership organizations
8700	Engineering and management services

J. Public Administration

K. Nonclassifiable Establishments

INDEX

ABC system, 180
Accountants
  in acquisition process, 15, 75, 178
  in negotiations, 178, 180, 183
Accounting principles, 197–198
Acquisitions. *See also* Buyers; Deals; Negotiations;
  Purchase investigation; Sellers
    auction process, 183–186
    confidentiality agreements, 237–240
    contract issues, 206–209, 224–225
    deal stream statistics, 72
    deal structures, 192–194, 205–208, 209
    defining needs, 73–75
    documents, 224–225
    driving forces, 6
    failures, 110, 111–112, 113–116
    focus matrix, 33, 35–38
    growth in, 1–2, 6
    industries targeted, 14,33
    legal counsel, 178,184
    locating companies for, 71–93
    middle-market companies, 8
    number of, 5
    officer in charge of, 76–78
    pitfalls, 227–229
    price of, 3,4,5,8,9,26,141–153
      auction process, 183–186
      cash flow, 146–150
      concept of golden handcuffs, 209–211
      deferred payments, 212–216
      methods for setting, 142–153
      payback, 132–133
      pool of forgiveness in, 208–209
      premium over quoted market price,
        145
      price earnings ratios, 3, 4, 9, 145–146
      public vs. privately held companies, 5, 26
      use of leverage, 136–137, 139
    postclosing issues, 225–227, 229–230
    process of, 24–25
    purchase investigation, 94–116
    reason for seeking, 1–2, 6, 13
    reference books, 54
    representations and warranties, 245–247
    specifications, 38–44, 87–88
    statistics of, 3,4
    strategic plan, 26–30
    structure, 192–194, 205–208, 209
    success and failure of, 31–32, 110, 113
    team, 156–158
      dealmaker, 76, 158–159
      directors, 159–160, 173–174

      financial and accounting expert, 166
      insurance expert, 168
      legal expert, 167–168
      marketing and sales expert, 165–166
      operations expert, 162–164
      president, 16—162
      taxation expert, 167
    timing of, 85, 86
Antitrust laws, 2

Bankers
  in acquisitions, 6, 10
  foreign, 48
Blum, Stephen B., vii-viii
Break-even, 106, 107–109, 144
Business culture, 16–23
  compatibility of, 19
  identities, 19
  issues to look for, 22
  prime objective, 21
Buyers
  assets, 205
  auction process, 183–186
  brochure for, 87–92
  capital stock, 205
  closing process, 246
  concept of golden handcuffs, 209–211
  default, 243
  foreign, 7, 11
  in foreign markets, 12
  problems of, 188–190
  purchase, 196, 197–198, 205–208
  screening, 61, 72–73, 92, 104–105
  time lines for, 85–86
  use of intermediaries, 79, 80, 81–84
  what they look for, 96–99
  wants and needs, 194–195

Case studies, 138–155
Cash flow
  break-even analysis for, 106
  company valuation, 118, 144, 146–150
  definition, 106, 121
  seller's prospectus, 64
Cavanagh, Richard E., 31
Clifford, Donald K., Jr., 31
Closing
  acquisitions, 217–220
  conditions, 246
  hiatus period, 220–222
  post-closing review, 229–230
  who manages after, 225–227

298